Writing as a Way of Healing

Also by Louise DeSalvo

Virginia Woolf

Conceived with Malice

Vertigo: A Memoir

Breathless: An Asthma Journal

Territories of the Voice

Louise DeSalvo, Ph.D.

Writing
as a Way
of Healing

How Telling Our Stories

Transforms Our Lives

HarperSanFrancisco
A Division of HarperCollins*Publishers*

While the descriptions of classes and student work are as accurate as memory and transcription allow—though condensed and edited—students' names have been changed to honor their privacy.

Grateful acknowledgment is made to the following publishers for permission to quote from their publications.

Aunt Lute Books for *The Cancer Journals* by Audre Lorde, copyright 1980 by Audre Lorde.

Beacon Press for *Ordinary Time* by Nancy Mairs, copyright 1993 by Nancy Mairs.

Capra Press for *Zen in the Art of Writing* by Ray Bradbury, copyright 1990 by Ray Bradbury Enterprises.

Farrar, Straus and Giroux for *My Brother* by Jamaica Kincaid, copyright 1997 by Jamaica Kincaid.

Harcourt Brace Jovanovich, publishers for "A Sketch of the Past," in *Moments of Being* by Virginia Woolf, copyright 1985, 1976 by Quentin Bell and Angelica Garnett.

Harper Collins Publishers for *Heaven's Coast: A Memoir* by Mark Doty, copyright 1996 by Mark Doty.

Harper Collins Publishers for *Paula* by Isabel Allende, copyright 1994 by Isabel Allende, translation copyright 1995 by Harper Collins Publishers.

Penguin Putnam, Inc., for *Two or Three Things I Know for Sure* by Dorothy Allison, copyright 1995 by Dorothy Allison.

The University of Arizona Press for *Plaintext* by Nancy Mairs, copyright 1986 by The Arizona Board of Regents.

W. W. Norton & Company, Inc. for *Recovering: A Journal* by May Sarton, copyright 1980 by May Sarton.

William Morrow and Company, Inc., for *Opening Up: The Healing Power of Confiding in Others,* by James W. Pennebaker, Ph.D., copyright 1990 by James W. Pennebaker, Ph.D.

HarperCollins books may be purchased for educational, business, or sales promotional use. For information please write: Special Markets Department, HarperCollins Publishers, Inc., 10 East 53rd Street, New York, NY 10022.

HarperCollins Web Site: http://www.harpercollins.com

HarperCollins,® ☕®, and HarperSanFrancisco™ are trademarks of HarperCollins Publishers, Inc.

FIRST EDITION

3 1571 00320 5724

Library of Congress Cataloging-in-Publication

DeSalvo, Louise A.
    Writing as a way of healing : how telling our stories transforms our lives / Louise DeSalvo. — 1st. ed.
      ISBN 0–06–251519–5 (cloth)
      ISBN 0–06–251520–9 (pbk.)
      1. Authorship—Psychological aspects.   2. Diaries—Authorship.   3. Healing.
  I. Title.
PN171.P83D47   1999
808'.02'019—dc21   98–35064

99 00 01 02 03 ❖ RRD(H) 10 9 8 7 6 5 4 3 2

For Ernest J. DeSalvo, Edvige Giunta,

Catherine Kleinpeter, Geri Thoma,

and my Hunter College students

So while our art cannot, as we wish it could, save us from wars, privation, envy, greed, old age, or death, it can revitalize us amidst it all. . . .

Writing is survival. . . .

Not to write, for many of us, is to die.

I have learned, on my journeys, that if I let a day go by without writing, I grow uneasy. Two days and I am in tremor. Three and I suspect lunacy. Four and I might as well be a hog, suffering the flux in a wallow. An hour's writing is tonic. I'm on my feet, running in circles, and yelling for a clean pair of spats.

RAY BRADBURY
Zen in the Art of Writing

Contents

Acknowledgments

Virginia Woolf said that no author is singularly responsible for bringing a book into the world; the work depends on the efforts of many. This is certainly true for me.

First, I must thank my writing students at Hunter College. They taught me much of what I've learned and I'm grateful to them for sharing their work and their stories. I am especially grateful to former students Julia Raynor, Catherine Kapphahn, Elizabeth Primamore, Pearl Abraham, Marika Brussel, Scott Bane, John Champagne, Louisa Costa, Delia Doherty, Tim Elhajj, Elena Georgiou, Leota Lone Dog, Juliet Marinelli, Joe Miserendino, Pamala Renée McCormick, David Mann, Juliet Marinelli, Alison Marek, Charles Naylor, Nancy Park, and Cynthia Ward for sharing their ongoing challenges and triumphs.

A portion of this book was written while I was on a sabbatical leave from Hunter College, The City University of New York. I thank Professor Richard Barickman, chair of the Department of English, and Professor Allan Brick, former chair, for their support. I thank, too, my colleagues at Hunter College for their generosity and for reminding me daily of the powerful positive impact that good teaching (which respects students and their stories) has on people's lives: Meena Alexander, Fred Bornhauser, Harriet Luria Johnson, Estella Majozo, Donna Masini, Nondita Mason, Regina McBride, Karen Greenberg, Teri Haas, Ann Raimes, William Pitt Root, Jenefer Shute, Trudy Smoke, Suzanne Stein, Neil Tolchin, Sylvia Tomasch, Barbara Webb, and David Winn.

While this book was in process, UNICO National awarded *Vertigo* the Gay Talese Award for Literature. This aided the writing of this book immeasurably.

Members of the Biography Seminar at New York University and the Women Writing Women's Lives Seminar (among them, Louise Bernikow, Sallie Bingham, Rachel Brownstein, Mary Ann Caws, Norah Chase, Ellen Chesler, Bell Chevigny, Blanche Wiesen Cook, Elizabeth

Harlan, Dorothy O. Helly, Gail Hornstein, Temma Kaplan, Carol Klein, Nancy Matthews, Honor Moore, Dona Munker, Nell Painter, Nancy Rubin, Stacy Schiff, Patricia Bell Scott, Sue Shapiro, Alix Kates Shulman, Ann Snitow, Carol Stanger, Meena Alexander, Gloria Erlich), with their unflinching discussions of their writing process and their generosity, too, in sharing information about their subjects through the years, have exerted a profound ongoing influence on my thinking.

Researchers, writers, friends, and colleagues have been generous in their support, or in sharing stories of their artistic or writing processes. I would like to thank Mandy Aftel, Rosemary Ahern, Ken Aptekar, Helen Barolini, Regina Barreca, Evelyn Bassoff, Mary Beth Caschetta, Robert Cormier, Susan Cygnet, Beth Rigel Daugherty, Rose Di Poto, Erika Duncan, Janet Emig, Joshua Fausty, Patricia Foster, Kennedy Fraser, Kenny Fries, Fred Gardaphé, Audrey Goldrich, Diana Hume George, Sandra Gilbert, Alison Glenny, Alex Goren, Joanna Herman, William Herman, Norbert Hirschhorn, M.D., Mark Hussey, John Koster, Craig Kridel, Burgess Levin, Jane Lilienfeld, Arnold Ludwig, M.D., Nancy Mairs, Jane Marcus, Michael Marcus, James McCourt, Roger McIntyre, Frank McLaughlin, Toni McNaron, David Mitchell, Carol Newman, Paul Newman, Jay Parini, Canio Pavone, James W. Pennebaker, Kate Probst, Mary Saily, Susan Fromberg Schaeffer, Vanessa Smith, Gay Talese, Maria Terrone, Vincent Virga, Robert Viscusi, Jeanette Vuocolo, Ann Warnick, Robert Warnick, Robert White. Mary Capello, Brooke Kroeger, Kate Probst, and Eunice Lipton were especially helpful, providing ongoing challenging conversations and warm friendship.

I would like to thank those at Harper San Francisco who helped make the dream I had of this book real. My editor, Mark Chimsky, was enthusiastic from the start; he always said the right thing at the right time and sent me back to work knowing exactly what I needed to do; his editorial acumen and vision of the book kept me on track. Editorial assistant Eric Hunt helped with many important details and was cheerful and helpful on days when I needed a boost. Copyeditor Priscilla Stuckey untangled my prose. Production Consultant Lisa Zuniga understood what needed doing near the end of the process.

Laura Beers, art director, translated my words into a beautiful design with a perfect cover. Margery Buchanan, marketing manager, took a keen interest in this project from its inception, and I thank her for it.

Finally, I want to thank my family and those to whom this book is dedicated. Deborah DeSalvo, Jason DeSalvo, Justin DeSalvo, Millie Sciacchetano, and Louis Sciacchetano provided love, care, and comfort. Steven DeSalvo gave me more pleasure than I can say and underscored the tremendous healing potential of story for the very young.

That this book was written at all is largely due to my husband, Ernest J. DeSalvo, who each day listens to my thoughts, feelings, challenges, and triumphs. At a critical juncture, he knew exactly what I needed to do next. Edvige Giunta, professor of English at Jersey City State College, helped me conceptualize this book; she generously shared with me her experiences as a writer of memoir and poetry and as a teacher of memoir writing. Catherine Kleinpeter assisted me with the research; she discovered a myriad of sources that enrich this book. Geri Thoma, my agent, understood how important it was for me to write this; she has been an unfailing source of support and good cheer for a decade. And my Hunter College students have taught me much of what I know about the writing process.

Part One

Writing as a
Way of Healing

Chapter One

Why Write?

I believe that writing is an
account of the powers of extrication.

JOHN CHEEVER, *Journals*

What is healing, but a shift in perspective?

MARK DOTY, *Heaven's Coast*

I am the only one who can tell the story
of my life and say what it means.

DOROTHY ALLISON,
Two or Three Things I Know for Sure

Writing has helped me heal. Writing has changed my life. Writing has saved my life.

How often have I uttered these words, and meant them, or written them into my journal since I started writing? A hundred times? A thousand?

And how often have others—acquaintances, friends, students, published writers—told me that writing has helped them heal from loss, grief, or personal tragedy, that writing gave them unimaginably plentiful spiritual and emotional advantages? That writing has changed them, has helped them come to terms with something difficult, that writing has saved their lives? Often.

How often have I been reading a writer's published journal or letters and stumbled upon an admission that, for this author, without writing, life just wouldn't be worth living, that writing has given purpose and meaning to life? Times too numerous to remember. While I've been reading the words of Alice Walker, James Baldwin, Virginia Woolf, Elizabeth Bishop, Anaïs Nin, Alice James, Charlotte Perkins Gilman, Henry Miller, D. H. Lawrence, Djuna Barnes, Toni Morrison, Isabel Allende, Alice James, Dorothy Allison, Kenzaburō Ōe, countless contemporary memoirists—the list goes on.

These writers describe how they have consciously used the writing of their artistic works to help them heal from the thorny experiences of their lives, especially from dislocation, violence, racism, homophobia, anti-Semitism, rape, political persecution, incest, loss, illness.

The writer H. D., in *Hermetic Definition,* phrased it most succinctly: "Write, write, or die." And Henry Miller, the working-class writer who began his first novel after taking numerous odd jobs (selling newspapers, selling candy, working at Western Union), once admitted in a letter published in *Art and Outrage,* how much writing had changed him. "The more I wrote," he said, "the more I became a human being. The writing may have seemed monstrous (to some), for it was a violation, but I became a more human individual because of it. I was getting the poison out of my system." My student Melanie, a former emergency room nurse, told me that for her, now, writing was "a necessary life-support system." And my student Homer, who came to the United States from a country in the throes of upheaval, where he was persecuted, said, "Through my work, I rejoin the world."

Wounds, Shocks

In *Legacy of the Heart,* Wayne Muller observes that "our own wounds can be vehicles for exploring our essential nature, revealing the deepest textures of our heart and soul, if only we will sit with them, open ourselves to the pain, . . . without holding back, without blame." For many years now, I have been using writing in this way, and I have taught scores of students to use writing in this way, too. Inevitably, healing shifts in perspective occur.

Virginia Woolf said that the moments of profound insight that come from writing about our soulful, thoughtful examination of our psychic wounds should be called "shocks." For they force us into an awareness about ourselves and our relationship to others and our place in the world that we wouldn't otherwise have had. They realign the essential nature of our being.

In my case, these healing shifts in perspective often came from writing about my childhood—a wrenching separation from my loving and caring father, who spent the war years in the Pacific, and then his return from the war, a very changed, volatile, highly strung, and angry man; my life as the daughter of a depressed mother who was often unable to care for me; a jolting move from an Italian working-class neighborhood in Hoboken, New Jersey, which I loved, to a suburb, in which I felt like an outsider; the abuse of a caregiver. The shifts in perspective came, too, from writing about profound losses in adulthood—my mother's and my sister's deaths.

But healing flashes of insight often came, too, when, during a day's writing, trying to link current feeling with past event, I stumbled into a "moment of being" that I had forgotten. Often it was one that signified much. One—the comfort and joy of my mother reading to me in her rocking chair at the end of the day during the war, when she would take my index finger and guide it under the words she read. This was the source, I'm certain, of my deep and abiding love of reading, of why, to me, it's as essential to my well-being as food and water. A second—my father building me my first desk so that I could give my homework proper attention and then selecting and buying, for the drawer pull, a handle of brass beyond what he'd budgeted. Is it any wonder I'd rather be at my desk than anywhere else in the world? A third—the taste of homemade peach ice cream fresh from a hand-cranked freezer on a holiday at Lake George at the end of the day when my father urged me to swim as far as I could across the lake as he rowed beside me to make sure I was safe. The source, I know, of my love of carefully prepared food; the source, too, of my ability to take on challenges.

These are some of my "shocks," my shifts in perspective that have come from writing. I've had many wounds to heal, and I've done much writing to heal them, and in the process I've discovered a rich, deeply textured life I hadn't before recognized.

The Necessity of Writing

Many people I know who want to write but don't (my husband, Ernie, for example) or who want to write more than they have but say they can't find the time (my friend Marla) have told me that taking the time to write seems so, well, self-indulgent, self-involved, frivolous even. And that finding the time to write—even a diary, much less fiction or memoir or poetry—in their busy schedules is impossible. "I'll write when I have the time," they say. "A Walter Mitty fantasy," someone I know calls it—thinking that the time to write will come along one day and poke you in the ribs and say, "I'm here; now you can write."

What, though, if writing weren't such a luxury? What if writing were a simple, significant, yet necessary way to achieve spiritual, emotional, and psychic wholeness? to synthesize thought and feeling, to understand how feeling relates to events in our lives and vice versa? What if writing were as important and as basic a human function and as significant to maintaining and promoting our psychic and physical wellness as, say, exercise, healthful food, pure water, clean air, rest and repose, and some soul-satisfying practice?

Writing as Fixer

The metaphor I use most frequently is of writing as a "fixer." As in photography, writing acts for me as a kind of fixer, like the chemical—the fixer—you use to stabilize the image. "Fixing things," I sometimes call it.

And it acts as another kind of "fixer," with all its healing implications. I use my writing as a way of fixing things, of making them better, of healing myself. As a compasslike way of taking a "fix" on my life—to see where I am, where I've been, and where I'm going.

Writing

Yesterday, when I was feeling sad, I took my diary off the shelf, picked up my current lucky pen, a gift from my student Andrew, and wrote.

I described what had happened the day before. How I had seen a young mother comforting her toddler when I was out food shopping. Suddenly, inexplicably, I found myself weeping and I rushed out of the store and into my car. The sight of her, bending over him, stroking his poker-straight hair, telling him that everything would be all right, left me feeling bereft.

I wrote how earlier the preceding morning, I had been cleaning out a closet in my basement. I found my mother's old red bathrobe, a gift I'd given her a few years before she died. After her death, I couldn't part with it; it bore her smell—the faintest hint of White Shoulders, the perfume she wore.

But now, years after her death, imagining I was well past my grieving, thinking I didn't need to keep this totem any longer, I'd put it into a bag of old clothes I was collecting for Goodwill that I dropped off on my way to the supermarket.

My grieving apparently, I understood as I wrote, wasn't over, perhaps would never be completely over. The sight of that mother and child keenly reminded me of my loss. It made me yearn, too, for an engaged, comforting mother—someone my mother couldn't be when she was depressed.

I wrote about my feelings about giving away my mother's bathrobe—how I longed for it as I longed for her. I wrote how, in that supermarket, grief felt like panic to me. Or like falling into a hole in the ground.

I wrote some reflections, too. About how my mother's reading to me while my father was away at war is a consoling, healing memory I return to often.

To close, as always, I wrote, too, about what I was grateful for—that the act of writing has been such a sturdy and dependable source of comfort for me through the years. And I wrote about what I was looking forward to—seeing my grandson, Steven, and making cornbread with him.

After twenty minutes of writing, though I was still sad, my feelings had undergone a subtle but real transformation. A baker friend of mine calls it feeling "yeasty"—alive and growing and changing. That's what I often feel after I write. Yeasty.

I'd examined my feelings, linked them to something that had happened, and to my past. My feelings of loss for my mother, though I still had them, no longer overwhelmed me. Now, I felt connected to my feelings and to my life story. I was aware that I had honored my feelings of loss, but that I had transformed them into language so that I held these feelings differently. I realized, too, that I am committed to writing and the nourishment it provides me.

Writing as Sturdy Ladder

Alice Walker, author of *The Color Purple,* sees her writing as necessary to her well-being, to her very existence. Writing, she once remarked, not only for her, but for us all, is "a matter of necessity and that you write to save your life is really true and so far it's been a very sturdy ladder out of the pit."

Writing as a *very sturdy ladder out of the pit.* I like that metaphor very much. For it says that though there's a pit, there's a way out that's safe and strong and dependable. That all you have to do when you're in the pit is to remember that writing's there. And use it as a way to reach freedom and safety.

Most writers I know or have read about use metaphors like Walker's sturdy ladder to describe the efficacious nature of their writing. "Picking and digging," my writing partner Edvige Giunta, who grew up in Sicily, with a garden out back and a grove of olive and lemon trees, calls it. "Balm on a wound," my student Susan calls it.

For me, writing has functioned in different ways at different times for different projects. Always, though, like Walker, my writing has been *necessary*. For without writing, I know, I would be lost, or worse.

An Invitation

This book is an invitation for you to use writing as a way of healing, as a fixer, as a sturdy ladder, as picking and digging, as balm on a wound—or whatever metaphor describes how the process works for you. This book is an invitation to engage with your writing process over time in a way that allows you to discover strength, power, wisdom, depth, energy, creativity, soulfulness, and wholeness, to "cultivate those qualities of heart and spirit that are available to you in this very moment," as Wayne Muller has phrased it. For, as he's observed, "your life is not a problem to be solved but a gift to be opened."

This book is an invitation for you to use the simple act of writing as a way of reimagining who you are or remembering who you were. To use writing to discover and fulfill your deepest desire. To accept pain, fear, uncertainty, strife. But to find, too, a place of safety, security, serenity, and joyfulness. To claim your voice, to tell your story. And to share the gift of your work with others and, so, enrich and deepen our understanding of the human condition.

WHAT YOU CAN DO NOW Do you have something you need to write about right now? Something that needs fixing? Can you write for, say, twenty minutes, a half hour, or so, and watch what happens? Find some paper. A pen. (Your lucky pen.) And begin.

After, think about this. What is *your* metaphor for the act of writing? What could writing mean to you? Write it down. Explore it. Remember it. Cherish it.

Creating an Image of Restitution

Once, when I was talking to Julia Feraca on Wisconsin Public Radio, we engaged in a dialogue about the healing potential of writing. She was intrigued by the implications of my work, that the act of writing can be personally helpful and healing. And she wanted to discuss, not only how this applied to "great and famous" writers, but how it might be useful to anyone who was willing to write steadily.

After we discussed some famous writers' lives, Julia Feraca focused on an idea from my work that intrigued her that she wanted me to explore more fully—that *the act of writing about something painful can help right a wrong that has been done to you.* It can be a form of restitution.

She told us of her life as her father's daughter—recounting the feelings of impotence that his authoritarian behavior engendered in her. Then she sketched how, when her father was incapacitated by a heart attack, she had written a poem about him. Through writing it, she said, she transformed her feelings about him and about herself. And it changed her relationship to him. It enabled her to care for him in a way she hadn't before.

Writing changed the way she felt about her father—she no longer feared him; she understood him, even pitied him. Writing changed the way she felt about herself—she became immune to his onslaughts.

A central, stunning image in the poem, which Julia Feraca read for us, was that of her father's frayed and tattered trousers. Creating that image, we agreed, "defrocked" her father, robbed him of the power he had wielded over her. But it also informed her that her father's spiritual and emotional being was damaged, wasn't whole. (As Julia Feraca read her poem, I remembered how the writer Djuna Barnes once used the image of a "midge" to cut her abusive father down to size.)

Writing those lines, Julia Feraca said, made it feel like the balance of power in their relationship had tilted in her favor. And this change, she shared, has been long-lasting. For the poem was among the first she wrote.

Julia Feraca's story shows how a beginning writer can engage in a significant moment of self-healing that initiates a new sense of understanding, vitality, power. For writing can change the past; it can change our personal history.

We are the accumulation of the stories we tell ourselves about who we are. So changing our stories, as Mandy Aftel, Daniel Goleman, Jay Martin, Martin E. P. Seligman, Ph.D., and others have shown, can change our personal history, can change us. Through writing, we revisit our past and review and revise it. What we thought happened, what we believed happened to us, shifts and changes as we discover deeper and more complex truths. It isn't that we use our writing to deny what we've experienced. Rather, we use it to shift our perspective.

Witnessing Healing Transformations That Occur Through Writing

As a teacher of writing, I regularly witness the physical and emotional transformation of my students. I see how they change physically and psychically when they work on writing projects—diary, memoir, fiction, poetry, biographical essays—that grow from a deep, authentic place, when they confront their pain in their work. Through reading scientific studies, I have learned that writing can help anyone—not just people who consider themselves writers—significantly improve their psychic states and also their physiological well-being. I wasn't surprised to learn this, for I and other writers have known it either intuitively or by reflecting upon our writing processes.

"Why is it that I always get sick *after* I finish a book, and not while I'm writing?" a friend recently asked. "Crazy as it sounds," she concludes, "it must be that writing keeps me healthy."

That writing keeps her healthy isn't a crazy, off-the-wall belief. It's true. And although writing can't cure us (eradicate whatever it is we're suffering from), some studies suggest that it might prolong our lives. And it certainly can help us heal. It can enable us to accomplish that

shift in perspective marked by acceptance, authenticity, depth, serenity, and wisdom that is the hallmark of genuine healing.

This applies, too, to those of us with serious challenges. I have
taught people who are disabled, who live with chronic illness and with
terminal illness; people who are crippled (their word) and blind; people
who have been raped, assaulted, seriously neglected, and tortured;
people who are the victims/survivors of incest, political persecution,
racism, sexism, homophobia. All have been profoundly changed by
writing. Their work does not make their pain disappear, but they say
they have a different relationship to it. As the poet Audre Lorde once
said to me, "You'll always *have* the pain, so you may as well *use* it."

Over the years, in my classes, Barbara grappled with the aftermath
of having had three abortions, something that she avoided thinking or
writing about for a long time. Eric began to examine his adult-onset
blindness and his father's difficult death from cancer. Maria wrote of
her battle against anorexia, bulimia, and drug use. James for the first
time explored what it was like to grow up with the violence of his father's alcoholic rages. Genevra examined her complex feelings about
her mother's devotion to a murderous, violent, and drug-abusing
uncle. Trina has written of the anguish of leaving her aging grandmother in the urban war zone of Caracas, Venezuela, to come to the
United States to study dance.

If I took one photograph on the first day of class and another on
the last and showed you, you, too, could *see* the difference. By the end
of their work, these beginning writers look better, they feel better.
They stand taller, they inhabit their bodies in a more comfortable way,
their voices are stronger, they smile more, they seem more serene.
They're physically healthier, too. And they will tell you, should you ask
them, that though their work has entailed living with and through
painful, often troubling, feelings, they *are* much better.

Here's how Trina phrased it in a letter she wrote after class ended.
"I don't feel like I'm the same person I was. Now, I own my life, my
story, because I know what it means. I feel more deeply—the pain, but
the pleasure, too. Writing about my grandmother gave me something I

lost. Though, surely, it can't replace losing her. But now my missing her seems bearable."

What I've learned through the past twenty years, through reflecting on my experience as a writer, through the lives of the writers I've studied, and through my students, is that the writing I describe in this book can be a very powerful way of healing. I've learned how, for example, Virginia Woolf, Djuna Barnes, and Henry Miller wrote their way out of suicidal or homicidal episodes. How they transformed their traumatic past into works of art. How the wisdom of these works of art benefited others.

Why Write?

Writing is cheap. You don't need special equipment to begin. Only some paper and a pen. Henry Miller often "borrowed" butcher paper to work on; Vladimir Nabokov used notecards; Jack Kerouac, little notebooks.

Writing doesn't need to take much time. Though we can take as long as we choose (or as we have), we can write for, say, only twenty minutes or so every day or whenever we can, and we can continue to reap the benefits of writing while we keep at it fairly frequently.

We can write during tiny pockets of time throughout our day, if that's all we have. Audre Lorde often scribbled away at her poems while waiting in supermarket checkout lines. Nobel laureate Toni Morrison, when she started, wrote stretched out on her sofa, "around the edges of the day," while working full-time to support a family as a single parent. (Once, her son came over to her and tried to get her attention by tugging on her ear while she was in the middle of an extremely important sentence. He vomited on the paper. But she was so involved she wrote around it, knowing that she could clean up later but that she might never get that particular sentence back.) I have written diary and works in progress while waiting for appointments and while stopped in traffic. My students write while waiting for class to start, during an idle moment at work, or on the subway while commuting.

Writing is self-initiated; writing is flexible. We can write when we can. We can write when we choose. We can write when we write best. My friend, the poet Maria Terrone, because she works full-time, writes propped up in bed very late at night or on weekends. Virginia Woolf wrote mornings, from ten to one. ("She wrote all those books working only three hours a day!" a student once marveled. "Yes," I replied, "and she took an 'official' month-long holiday, which nourished her, each year.") George Sand and Marcel Proust wrote in the middle of the night. I write three hours a day, during whatever hours I can manage. The prolific poet and novelist Joyce Carol Oates seems to write, always. ("Why aren't you writing?" she once admonished Gay Talese, while they were waiting together for an airplane. "You're wasting time.")

Writing is private, or you can share it. We can keep our writing to ourselves, as Virginia Woolf did when she kept her work in a locked diary when she was fifteen. As I keep my diaries private, though I draw upon them in my work. Or we can find a writing partner and share our work, as Henry Miller did with Anaïs Nin, as I do with Edvige Giunta. Eventually, you might consider sharing it, since sharing seems to confer benefits that keeping our writing private doesn't, though there are also risks in going public with our stories—ones that the writer Nancy Venable Raine addresses in *After Silence,* a memoir about her rape. But Raine writes, too, about the necessity of going public and of perhaps making people's negative responses to our work (they told her rape wasn't an agreeable topic) part of our story.

Writing is portable. It can be done practically anywhere. My student Leslie writes, balancing her notebook on her backpack, on her hour-long commute into New York City. Another student, Paul, writes outside, even in winter. Many years ago, in my backyard on a sultry summer afternoon, I wrote at my first book while my two babies splashed away in a tiny plastic wading pool. (The water marks on those sheets stand as reminders.) And there was Henry Miller, at his favorite café, the Dome, in Paris, or working, hunched over a borrowed typewriter in a borrowed apartment in Paris, surrounded by the noisy revelry of his friends having a drunken party. Ernest Hemingway at the Closerie de Lilas. D. H. Lawrence, propped against a granite boulder in Cornwall, scribbling *Women in Love* into a little notebook. Djuna Barnes, dressed in her most glamorous nightgown, writing *Nightwood* in bed in a lavishly decorated bedroom at her friend Peggy Guggenheim's house on the edge of Dartmoor in England. George Sand, at her desk in Nohant in the middle of the night, her lovemaking finished for the day, munching on the expensive chocolates she ordered from Paris to keep herself awake, and writing.

Writing can be done whether we're well or ill. Marcel Proust wrote all million and a quarter words of *Remembrance of Things Past* in bed, while he was seriously asthmatic. Alice James, in the days before her death from cancer, continued to fashion sentences for her diary. Harold Brodkey reflected on his life as he was dying of AIDS. Elizabeth Bishop wrote a poem about breathing while she was having an asthma attack. Flannery O'Connor wrote some of the best stories of her career as she was dying from lupus. New Zealand writer Janet Frame wrote prizewinning work while institutionalized.

Writing to heal requires no innate talent, though we become more skilled as we write, especially when we pay careful attention to the process of our writing. Every published writer was once a beginner. Even seasoned writers, facing a new project, must start anew, begin again. The writer Eudora Welty once remarked, "Each story teaches me how to write *it* but not the one after it." My beginning writers at Hunter College, where I teach—"baby writers" I call them—write important meaningful work from the start. And the writing I suggest here we all can manage. Learning something about the writing process, and learning to witness our writing practice (as I describe in part 2), enables us to use writing in a deeper way.

WHAT YOU CAN DO NOW Start writing.

Write by hand. In a beautiful notebook you buy expressly for this purpose or make for yourself, or on whatever you have handy. Notecards, say.

Or write on a typewriter or on a computer—but print what you write so you can touch it, see it, read it.

Write for about twenty minutes a day. But write more if you want, or less. Try not to censor yourself. But if you're not ready to write about something, don't, yet; you will when you're ready.

Write what you need to write or want to write. Or write what you don't want to write.

Write what troubles you or what delights you. Can you link these feelings to events in your life? Write what you see, smell, taste, touch.

Write quickly if you choose, or write slowly and deliberately.

Write in long elegant sentences with lots of commas and semicolons (like William Faulkner). Or in short, choppy sentences (like Ernest Hemingway). However you write is fine.

Write without knowing what will be next. Write to surprise yourself. Or write and ponder and write and ponder some more.

Write outside or inside. Write leaning against a rock, a pad on your knees, or write at the kitchen table late at night after a long day's work.

Write in the morning or in the afternoon or in the middle of the night. Write when you're feeling rested or when you're exhausted after a long day's work.

Write when you're sick or when you're well. When all's serene or when it's chaotic.

Write lying on a sofa or propped up in bed or in the bathtub. Write in a library or on a subway or a bus or in a car sitting in traffic (like Isabel Allende did when writing her story "Two Words").

Save everything you write in a safe place. Read it, or don't. At first, it's probably best not to show your writing to anyone. Writing only for yourself will let you write more freely.

Chapter Two

How Writing Can Help Us Heal

The Health and Emotional Benefits of Writing

I became a writer out of desperation. . . .
When I was young, younger than I am now,
I started to write about my own life and I
came to see that this act saved my life.

JAMAICA KINCAID, *My Brother*

While my mother was dying, I walked into a bookstore to look for something to read as I sat next to her on my daily visits. Reading made the time pass. Reading made the time easier. I wanted to find something that would help me handle my complicated feelings.

During this difficult time, I had been writing in my journal to help ease the pain. I free-wrote whatever came to mind. Some days I described my writing (I was working on a novel). Or I wrote about daily events—meals made, friends seen, special moments or arguments with my sons, books read, my trip to the hospital. Other days I wrote about my feelings. Poured out my sorrow (about my mother's illness), anger (that my mother was dying), grief (over my mother's loss and over my feeling that, because of her depression, I'd never really had a mother). Though I felt compelled to recount troubling events from my childhood, I deliberately avoided revisiting my past in any detailed way in the pages of my journal. To do so, I thought, would make me feel worse, would bring unbearable pain.

I didn't yet know that though I was journal-writing to try to help myself during this difficult time, my writing—just describing what I was doing or thinking or dumping my feelings onto the page—wasn't helping me. It was probably even making me feel worse. I wrote in my journal that I was depressed. I wrote, too, that "I don't want to write about it." Beyond this, I said little about my current feelings. (Writing "I am depressed" was as good as saying nothing about how I was feeling, about what I needed to say if I was to stop being depressed. Depression, I have recently come to believe, is a complex story that hasn't yet been told.)

I had been reading D. H. Lawrence's letters and several biographies about him. I learned how Lawrence wrote poems about his mother as he sat by her bedside while she was dying. He also began drafting an early version of *Sons and Lovers,* his novel exploring their complicated, loving, but painful, all-too-close relationship. This suggested that I, too, could begin writing about my mother, that I could draft some scenes from my childhood with her now, as I wanted to.

A line in one of Lawrence's letters captured my attention. "One sheds one's sicknesses in books—repeats and presents again one's emotions, to be master of them." Lawrence was saying that you could *use* your difficulties in your work and master your emotions if you represented them in your writing. "Representing," of course, means "describing." But it also means "re-presenting"—presenting scenes from the past as if they were presently occurring. This would undo, remedy, or rectify the effects of early experiences.

I was still, however, using my writing to fight the feelings I was having, to try to make them go away rather than representing them. I wasn't letting myself feel them deeply, explore them, understand them, learn their source, and link them to past and present events in my life. I was evading the narrative and emotional truth of my life. So my journal wasn't helping me understand and integrate my feelings during this complex time. I was stopping myself from writing my own life story. I feared I would find it unbearable.

As I searched the bookstore for works on grieving, on death and dying, I spotted James W. Pennebaker's *Opening Up: The Healing Power of Confiding in Others.* On impulse, I bought it. And I was grateful. For I found this book exactly when I needed it—both for my life and for my work.

As I sat next to my mother, I read Pennebaker. He described a special kind of writing I could use to deal with painful life experiences—with loss, death, abuse, depression, and trauma. I began to use it immediately in my journal writing, in the sketches I started penning of my early life. Later, I used what I learned, too, as I wrote my memoirs, *Vertigo* and *Breathless,* and all my subsequent work.

Learning to open up about everything in my past in the healing way Pennebaker described didn't happen all at once. Slowly, surely, though, I made important changes in how I wrote, in what I wrote, and, perhaps even more important, in how and what I felt as I wrote.

Opening Up summarizes ten years of scientific research into the connection between opening up about deeply troubling, emotionally difficult, or extremely traumatic events and positive changes in brain and immune function; it remains the best layperson's introduction to this research. (See the note at the end of this chapter for other sources.) Pennebaker's work on the relationship between suppressing our stories and illness, on the one hand, and telling our stories and increased health, on the other is well respected and pathbreaking in the field of psychology although not widely known by writers and would-be writers. In carefully controlled experiments, done while he was professor of psychology at Southern Methodist University in Dallas, Texas, Pennebaker and his associates made the extremely important discovery that "writing can be an avenue to that interior place where . . . we can confront traumas and put them to rest—and heal both body and mind." Writing, then, seems to improve physical and mental health. But not just any kind of writing. Only a certain kind of writing will help us heal.

The Health and Emotional Benefits of Opening Up Through Writing

Pennebaker and his associate, Sandra Beall, tested the relationship between writing and wellness in the students they studied. All students were told to write in a journal for about fifteen minutes a day over a four-day period.

The first group was instructed to write about a trivial topic—a description of their living room, say.

The second group was instructed to write about their traumatic experiences. But they were subdivided into three groups to test three different ways of writing about trauma: (1) just venting emotions; (2) just writing what happened; (3) writing about events and emotions at the same time.

Those students writing about events *and* emotions about a trauma were told to "write continuously about the most upsetting or traumatic experience of your entire life," something that "has affected you very deeply." Ideally, it should be about something that the students hadn't talked about with others in any great detail. Students were told not to worry about "grammar, spelling, or sentence structure." But it was "critical" that "you let yourself go and touch those deepest emotions and thoughts that you have. In other words, write about what happened and how you felt about it then, and how you feel about it now."

Pennebaker and Beall learned that most students in this group reported they *had* experienced significant trauma in their lives; undisclosed trauma is not uncommon. When students' experiences in writing about events *and* feelings were evaluated—by taking students' blood pressure, reading their journal entries, studying follow-up questionnaires about their entries and their emotions—Pennebaker and Beall discovered that the impact of writing about trauma was "far more powerful" than they had predicted.

Students wrote quickly and at length. Many students "cried as they wrote." Many reported "dreaming about their writing" over the four days of the study. Many revealed "intimate feelings" they hadn't before shared.

Many depicted "profound human tragedies"—some that hadn't before been revealed. One student remembered the "hot summer night" his father took him into their backyard to tell his nine-year-old son that he was divorcing the boy's mother because "things haven't been the same since you and your sister were born." Another wrote of how, at ten, she hadn't picked up her toys when told to do so by her mother and how her grandmother had fallen, broken a hip, and died a week later during surgery. A third wrote of her complex feelings of being sexually abused by her grandfather when she was a teenager and of the "terrible conflict" she faced, for she felt physical pleasure and intense love for him, yet betrayal and violation. Other students wrote of the death of a family member or friend, interpersonal and family conflicts and family abuse, being gay, alcoholism, suicide attempts, illness or injury, anger at parents' divorces, public humiliations. Many reported feeling saddened, troubled, and dismayed by their writing.

Pennebaker and Beall were initially discouraged that the writing had stirred such negative feelings in these students, especially because students in the other groups (those who wrote about trivial subjects or who wrote only about emotions or events) initially felt more positive about their writing. They were concerned that the students linking events and feelings about trauma didn't immediately feel better, as they had anticipated. (Students, though, were reporting *appropriately* difficult feelings about the traumas they were describing; there is nothing wrong with having difficult feelings about something bad you've experienced.)

Four months later, though, the students writing about events and feelings reported that their spirits had improved significantly—that their writing had helped them resolve a difficult issue. "Writing about their deepest thoughts . . . resulted in a more positive outlook."

The important discovery Pennebaker and Beall had made, then, was that *to significantly improve your spirits long-term, you must endure difficult feelings initially.*

Six months after the experiment, Pennebaker and Beall studied the health of these students by counting visits made to the student health service before and after the writing days.

Before writing, all students visited the health center at the same rate. After writing, visits by students who wrote about superficial topics or *only* about their emotions or *only* about traumatic events (without describing feelings) were roughly the same. But after writing, visits by students who wrote about both what happened and how they felt about it dropped by 50 percent.

Pennebaker and Beall reached their landmark conclusion (later replicated by other investigators and confirmed in more sophisticated follow-up studies) that simply writing about trivial topics or only venting one's feelings about trauma or only describing traumas isn't sufficient to improve health. *To improve health, we must write detailed accounts, linking feelings with events.* The more writing succeeds as narrative—by being detailed, organized, compelling, vivid, lucid—the more health and emotional benefits are derived from writing.

Through writing, these students had achieved a cathartic discharge of complex, pent-up feelings. But, too, they had reflected upon the significance of these events, attaining insight into their traumas and achieving some distance from them. Through writing about events *and* feelings, students integrated the two; they understood what had occurred and what they felt about it, and they assimilated the meaning of this event into their lives, thereby diffusing its power over them.

One student wrote, "Although I have not talked with anyone about what I wrote, I was finally able to deal with it and work through the pain instead of trying to block it out. Now it doesn't hurt to think about it." Another: "I had to think and resolve past experiences. . . . One result of the experiment is peace of mind, and a method to relieve emotional experiences. To have to write emotions and feelings helped me understand how I felt and why."

Another, later study ("Confession, Inhibition, and Disease") examined brain wave activity in people confronting traumas. Pennebaker discovered that for students who explored feelings about traumatic events as they wrote, there was a congruence in brain wave activity between the left and right hemispheres, indicating that both emotional and linguistic information was being processed and integrated simultaneously. This, then, in terms of brain function, is what achieving "integration" means.

Other experiments established that people who linked traumatic events and feelings in this way had "T Lymphocytes [that] were more 'energetic' than the control group." Their bodies, then, were more able to fight infection (having greater antibody response to Epstein-Barr virus and hepatitis-B vaccination, for which they were tested) than before writing. Their heart rates lowered. Other tests showed, too, that they were in a more relaxed physiological state.

The act of linking feelings with troubling events, then, makes our bodies display responses associated with yoga and meditation. This explains why writers who stop work soon feel out of sorts—why they become edgy, irritable, anxious, even depressed. This explains, too, why people who begin writing report feeling a greater sense of well-being— why they become calmer, more capable of coping with stress, more serene, even when facing life's challenges, than they'd been before.

Writing thoughtfully and emotionally about traumatic experiences, rather than writing about superficial topics or venting feelings or simply describing what happens, seems to improve our immune system. And this improvement, in Pennebaker's subjects, tended to last for six weeks.

Further experiments with other groups of students and people in distress (people laid off from jobs; people whose spouses had died tragically; people with illnesses) showed that substantial behavioral changes are also associated with this kind of writing. Students' grades improve. People get new jobs more quickly. People are absent from work less. Grieving people are healthier. Sick people are somewhat healthier; if they are terminally ill, they seem, nonetheless, to be in a state of emotional and spiritual healing—more accepting, secure, serene.

Pennebaker and his associates had tested the theory that *repressing* thoughts and feelings about traumatic or distressing events might be linked to illness and that *expressing* thoughts and feelings through writing about traumatic or distressing events might prompt significant improvements in health.

Over time, Pennebaker explains, the work of inhibiting traumatic narratives and feelings acts as an ongoing stressor and gradually undermines the body's defenses. Like other significant stressors, inhibiting our stories and our emotions can adversely affect immune function— "the action of the heart and vascular systems, and even the biochemical workings of the brain and nervous systems."

Many researchers have observed that survivors of childhood sexual abuse and other traumas (like rape) or the suicide or accidental deaths of people close to them, if they do not discuss these events, tend to develop more major illnesses than people who do express their feelings. Often, though, the trauma remains undisclosed because, though people would like to discuss it, they can't or won't because they fear punishment, embarrassment, or disapproval or because they can't find an appropriate audience. So, many people actively stop themselves from telling their stories; they inhibit their need to tell their traumatic narratives. This, though, "deplete[s] immune functioning, and increase[s] incidence of physical illness."

Confronting the chaos of our most difficult memories and feelings, though, and translating them into coherent language can have "remarkable short- and long-term health benefits." For when we deal with unassimilated events, when we tell our stories and describe our feelings and integrate them into our sense of self, we no longer must actively work at inhibition. This alleviates the stress of holding back our stories and repressing or hiding our emotions, and so our health improves.

What Kind of Writing Helps Us Heal?

Writing that describes traumatic or distressing events in detail *and* how we felt about these events then and feel about them now is the only kind of writing about trauma that clinically has been associated with improved health. Simply writing about innocuous subjects (like what we did throughout our day) or simply writing about traumatic events or venting our feelings about trauma without *linking* the two does not result in significant health or emotional benefits. In fact, in one experiment, it was found that simply venting feelings might have made the writers somewhat sicker.

In other words, we can't improve our health by free-writing (as I had been using my journal) or by writing objective descriptions of our traumas or by venting our emotions. We cannot simply use writing as catharsis. Nor can we use it only as a record of what we've experienced. *We must write in a way that links detailed descriptions of what happened with feelings—then and now—about what happened.*

Both thinking and feeling are involved. Linking them is critical. Feelings about the traumatic event in the past and the present are expressed and, perhaps, compared so that the writer unravels how the past impinges on the present but how, too, it's different.

In controlled clinical experiments, then, only writing that describes *traumatic events and our deepest thoughts and feelings about them, past and present, is linked with improved immune function, improved emotional and physical health, and behavioral changes indicating that we feel able to act on our own behalf.* And this was accomplished in the experiments by only one hour of writing—fifteen minutes a day—over a four-day period!

Later studies showed that the more days people wrote, the more beneficial were the effects from writing. And these benefits occurred despite educational level: people with sixth-grade educations benefited as much as those with advanced degrees. "Sickly" people benefited more perhaps than "well" people. Women benefited more perhaps than men. And the positive effects of writing did not depend upon getting any feedback on the writing or even upon anyone reading what was written.

If the positive effects of writing over four days lasted for six weeks, and the benefits of writing for longer periods lasted longer, then it seems evident (though Pennebaker never makes this connection) that engaging in an ongoing writing program—even a simple one—can provide ongoing health and emotional benefits.

Guidelines for Confronting Trauma in Writing

Soon after reading Pennebaker, I wrote some guidelines, derived from *Opening Up,* that I copied onto an index card and used as a place marker in my diary. I still use them to remind me how to write in a healing way.

Do's

1. Write twenty minutes a day over a period of four days. Do this periodically. This way you won't feel overwhelmed.
2. Write in a private, safe, comfortable environment.
3. Write about issues you're currently living with, something you're thinking or dreaming about constantly, a trauma you've never disclosed or discussed or resolved.
4. Write about joys and pleasures, too.
5. Write about what happened. Write, too, about feelings about what happened. What do you feel? Why do you feel this way? Link events with feelings.
6. Try to write an extremely detailed, organized, coherent, vivid, emotionally compelling narrative. Don't worry about correctness, about grammar or punctuation.

7. Beneficial effects will occur even if no one reads your writing. If you choose to keep your writing and not discard it, you must safeguard it.
8. Expect, initially, that in writing in this way you will have complex and appropriately difficult feelings. Make sure you get support if you need it.

On the other side of my notecard, I wrote a set of warnings I'd gleaned from Pennebaker:

Don'ts

1. Don't use writing as a substitute for taking action.
2. Don't become overly intellectual.
3. Don't use writing as a way of complaining. Use it, instead, to discover how and why you feel as you do. Simply complaining or venting will probably make you feel worse.
4. Don't use your writing to become overly self-absorbed. Over-analyzing everything is counterproductive.
5. Don't use writing as a substitute for therapy or medical care.

Beginning to Write in a Healing Way

Since reading Pennebaker, I have applied what I learned about confronting my early traumas and my present difficulties. I had feared that writing about what had happened to me as a child, and my feelings about it, would make me feel worse. I had feared that examining present problems would intensify my negative feeling. I learned, though, that writing about traumatic or difficult or complex events *and* feelings as described here helped me immeasurably. In my lifelong project of using my writing to unravel the meaning and the feelings about my past, I have revisited my past one moment at a time. Doing so has recast the meaning and significance of my life, has helped me heal.

WHAT YOU CAN DO NOW Try enacting the writing plan outlined here. Remember to link events with feelings; to write in a detailed way; to tell a complex story; to describe feelings in the past and in the present.

Do this on four or more successive days. Remember that, like Pennebaker's subjects, you might have some difficult feelings. Make sure you have someone with whom to discuss them, if necessary. You can write, too, about the feelings raised by your writing.

Initially, it's probably best not to share your work or to reread it.

Note: James W. Pennebaker's *Opening Up* was originally published in 1990 by William Morrow and was intended for the general reader. His prior works included *The Psychology of Physical Symptoms* and *Mass Psychogenic Illness.* The specialized books and scores of articles that Pennebaker used to write *Opening Up* (many of which I've subsequently read, some of which are in my Sources and Further Reading) are listed in his "Notes" to the volume. *Opening Up* remains the best general and most readable introduction to this research. Pennebaker's study linking left- and right-brain wave activity is "Confession, Inhibition, and Disease."

After the publication of *Opening Up,* many major periodicals reported on the significance of Pennebaker's findings. Articles appeared in *American Health, Omni, Psychology Today, The New York Times, Prevention.* A subsequent excellent rethinking of the issues in *Opening Up* can be found in Kent D. Harber and James W. Pennebaker, "Overcoming Traumatic Memories," in *The Handbook of Emotion and Memory: Research and Theory,* ed. S. E. Christianson (Hillsdale, NJ: Lawrence Erlbaum, 1992).

Dr. Edward J. Murray, professor of psychology at the University of Miami, in a March 7, 1991, *New York Times* article said that though he initially questioned Pennebaker's findings, his own follow-up work showed that "writing seems to produce as much therapeutic benefit as sessions with a psychotherapist."

Chapter Three

Writing as a Therapeutic Process

How Writers See It

Two or three things I know, two or three things I know for sure, and one of them is that to go on living I have to tell stories, that stories are the one sure way I know to touch the heart and change the world.

DOROTHY ALLISON,
Two or Three Things I Know for Sure

Give sorrow words. . . .

WILLIAM SHAKESPEARE

When I was in high school (a million years ago, as my son Justin always informs me), we used a literature textbook remarkable not so much for what it contained, but for what it didn't. In its five hundred pages, there was no photo, no realistic portrait, to suggest that the works we read had been written by living, breathing, feeling, thinking writers. There was nothing to indicate that "real" writers often wrote to heal their emotional wounds and that I, too, could write to help myself in this way.

The most human representation of the writer that we saw was the familiar etching of William Shakespeare that had originally graced the title page of the first folio. I remember myself at fifteen, staring at it, trying to penetrate the mystery of how that frozen being could have penned works of majestic power, of longing and yearning. I wanted to know what his life had been like and what had happened to him that needed to be expressed, so I embarked on a long, self-initiated research project to learn whatever I could about his life. It wasn't much.

Still, audacious as it seems, I identified with Shakespeare, and with other writers, too. I wanted to scribble impassioned sonnets about how you could never truly possess someone you loved, about the effects of the passage of time, about how our desires are often thwarted by circumstances beyond our control. I wanted to record in my black-and-white speckled notebook my reflections about love lost and love found. I wanted to write about how much I hated my father, how much I resented taking care of my sister, how my grandmother and mother were always fighting, how my mother was often depressed. I wanted to write memories of Hoboken, the place we'd moved from, the only place I'd felt at home. I wanted to write how I thought the suburb of Ridgefield, New Jersey, was the most boring place on earth.

But I never got past filling the first several pages. For what I wrote seemed awful, nothing like the perfect essays and stories we were reading in school. True, I'd won an award for my writing in grammar school for an essay called "Safety in the Home, Street, and School." But that writing was different. It wasn't about my personal life. It wasn't about "the real me," as I liked to call the person I believed was my essential self.

The truth was that I didn't believe a person as ordinary as I was could ever write anything of significance—even anything that could be personally useful, that might enrich my being. But I had a *need* to write. It grew from my pain in living in a difficult household, my sense of difference, my internal, perpetual gloom from the events of my childhood, which couldn't be driven away no matter how hard I tried.

Had I known that famous writers often started their work out of the same sense of desperation, grief, loss, and longing that I felt, I might have permitted myself to begin writing. And to continue writing. And my days might have been more vivid, less cloudy.

Secretly, though, I hoped that someday, by some miracle, I might become a writer. I prayed to become a writer in the same way that I prayed to have big breasts. I hoped that I'd wake up on my sixteenth birthday with both wishes fulfilled.

I had no model, though, for what the act of writing was like. In school we were given writing assignments to do at home, which the teacher marked (one grade for content; another for grammar and style). But there was no talk of the "writing process"; no instruction in the creative stages of bringing a long work to fruition; no discussion about how writers used their work to explore traumatic events. As with so much else, we were on our own.

I didn't know that if you want to write, you must follow your desire to write. And that your writing will help you unravel the knots in your heart. I didn't know that you could write simply to take care of yourself, even if you have no desire to publish your work. I didn't know that if you want to become a writer, eventually you'll learn through writing— and only through writing—all you need to know about your craft. And that while you're learning, you're engaging in soul-satisfying, deeply nurturing labor. I didn't know that if you want to write and don't, because you don't feel worthy enough or able enough, not writing will eventually begin to erase who you are.

I didn't know that the writers whose works we read harbored hopes and dreams like mine when they were young but that they acted on their desires, whereas I wasn't acting on mine. I didn't know that they kept writing notebooks as children and as adolescents; that their youthful attempts at keeping journals, at constructing essays, poems, and stories, were as flowery or pompous or inept or as full of promise as my few aborted attempts. And so my need to use writing as a process of self-discovery, self-enrichment, and self-healing was derailed for twenty years.

Telling the Story That Must Be Told

The writer Nancy Mairs, who grew up when I did, had the same experience, the same feelings. In a diary she kept in 1958, she wrote, "I want so desperately to express myself. I can't stand this suppression. I want to write, to act, to sing, anything. I can't. I can't." In 1959 she wrote, "I am so empty, so hungering. I know that deep within me lies something but I see it in comparison with the talents of others & it is so pitifully small."

Mairs believes repressing her desire to write exacerbated the suicidal depression that she survived as a grown woman and that, eventually, writing helped her understand. I, too, now believe that the way out of depression lies in finding the story that hasn't been told, that must be told, and in exploring the feelings that narrative engenders—in writing it down.

Like so many young people, neither Mairs nor I was encouraged to follow our desires to write. There are few parents like the New Zealand writer Janet Frame's mother, who ask their children for poems, or like Virginia Woolf's mother, who encourage their children to publish a family newspaper. Often, when I wrote as a child, I was interrupted, told to "get busy," do my homework, help with the dishes, play Monopoly with my sister. I didn't know that for all writers there is an apprenticeship period and that the sooner we begin, the better. Virginia Woolf started taking herself seriously as a writer when she was fifteen, though other writers, like Harriet Doerr, author of the novel *Stones for Ibarra,* or like the poet Amy Clampitt, didn't begin writing or publishing until they were elders.

If we commit ourselves to engaging in the process of writing, our work will evolve and mature. Becoming competent takes time, and we all have within ourselves the capacity to do it. Yet instead of being helped to achieve this healing insight, I was taught that, in the words of one of my English teachers, when it comes to being a writer, "you either have it or you don't."

This simply isn't so.

Works of literature were created, I was told, because the writers wanted to make objects of beauty, not because they needed to understand life's difficult, perplexing, or traumatic moments. Art for art's sake, I thought, not art for the sake of life. As a young woman, I didn't have the opportunity to learn what I needed to know: that famous writers had written the stories they needed to tell in order to help themselves heal from the traumatic events in their lives. And that I, too, could help myself immeasurably by writing about my pain.

Honoring the Desire to Write

What aspiring writers need to begin and continue writing is unconditional acceptance of their *desire* to write. And they need to honor that desire. Aspiring writers must understand that if you want to write for an audience, learning to write, just like learning anything else, takes time and that we must be realistic and patient with ourselves while we're learning. Meantime, the very act of writing will dispense its curative benefits. Neither Nancy Mairs nor I was taught this when we were young, hopeful writers.

A Few Words About Thwarted Desire

Desire. If we have always wanted to write—something, anything—and if we haven't, our desire won't disappear. Our need won't dissipate. Our stories won't go away. Our traumas won't heal themselves.

Each time we think about our unenacted desire, we will feel thwarted, diminished, unfinished, incomplete. Repressing our stories can harm us, as Nancy Mairs's experience proves.

As a girl, my mother wanted to become a writer, but she never realized her desire. I don't know much about her early life. But I think what she needed to explore was the profound impact of her mother's death from influenza, the near-lethal abuse and neglect of her caregivers, the damaging effect of a life lived in extreme poverty with a father whose railway work took him away for long periods, and the hatred of her stepmother. Not writing about this negatively affected her, I'm sure, for she had no outlet for her complex emotions.

Though she wanted to write, it was the thirties, and money was scarce, and her income from selling shoes was needed by her family. She couldn't use the scholarship she was awarded to go to college.

Throughout my youth, my mother let me examine the medal, engraved with her name, that she had been awarded for her writing in high school. She wore it on the lapel of her Sunday suit throughout her life. Seeing it made me sad. It became the image of what my mother wanted but didn't pursue. Though she was the best writer in her class, the only writing she managed in adulthood were exquisitely phrased, weekly letters to my children while they were in college. She wrote about how everyone in the family was doing; she even wrote about our animals. She never wrote about herself.

"I've *always* wanted to write a novel; I'll get around to doing it one of these days," a man I know often told me. Once, exasperated—for by now he was in his fifties, with a heart condition, and he had been complaining for fifteen years about how unfulfilled he felt—I told him, "Look, you must think you're immortal. You're acting like you're going to live forever. You're not getting any younger. If you want to write, you better start today or your time might run out."

And he did. Writing reinvigorated his life, for he began to liberate the stories he'd held captive within him—about his longing for fatherly love, about his orphanhood and his lifelong sense of isolation, loneliness, and unworthiness. He started traveling to the remote Australian locations he wanted to use in his work, studying the habitats of wildlife, trekking in the wilderness, making new friends, sharing his newfound passions with his wife.

Writing as Symbolic Repair

In *Creativity as Repair*, Andrew Brink has observed that the impulse to create usually comes from some early damage to the self. Doubt, pain, trauma, insecurity, uncertainty—these feelings are the fuel that drive the creative process. This wound or loss initiates a life's work of healing, "of trying to make right what early went wrong." Writing, then, uses language to repair psychic wounds.

David Aberbach, in *Surviving Trauma: Loss, Literature, and Psychoanalysis,* says something similar. Creativity, he has discovered, more often than not is spurred by painful loss and unresolved or thwarted grief. In his study of the writing done by survivors of the Holocaust and of post-traumatic stress disorder, Aberbach has found that writing is a significant way "to . . . master trauma in all its horror and overcome it" and "to complete the work of mourning." Trauma and loss are both the subject of the writing and the motive behind doing the work.

Recently, I've read many literary works that, according to their writers, were written expressly so that their authors could heal from a psychic wound. In her memoir, *Two or Three Things I Know For Sure,* Dorothy Allison describes how her writing *Bastard Out of Carolina* evolved from her need to tell the story of how she was raped by her stepfather when she was five years old. "When I began," she wrote, "there was only the suspicion that making up the story as you went along was the way to survive." Junot Díaz, author of *Drown,* a montage of stories set in Santo Domingo's Barrio XXI and in London Terrace near Perth Amboy, New Jersey, has said in an interview that he wrote to overcome the losses he incurred by living through colonialism, emigration, and poverty and his grief at his brother Rafa's illness. Díaz began by "scribbling long letters to Rafa" when he was hospitalized. In his memoir, *Imagining Robert: My Brother, Madness, and Survival,* Jay Neugeboren relates how writing helped him manage his feelings about his brother's mental illness by helping him bring order to his chaotic experience; he eulogized, too, the brother that illness had robbed from him. In *My Dark Places: An L. A. Crime Memoir,* James Ellroy says he became a writer because his mother was murdered, an event that left him obsessed with crime and crime novels; by writing, he tried to discover what happened to her and to deal with his often self-destructive grief and rage. In Renée Roth-Hano's autobiographical novel *Touch Wood: A Girlhood in Occupied France,* the author describes how the magnitude of her losses propelled her to write about her pain as a survivor of the extermination campaign of the Nazis; about her life as a hidden child in a convent in Normandy during the Nazi occupation of France; about her separation from her parents, terror of discovery, and grief almost beyond words at losing the eighty-nine people she knew who were killed by the Nazis and also at the loss of her father, who died shortly after the war.

Writing from Grief

In Isabel Allende's *Paula* (a memoir about her daughter's terminal illness and death), Allende describes how she began writing *House of the Spirits,* the novel that catapulted her to fame. Not meant to be a work of fiction, intended for publication, the book was written more personally, because of her profound grief.

She started it as a letter to her grandfather when he was nearly one hundred. He was dying in Chile in the Santiago mansion where the novel is set. Allende was raised there but couldn't return to keep her promise to attend him, for she was in exile in Venezuela after the murder of her uncle, the former Chilean president Salvador Allende.

Until she began this "letter" to her grandfather, Allende didn't believe she could be a writer. For she had been trained to think women weren't supposed to be creative. But after learning of his impending death, she needed "to say good-bye" in writing.

He had been a "conservative, a patriarch, a very violent person," but she "loved him dearly." Allende wanted to assure him that his history wouldn't be obliterated. She would record the stories he'd told her. The first, which begins *House of the Spirits,* was "an anecdote about my great-aunt Rosa, my grandfather's first sweetheart, a young girl of almost supernatural beauty who had died in mysterious circumstances shortly before they were to marry."

As the stories poured out, Allende wrote as if in a trance. She felt she was "unwinding a ball of yarn."

That personal letter to her grandfather grew to a five-hundred-page manuscript that Allende carted in a canvas bag everywhere she went. Still, though, she couldn't admit she had begun a novel. That idea "seemed presumptuous."

Writing *House of the Spirits,* says Allende, "saved my life." She began her career for the purely private motive of expressing her grief, as a form of self-care. Through writing, she said, "the world became more tolerable. Living with myself was more tolerable too."

Writing to Give Form to Devastation

After Allende's daughter, Paula, lapsed into a coma, apparently because her treatment in a Spanish hospital during an attack of porphyria had been bungled, Allende rarely left her daughter's bedside. Carmen Balcells, her literary agent, sensing Allende's desperation and pain, arrived at the hospital one day, bearing gifts. Dozens of red roses. Nougats from Alicante. An "obscene-looking sausage." And, most important, "a ream of lined yellow paper," which Carmen deposited into Allende's lap.

"My poor Isabel," Balcells said. "Here, take this and write. Unburden your heart; if you don't you are going to die of anguish."

"I can't," Allende protested. She told Balcells that something inside her had "broken," that she felt she'd never write again.

But Balcells commanded Allende to "write a letter to Paula. It will help her know what happened while she was asleep." She told her to write instead of suffering wordlessly, insisting that her friend avail herself of the help that writing had offered her in the past. Balcells knew that without the release of words, Allende's health would be seriously compromised, that she was herself, literally, in mortal danger, for the chance of getting a serious illness in the wake of a family member's serious illness is very high.

And so Allende began writing a letter to her comatose daughter, Paula, to tell her about the life she was missing: "this is how I entertain myself in the empty moments of this nightmare."

"My soul is choking in sand. Sadness is a sterile desert," Allende wrote. "I plunge into these pages in an irrational attempt to overcome my terror. I think that perhaps if I give form to this devastation I shall be able to help you, and myself, and that the meticulous exercise of writing can be our salvation."

The personal letter Allende wrote to Paula soon grew into a more ambitious undertaking: to explain herself and her past and their family history of political oppression and exile to her daughter when she awakened. And to explain it, too, to herself. For although Allende had written of her past fictionally, she hadn't yet taken time to discover her feelings about past events in a way that would allow her to understand and integrate the terrible, ongoing losses she had sustained—of a country, of friends and family through political persecution, of landscape, of language, of cherished personal possessions.

Her daughter's illness impelled her to understand her life differently. "You, Paula," Allende writes, "have given me this silence in which to examine my path through the world, to return to the true and the fantastic pasts, to recover memories others have forgotten, to remember what never happened and what still may happen. Mute, paralyzed, you are my guide. . . . I spend my hours by your side, writing."

Allende describes her work as "therapy." Other people "go to a therapist . . . to talk about the world and about life and the pain of living. I do it through my writing." (Since Paula's death, though, Allende has begun therapy to help her with her loss.)

Before, Allende believed her past had "little meaning"; "I can see no order to it, no clarity, purpose or path, only a blind journey." After, though, Allende realized her life had been one of perpetual loss that began with the disappearance of her father after a sexual scandal—he was caught wearing women's clothes making love to a man—when she was three. She examines the end of her innocence—how, at age eight, being molested by a fisherman whom the next morning she found dead from a blow on the head had "left a scar" she never before understood.

But throughout her life, painful events had always been muted by the act of storytelling—first, her mother's compensatory stories of "an imaginary world where we were all happy," then, later, her own.

Though Allende could not save her daughter—she died a year later in Allende's arms—giving form to her pain allowed Allende to feel her despair, allowed her to connect it to the events in her life that occasioned it, even as it kept her despondency manageable.

"I had a choice," Allende says. "Was I going to commit suicide? . . . Or was I going to write a book that would heal me. . . . I went on writing because I could not stop. I could not let anger destroy me." So, through writing, Allende chose to live; through the act of writing, she began to integrate this and other traumatic experiences into her life. She believed, too, that there was a lesson in Paula's dying that she learned as she wrote: the virtues of "patience, courage, resignation, dignity in the face of death."

"To lose Chile and all of my past because of the military coup and being forced into exile pushed me to write *The House of the Spirits.*" Losing her political innocence, becoming aware of "the disappeared, the tortured, the dead, the brutal repression throughout Latin America, impelled me to write *Of Love and Shadows.*" And losing her daughter impelled Allende to write *Paula.* Writing, though, for Allende, "is a way of recovering what is lost." Though all Allende's writing comes from painful, deep, long-standing emotion, she says "the process of writing even if the theme is heavy is *wonderful.*"

Allende's work shows how creative writers use writing as a way of healing, of transforming despair into understanding and (in time) acceptance. It shows how writing that springs from intensely personal motives can be useful to others. For loss is a universal human experience, something we all must learn to deal with. Sharing our stories of loss, and accepting loss as a common feature of life, Allende says, helps us "enjoy the good moments all the more." As the novelist Amy Tan observed, Allende isn't "simply a story teller, she's a story giver."

Freedom. Autonomy. Power. Wisdom. Soulfulness. These words recur when writers speak of the effect of doing their work, of writing about the traumatic moments in their lives. As a writer like Isabel Allende shows us, we, too, can write to heal ourselves if our writing comes from a deep, authentic need. If we write about our pain, we heal gradually instead of feeling powerless and confused, and we move to a position of wisdom and power.

Writing as Self-Analysis

In Virginia Woolf's memoir, "A Sketch of the Past," there is an unequivocal statement about how her need to write came from the pain she'd experienced in childhood. By writing her autobiographical novel, *To the Lighthouse,* Woolf says, she "rubbed out" the impact of her father's violence by writing about it, and she quelled her mother's voice— the one telling her that the only proper role for women was to serve men—which formerly had obsessed her. Woolf believed that by writing "I did for myself what psychoanalysts do for their patients. I expressed some very long and deeply felt emotion. And in expressing it I explained it and then laid it to rest." The process wasn't simple or easy. It involved reexperiencing her past in a new way. But she *deliberately* used her writing as self-analysis to examine and integrate deeply felt yet unexpressed emotions linked to the troubling events of her past.

A Caveat

Many writers, like Woolf, describe their work as a form of analysis or therapy. And in the days before treatment was generally available, we know that many other writers used their work in this way. Many writers now also do their work without therapy or analysis; some fear that entering therapy might rob them of their creative drive. But although I, too, have found my work to be immensely beneficial and therapeutic, I personally believe it is essential for people wanting to write about extreme situations to have skilled professional support while writing or to attend a reputable support group.

In my writing groups, and with peers, I always strongly urge that while we're confronting trauma through our writing, we do it with the help of support and guidance. Some people I know have chosen to attend support groups like bereavement groups, Alcoholics Anonymous, incest survivor groups, or cancer survivor groups rather than enter therapy.

Some forms of therapy even employ writing. I have discovered in my own work that these processes are mutually beneficial; my work deepens because of my therapy; but my therapy progresses because of my work.

As David Aberbach has warned, writing, though it may be therapeutic, isn't therapy. But keep in mind as well that therapy isn't writing.

Why, then, should we write? Because writing permits the construction of a cohesive, elaborate, thoughtful personal narrative in the way that simply speaking about our experiences doesn't. Through writing, suffering can be transmuted into art. And writing permits us to use our writing as a form of public testimony in a way that the private act of therapy doesn't.

Finding Order Through Writing About Trauma

In her memoir, "A Sketch of the Past," Woolf used writing to heal. She started "without stopping to choose my way, in the sure and certain knowledge that it will find itself."

She began with some early memories: of sitting on her mother's lap; of "lying half asleep, half awake, in bed" in the nursery at Talland House, St. Ives, the family's country house in Cornwall.

But she soon found herself exploring some difficult feelings—what she called her "looking-glass shame," how looking in a mirror and seeing her reflection made her feel worthless. This feeling she traced to the looking glass in the hall at St. Ives and how, as a child, she was ashamed or afraid of her body, of seeing it in the mirror.

Through writing, she linked her feeling of shame with the memory of an important event that she was probably recalling for the first time —of how, at six or seven, she was sexually assaulted by her half-brother

Gerald Duckworth on the ledge in the same hall where the mirror hung and how she probably watched herself being violated in the mirror.

She describes how Gerald lifted her onto the ledge, and "as I sat there he began to explore my body. I can remember the feel of his hand going under my clothes; going firmly and steadily lower and lower. I remember how I hoped that he would stop; how I stiffened and wriggled as his hand approached my private parts. But it did not stop. His hand explored my private parts too." Recapturing what she felt then, she says she remembers "resenting, disliking" it. She felt, too, that "it is wrong to allow" parts of the body "to be touched," indicating she felt responsible for what happened and, perhaps, as a grown woman, still did.

In writing "A Sketch of the Past," Woolf wanted to recreate, in detail, the events of her childhood and to explore her feelings about these events. She had given herself precisely the task James W. Pennebaker gave his student subjects. She gave herself permission to remember, to feel, to articulate her recollections.

She wanted to explore what she felt now and what she *remembered* feeling. She wanted to link these feelings to events by taking herself back in time to specific "moments of being." Through describing them, she would discover the key to her development.

She wanted to discover the source of her difficult adult feelings and character traits: her hopelessness, despair, shame, depression, but also her creativity, resilience, strength, intellectual curiosity, integrity, and courage. What she discovered was that *through writing* she transformed the effects of harmful events into something meaningful.

Writing was Woolf's way of constructing reality, of redefining herself. She found the underlying patterns of life that hide behind appearances. This changed her view of the world from one of a chaotic place to one that was orderly though in need of change. "It is only by putting it into words that I make it whole," Woolf said. "This wholeness means that it has lost its power to hurt me; it gives me, perhaps because by doing so I take away the pain, a great delight to put the severed parts together. From this I reach what I might call a philosophy; . . . that we—I mean all human beings—are connected with this; that the whole world is a work of art; that we are parts of the work of art."

The Therapeutic Process of Examining Our Pain

The therapeutic process of writing goes something like this:

We receive a shock or a blow or experience a trauma in our lives. In exploring it, examining it, and putting it into words, we stop seeing it as a random, unexplained event. We begin to understand the order behind appearances.

Expressing it in language robs the event of its power to hurt us; it also assuages our pain. And by expressing ourselves in language, by examining these shocks, we paradoxically experience delight—pleasure, even—which comes from the discoveries we make as we write, from the order we create from seeming randomness or chaos.

Ultimately, then, writing about difficulties enables us to discover the wholeness of things, the connectedness of human experience. We understand that our greatest shocks do not separate us from humankind. Instead, through expressing ourselves, we establish our connection with others and with the world.

Writing and Psychic Growth

Henry Miller is as different a writer from Virginia Woolf as one can imagine. Yet in reading his work I learned that he conceived of his writing in similar terms.

The shock Miller responded to in his writing, which occurred in his adult life, was his wife June Miller's leaving him for a woman, their mutual friend, Jean Kronski. After June and Jean fled to Paris, Miller became seriously suicidal, for he believed he could never sustain the loss of June. He even wrote June a suicide letter.

But then one night, after he was finished with his work for the day at the Office of the Parks Commission, in Queens, New York, in a mood of "utter despair," he sat in front of a typewriter and, without knowing what he was doing, began to outline a work about their lives together and how June had betrayed him.

He would begin the work with the first time he saw her at a taxi-dancing hall in Times Square and he was immediately captivated by her beauty and sensuousness and he knew he would have to leave his wife for her. He would describe leaving his first wife, Beatrice, and their divorce and his guilt feelings about leaving his young daughter; his and June's abortive attempts to earn money; June's "gold digging" and whoring for him; Henry's early amateurish attempts at fiction; Jean's entrance into their lives; their drugged-out ménage à trois; and how Jean and June ran out on him.

Miller worked through the night. By morning a stack of thirty-two closely typed pages sat on his desk. *June,* he labeled it. It was the outline for *Tropic of Cancer, Tropic of Capricorn, Sexus, Nexus,* and *Plexus,* the books that he would write over the next thirty years!

He realized, when finished, that he was exhausted, but, "no longer wracked by emotion, he was strangely calm." He decided that after resting he would cable June to disregard his suicide note: instead of killing himself, he would write his way out of pain; in only outlining his book, he had "achieved some peace."

All Miller's novels were prompted by the shock of his losing June. But he believed his work matured because of his loss. Without this trauma, he said he would have had nothing substantial to express. For what he embarked upon was a period of intense soul searching. Before his loss, he lived his life unconsciously. After, in writing *Tropic of Cancer,* he discovered who he was, and he created a personal mythology about his role in life as an anarchic, iconoclastic, virile, tough, tender-hearted, working-class intellectual—a personal myth that could sustain him. Before writing about June, he thought himself a failure; after, he believed that his struggle and success in expressing himself, in breaking the silence of men like himself who hadn't been educated past high school, was heroic and that June's sacrifices had, in fact, enabled his work.

Through the years, Miller developed a profound and important philosophy about the creative process that he expounded in his novels, in letters to friends, and in nonfiction works like *The Cosmological Eye* and *The Books in My Life.* While Virginia Woolf believed that creativity required "a room of one's own," Henry Miller said he'd settle for a chair, and he charted how he wrote his work despite (or perhaps because of) leading a vagabond life in Paris, unattached to money and what it bought, yet free to practice his art.

For Henry Miller, writing was like "sewing up a wound," the wound inflicted by June's betrayal, which repeated a pattern of childhood betrayals—his life with a physically abusive mother and an alcoholic father and the sexual abuse of a trusted older man.

Lawrence Durrell, in *Art and Outrage,* described why he thought his friend Henry Miller used metaphors of healing in describing his writing. Durrell said that Miller retained a "large part of his childhood phantasy-life intact—with all its wounds." But Miller had "written it all out," providing himself and his readers, too, with "a catharsis." Through writing, Durrell said, Miller "cuts open the abscesses. . . . The pus and blood gushes out. But if any wound remains, it is clean, and can heal" and not continue to fester.

Writing, then, holds the key to how we all can achieve psychic growth, despite our pain and despair, and how we can imagine a hopeful future. Writing—organizing our thoughts, venting our feelings, and expressing ourselves in a complex way—Durrell thought, ultimately makes us hopeful, though the act of writing itself might cause us temporary pain.

Through writing, we change our relationship to trauma, for we gain confidence in ourselves and in our ability to handle life's difficulties. We come to feel that our lives are coherent rather than chaotic. We see ourselves as able to solve problems rather than as beset by problems. We enjoy a heightened sense of self. We become more optimistic. We recast our recovery from trauma as something we can accomplish rather than seeing our ordeal as something to be passively borne. Writing supplants our feelings of hopelessness, helplessness, and victimization about a traumatic event.

When I was first writing about my recollections of the sexual abuse I had experienced as a girl, I used a metaphor similar to Henry Miller's. I believed that I was using my writing as a kind of scalpel to cut out the growth festering inside me—my story—which was making me sick. It was an instrument that I had to wield with great care and skill for the excision to be successful, for the wound to heal. Without telling my story, I thought, I would stay sick; I even might die.

This is how Henry Miller describes why writing is therapeutic: "The work which was begun as a refuge and escape from the terrors of reality leads the author back into life, not *adapted* to the reality . . . but *superior* to it. . . . He sees that it was not life but himself from which he had been fleeing. . . . The whole past life resumes its place in the balance and creates a vital, stable equilibrium which would never have resulted without the pain and the suffering. . . . [Writing] lifts the sufferer out of his obsessions and frees him for the rhythm and movement of life by joining him to the great universal stream in which we all have our being."

WHAT YOU CAN DO NOW You might begin a letter to someone, as Isabel Allende did. Can you transform it into a story, even a novel?

What were your earliest stories, essays, or poems like? Did you keep a diary? Do you have them? What do they tell you?

Can you recall some early, significant childhood memories? Can you write a sketch of your past? Be sure to read the "Caveat" in this chapter if you choose to do this.

Are there any significant losses in your life you feel compelled to write about? Can you begin writing or sketching the shape that a long work, or a life's work about this loss, might take?

Chapter Four

Writing Pain,
Writing Loss

Qualities of a Healing Narrative

The only way through pain . . . is to absorb, probe,
understand exactly what it is and what it means.
To close the door on pain is to miss the chance for
growth. . . . Nothing that happens to us, even the
most terrible shock, is unusable, and everything has
somehow to be built into the fabric of the personality.

MAY SARTON, *Recovering: A Journal 1978–1979*

Last week I got a package in the mail from my writer friend Robert Cormier. Bob is best known for his novels about adolescents that "changed the direction of young adult fiction"—*I Am the Cheese, The Chocolate War, Beyond the Chocolate War,* and *After the First Death.* For many critics, his only rival is J. D. Salinger in portraying realistic, uncompromising, exquisitely wrought sagas of the cruelty and betrayal of young people.

Though we have met each other only once, we have had a long-standing correspondence. It never occurs to me to call Bob on the phone when I can write him and then await his splendid letters. Shortly after each book of mine has been published, I've received a generous, typewritten response from Bob composed on his ancient manual typewriter (he only recently switched to computer). He tells me what he likes, and he examines the mysterious congruence of our work—our portraits of childhood and adolescent suffering, loss, loneliness, and plucky stalwartness, resistance, resilience, and hope, even heroism, in facing life in a very difficult world.

Recently, we exchanged our latest works—his *Tenderness* for my *Breathless*—and I wrote him about this new book I am writing, asking whether the composition of any of his novels was healing in any way he would be willing to share.

He writes that though he thinks my premise—the connection between writing and healing—is "intriguing," he is sorry he can't help me out, can't "cite any direct, specific healing incidents" that occurred as he worked. His writing functions differently for him, "as an escape, a secret love, an extra richness and dimension in my life."

Okay, I think. Bob is a notable exception, though I know he once remarked, "It is the things that make me unhappy that send me to the typewriter."

I knew next to nothing about Bob's life when I encountered his work, though, on no evidence, I imagined a complex and difficult childhood for him that might have prompted the immensely realistic, nonromanticized portraits of pained and troubled adolescents that he skillfully develops in his novels. I later learned, though, through published interviews, that he grew up during the Depression and that, though "the streets were terrible," his "home was warm."

Near the end of Bob's note to me, he scribbles a sudden thought. That just thinking about writing and healing makes him remember that, yes, once, "my writing really was therapy. Ah, one specific—my father's death devastated me, he was 60 and I was 35—and I wrote my first novel 'Now and at the Hour' as therapy while he lay dying. I wasn't conscious of writing a novel but wanted really, in my anger and frustration, to put the world in bed with my father and have them see how it felt to die. So, perhaps it was a kind of healing for me."

I am grateful to Bob for telling me how he came to write his first work—to assuage his pain, to communicate what he witnessed as his father was dying. For how often have I heard of a writer or would-be writer in the midst of a difficult situation—a child ill, a parent dying, a marriage falling apart, a job lost—who feels driven to write about it then, yet who is persuaded that some distance from the event is needed? For "emotion recollected in tranquillity"—to quote William Wordsworth—some people tell us, is the only kind of emotion worth exploring on paper. What if there's no tranquillity? What if our lives are consistently compromised by war, political upheaval, illness, loss? Are we then never to write? No, I think. Expecting tranquillity is expecting a certain kind of privilege many of us never have *until* we write.

Through writing about his father's dying, Cormier wanted to put the reader (and himself as writer) in bed with his father. He wanted to write, too, reflections about his father's life, one of hard work and thwarted desire. But in writing of his personal experiences, paradoxically, Cormier created a work recapturing those of many of his father's contemporaries, people who lived through the Depression and World War II yet who matured when manual laborers' contributions to society were devalued. His book is an elegy for his father's loss but a testimony, too, to the often unacknowledged contributions of working-class people.

A former student of mine, Catherine Kapphahn, who is writing "Finding Sleep," a chapter from a memoir-in-progress of her mother's death from uterine cancer, told me that she, too, wanted to put the reader and herself in her mother's place, by describing what chemotherapy had been like for her mother. In doing this, Catherine said, she could connect with her mother, now dead, and reimagine her. She could feel her pain and, paradoxically, transcend her obsession with her mother's suffering by concentrating upon it as she wrote.

Thinking about her mother's chemotherapy in this way, Catherine said, "calmed" her and put her in a "powerful position," for she could express feelings and thoughts she had previously repressed. By paying attention to her grief—by not running from it but, instead, exploring it deeply—Catherine preserved her mother's experience and, through writing what she witnessed or remembered, she regained (symbolically) what she had lost (in actuality). Catherine was forced, too, to think about her mother's difficult early life as a girl in Croatia—how she had nearly died from tuberculosis. Through writing of her mother's death, Catherine began to understand her mother's life.

Choosing to Write About Pain, Loss, and Grief

It is early in the semester of a memoir-writing class at Hunter College. Today, my student writers will choose the subjects they'll be working on for the rest of the semester. Some want to become professional writers; others are simply interested in writing. By the semester's close, though, all (but two who drop the course early) will have written a thirty-page, publishable memoir—the course's only requirement. Many, I can see, are anxious and fearful. Al is downright skeptical about my assurance that every writer who commits to the writing process I outline in class will do important, healing work.

Naturally, they're afraid. They readily admit it when I ask them. What they don't expect is my response. "I'm thrilled," I say. For anxiety and fear (even downright terror), I tell them, are the fuels that drive the creative process. Anxiety and fear are feelings we'll learn to tolerate, even welcome. They're signals, as Eric Maisel, Ph.D., has observed in *Fearless Creating,* that we're committed to the process; that we're doing significant work; and that we're growing and changing through our work. No growth, no change, occurs without them. If we aren't committed, if we haven't chosen something important to write about, I tell them, we'd feel nothing at all.

My students sit in a circle in our rather ramshackle classroom. I sit atop the teacher's desk. Today, we'll talk about their choice of subject. We've made an agreement, though, if anyone wants to keep their subject private, they can.

I've suggested that they select a subject to work on that they have returned to often in their thoughts or that they fear thinking about or that they are compelled to examine—one they can write about at sufficient length. I haven't stipulated that they choose painful subjects. I only say that their choices need to feel authentic and be *personally meaningful*. And that once they decide, they honor their subjects and trust that their choice will take them on a writing journey that will necessarily be a healing journey.

Though two women choose and reject a few topics before discovering their real subjects, other students tell me that they immediately knew what they would explore. As Al said when he told us he was writing about his homeless life in London, "It is *necessary* for me to write about this now; I can't avoid it any longer."

I've developed a teaching style for my writing classes that makes my student writers completely responsible for their work. This is because I believe, fundamentally, that writing is about cultivating and practicing autonomy. It is the way healing begins, especially if, in the past, our autonomy has been seriously compromised or even stolen from us. What we often explore in our writing is an assault on our integrity as people. Writing, then, enacts a freedom we often felt we didn't have.

Choosing—or rather, finding—our own subject, one that is personally, deeply significant, then, is the first step of the process. Others include learning to work, developing our own authentic voices, and deciding what form our work will take, when our work is finished, and under what conditions we'll share it. Throughout, I act as supportive coach, mentor, and guide.

And so we begin.

Lauren passes; her subject is private. Later, when she feels ready, she tells us she is writing about the year she spent in a treatment center for suicidal depression. Maria wants to write about her former drug use. Julia, her father's recent cancer diagnosis. Jessica, her uncle's murdering someone she knew and his subsequent incarceration. Ellen, a recent abortion. Mary, her parents' disintegrating marriage. Eric, his father's death from cancer and his own blindness. Jeremy, his father's death (we later learn, from AIDS). Lois, about being in exile. Elise, about her father's violence toward her after she discovered he was having an affair. Anna isn't sure; eventually she'll write about her exhibitionistic sex. Eleanor, about her brother's attempted suicide.

Entering Our Pain, Loss, and Grief

For our writing to be a healing experience, we honor our pain, loss, and grief. We learn what the process of writing will hold for us by learning from good mentors and guides. We go with our pain and into it; we observe it and examine it in detail. We try to find words to describe our sensations precisely, accurately, and without distortion. We observe our writing process. Because we understand that doing the work might be painful, we honor our feelings and witness them instead of denying them or ignoring them. In this way, we enable ourselves to tolerate them. After doing the work, we will most likely feel a shift in our perspective, an enlargement of our sense of self.

Creative Work as Elegy

Over the last twenty years, in each writing course I've taught, most of my students choose subjects that are connected to profound psychic pain, to deep and often unarticulated loss, to unresolved grief. Pain, loss, grief. Although initially I was surprised, now, after years, I'm not.

Like Elaine Scarry in her *The Body in Pain,* I now see pain, loss, and grief as the basis for virtually every act of cultural creation. And I believe that writing about these subjects is something we can deliberately choose to do as a "righting" process, engaging in an act of restitution for "righting" what profoundly disturbed us.

When Virginia Woolf contemplated the literary works she had created, she realized that in writing each she had tried to recover something or someone she had lost. Using the term *novel* for her creations, she realized, was inadequate. Instead, she believed each of her works, more properly, should be termed *elegy*—a lamentation for the dead.

In writing *Jacob's Room,* her third novel, in which she discovered her authentic narrative voice, she based Jacob, her central character, upon her brother Thoby, who, after a trip to Greece, died young from typhoid fever incorrectly diagnosed as malaria. To inspire her, and to record the source of her art, she copied into her notebook the last line of Catullus's elegy for *his* dead brother, "Ave Atque Vale" ("Hail and Farewell"), and then wrote the words "Julian Thoby Stephen 1881–1906."

As she worked, though, the novel became a remembrance, too, for all the young men of her brother's generation who died during World War I, a fate that Thoby Stephen was spared. For in her novel, Woolf imagines that Thoby/Jacob has died fighting for his country. Through writing *Jacob's Room* to honor her brother and lament his death, Woolf also created a profound work of cultural criticism, one that denounced war and mourned a generation of promising young men who had been eradicated.

In writing about Thoby, in meditating upon the details of his life—how he behaved to women, how he behaved at school—Woolf came to understand that her beloved brother himself believed that some people (white privileged men) are better than others (people of color, poor people, all women) and that some people (white privileged men) deserve to rule others (people of color, poor people, all women). Through writing about him, she stopped idealizing him, and she saw him more clearly, more honestly. This, then, helped her grief. For when we idealize the people we've lost, we can't get beyond our grief to reenter the world.

The Link Between Lamenting and Caring

May Sarton, in *Recovering: A Journal 1978–1979,* described how, in reading Henri J. M. Nouwen's book of sermons, *Out of Solitude,* she learned that the word *care* has its roots in the Gothic word *Kara,* meaning "lament." The "basic meaning of care," then, Sarton notes, is " 'to grieve, to experience sorrow, to cry out with.' "

We show we have cared about someone by letting ourselves engage in the act of lamenting their loss or death. But we show we have cared about someone, too, by "crying out with"—by using our grief to understand our connection to others, as Woolf did.

By engaging in lament, we care for ourselves. For not to express grief is to put ourselves at risk for isolation, for illness.

Nouwen believed we receive consolation and hope from reading authors "who, while offering no answers to life's questions, have the courage to articulate the situation of their lives in all honesty and directness. . . . Their courage to enter so deeply into human suffering and *to become present to their own pain* gave them the power to speak healing words."

Similarly, we receive consolation and hope from doing writing that enters deeply into our suffering, that articulates the situation of our lives with honesty and directness, that connects our situation to that of other people. Though our doing this will be courageous, we don't need courage to embark upon this healing journey; we will develop the requisite courage *as we work.* Genuine courage—"mettle," Winston Churchill called it, emphasizing its vigor and staying power—is doing something that needs doing that you don't quite think you have the courage to do but that you keep on doing regardless.

As Sarton read Nouwen, she underscored the words *to become present to their own pain.* And these words represented what Sarton herself tried to achieve in her journal *Recovering.* In writing this work, Sarton tried to become present to *her* pain; she undertook the task of entering deeply into the sources of her depression and her rage, rooted in the loss of a love that she had cherished.

In suggesting that we become present to our own pain, Nouwen hints at some characteristics of a healing work of art that I will explore further. First, we must become present to our own pain—we must not deny its existence, we must let ourselves feel it. Second, we must record it honestly—without hypocrisy, dishonesty, sentimentality, or idealization. And finally, we must recount it directly.

How Writing Creative Narratives About Pain and Loss Can Heal

Sigmund Freud, in *Beyond the Pleasure Principle,* observed that shell-shocked soldiers experienced repeated, detailed nightmares in which traumatic events were reenacted. This, too, has been observed of victims of abuse and torture. Lenore Terr, M.D., in *Too Scared to Cry,* has documented the art and stories of severely traumatized children—those, for example, of Chowchilla, California, whose school bus was abducted and buried. They later developed elaborate kidnapping scenarios to try to master their trauma.

Freud theorized that though these dreams were painful and upsetting, they nonetheless represented an unconscious attempt by people who had experienced extreme trauma to revisit it in all its complexity and to try to master its horror and so overcome it. Terr discovered that severely traumatized children use imaginative play earlier, longer, and more frequently than children who haven't been traumatized. Experiencing profound pain, then, seems to unleash our imaginations to try to overcome its harmful effects. It is essential, though, that this desire isn't inhibited, that it is instead acted upon.

Both Freud and Terr suggest, then, that we possess an emotional self-righting mechanism, akin to our body's innate ability to heal wounds. This is our creative imagination, our ability to take experience and reenter it and represent it after the fact in some kind of symbolic way.

With writing, this is, of course, through language. Freud believed that, although painful, the dreams of the soldiers held an important clue to how we can use creativity and our imaginative powers to confront painful and traumatic situations we've experienced. And Terr maintains that the inventive activity of traumatized children is testament to our innate drive to use imaginative work to try to heal ourselves. (With extreme and severe abuse, we will also need professional help.)

Characteristically, the dreams of the soldiers and the play of the children were vivid, detailed, image laden. Though the soldiers' nightmares were upsetting, and though they came unbidden, they suggest that one way we can confront painful and traumatic situations is to *consciously* engage in writing narratives that are vivid, detailed, and image laden.

David Aberbach, in *Surviving Trauma,* observes that creative work helps us deal with hurt and sorrow, for in many ways it mimics the work of mourning. Through writing, we allow ourselves to move through the most important aspects of mourning—but at a safe and symbolic distance. We use our imaginations to revisit difficult experiences deliberately in an attempt to master them. We engage in searching for exact, concrete details and language evocative enough to communicate.

This creative searching mimics the imaginative seeking of the lost person or self that is characteristic of mourning. It has been immortalized in myths—Demeter searching for her abducted daughter, Persephone, for example, as my writing partner Edvige Giunta reminds me—that depict characters searching for their lost loved ones and finding them, though perhaps only temporarily. Feelings of longing and yearning accompanying the mourning process fuel our search to find what we've lost. This longing and yearning also attend creative activity.

If we allow ourselves to spend sufficient time writing, we eventually find the right details, discover the appropriate phrase, and so our searching ends. We symbolically resolve the searching and the yearning stages of the mourning process into a "finding and having" stage—

a symbolic resolution. In this way, we recover the person or the self we've lost.

Because our writing, our work of art, is a concrete object, it becomes a memorial and a testimony to the resolution of the mourning process. And to the lost person and the lost self. By writing about them, we give them posthumous life. By writing, we celebrate, too, our courage and survival. Engaging in writing, in creative work, then, permits us to pass from numbness to feeling, from denial to acceptance, from conflict and chaos to order and resolution, from rage and loss to profound growth, from grief to joy.

The Qualities of a Healing Narrative

What are the transformative qualities we can aim for as we write?

A healing narrative renders our experience concretely, authentically, explicitly, and with a richness of detail.

It tells precisely what happened. It is accurate. It is rooted in time and in place. We describe when and where this happened. We describe the people who were involved fully; we do not idealize them or vilify them but instead present them as well-developed portraits. We describe things in way that is uniquely, authentically ours; our narrative can't sound as if anyone else could have written it or as if someone other than ourselves has written it. And we do this even if our subject is difficult.

Research has demonstrated that depressed and suicidal people are much less likely to report memories or happenings in an extremely specific way. Instead, recollections tend to be overly general and vague. It's possible that this is a strategy for avoiding pain or that the contents of memory are being censored. Still, when narratives are reported in an overgeneralized way, any situation seems more catastrophic than it really is.

Describing events and memories in a general way—"it was the most horrible time in my life," "I felt like such a failure then"—is nei-ther helpful nor therapeutic; it might even be damaging. Instead, re-counting concrete details of particular incidents—what happened, where it happened, when it happened, who was involved—is crucial if our narratives are to be healing. Using diaries and journals is particularly important here. Keeping them seems to encourage the specific recall of events.

"How much detail about what happened do you want?" my student Tony asks. "About a thousand times more than you think you need," is always my answer.

"How do I manage to write that much?" Tony says.

"By asking yourself, 'What more can I say about this?' each time you revise. You will unlock the details over time. One will lead to another and another and another."

In emphasizing the healing aspect of using a plethora of details, I speak of Maria Rosa Henson, the Philippine writer, author of *Comfort Woman: Slave of Destiny*, which relates how she had been systematically raped by Japanese soldiers during World War II. Henson described how she fought against her trauma by training herself to remember every detail of her abuse, which began when she was fifteen, when she was assaulted by as many as thirty men a day. "I learned to remember everything, to remember always, so that I will not go mad," she said. I speak of the preciseness with which Nancy Venable Raine narrates how she was raped in *After Silence* and how she believed it was necessary for her to do so. (Dr. Judith Lewis Herman's work with trauma survivors provides proof that specifically retelling each trauma is necessary for healing.)

Conversely, many researchers have observed that an inability to render pain and trauma *explicitly*, describing it instead in vague and general terms, signifies that the person has not yet entered the process of healing. The aim of some therapies is to invite the richness of detail that Henson believed was linked to her survival.

As my student Eric wrote about his father's death from cancer, he moved from standing outside his father's hospital room to moving inside to standing right next to the bed. Emotionally, too, he got closer. His details became more explicit: he started to describe what he saw, touched, smelled, felt. His ability to portray the telling detail that his father had been needlessly castrated, for he died soon after, signaled a shift into healing. Eric could show the reader how this proud man felt about what happened, how it shamed and humiliated him. He could write of his father's loss and of his loss, too. This was his narrative's most difficult, yet most reparative, moment.

A healing narrative links feelings to events.

It describes how we felt then and how we feel now. It compares and contrasts past feelings and current feelings about events. It charts the similarities or differences in our feelings over time.

If we felt nothing then, as often happens with people in acute crisis, we describe what feeling nothing felt like, when feeling started (if it did), and what it means not to have felt anything.

A healing narrative is a balanced narrative. It uses negative words to describe emotions and feelings in moderation; but it uses positive words, too.

It is important for us to describe our negative feelings. If we find ourselves writing about how our fathers or our mothers were saints, for example, we must ask ourselves if they were something more, too. If we find ourselves writing about how we're saints, we must be especially wary.

Because negative events and negative feelings seem more accessible when we're in emotional pain than do positive events and pleasant memories, it is especially important for us to report the positive aspects of our existence. When I remembered that a neighbor had given me a simple gift while I was severely depressed as a child—colored paper collected for me in a paper factory where the person worked—a significant shift occurred in my perception of my childhood. I realized that someone had tried to help me.

"How can we possibly write positively about a painful subject?" I've often been asked. "By describing what sustained us during that time," I say. I tell about Audre Lorde, who in *The Cancer Journals* wrote about how the love of women nourished her after her surgery; how her friends Blanche and Clare surprised her while she was in the hospital by appearing for a visit bearing a "gorgeous French rum and mocha cake with a marzipan banner that said 'we love you, audre,' outrageously rich and sinfully delicious." I relate how Mark Doty, writing of his lover's death in *Heaven's Coast,* also told how "joy sneaks in" even as we mourn: "listening to music, riding my bicycle, I catch myself feeling, in a way that's as old as I am but suddenly seems unfamiliar, *light.* . . . It comes back to me as if from a great distance, this old delight in the world."

After Eric wrote that difficult moment into his narrative, it unleashed a flood of positive moments—how his father gardened, how he made delicious pasta sauces from the many vegetables he lovingly tended. At first none of this positive material was included. Writing it, Eric said, gave him something back. And he closed his piece with a recipe for his father's sauce. On the day he presented his work to the class, he handed us a copy of the recipe. Now, when I make it, I think of Eric and his father.

A study by Pennebaker discovered that the more people described positive emotions in their writing, the more likely they were to be healthier afterward. But describing negative emotions either excessively or very little or not at all correlated with poorer health. Describing negative emotions in moderation correlated with improved health.

This suggests that we profit most from understanding an event's positive and negative aspects. We must not, of course, deny our negative feelings: we must express them. But neither must we deny our positive feelings: these also must be expressed. Balanced narratives make us feel hopeful.

If we find that we describe only our negative feelings, it will be worthwhile to revisit our experience to see if we can discover any positive moments, anything we learned from the events, or how we grew or changed in its aftermath.

A healing narrative reveals the insights we've achieved from our painful experiences.

A healing narrative doesn't just narrate what happened to us and how we feel. It is a way for us to reflect upon the significance of what happened. It connects our experience to other experiences in our lives or to those of other people or to society. It reflects upon cause and effect, illuminating why events may have happened as they did. Raine does this brilliantly in *After Silence* by contextualizing her rape: she writes about its prevalence, discusses attitudes about it, and shows how the subject is treated in works of literature.

A word of caution. Reflections about cause and effect that can harm us are based on questions like "Why did this happen to me?" "What did I do to deserve this?" "How did I invite this?" "Why was I singled out?" Questions such as these indicate that we are ready to blame ourselves for the trauma that occurred, and such self-blame is harmful. It is more helpful to examine our personal experience in a broader context. For example, it helped me understand my abuse by knowing that my abuser had been the daughter of a prostitute. Knowing this, I imagined that she herself had been violated by her mother's "tricks," which suggested why she might have abused me. I discovered a possible chain of cause and effect in my story without asking whether I'd caused the abuse, which would have been damaging.

A healing narrative tells a complete, complex, coherent story.

Someone who knows nothing about who we are should be able to understand the narrative fully by reading it. This, of course, is necessary when we publish our work. But even if we are writing only for ourselves, or for a writing group, to be healing, our stories must be conveyed so completely on paper that there are no gaps in the narrative. By writing our stories fully, we begin to understand what was formerly unclear.

Often, our narratives begin in chaos. They become healing narratives as we organize them, as we ask ourselves, "Then what happened?" "Who was there?" "Why?" "Did that happen before or after?"

I asked my student Marion to write about a profoundly significant moment in her life. She described herself coming home one day to find her house in flames. She told us what she saw. But the story was jumbled; none of us who listened could figure out exactly what was going on or why this event was so devastating. True, seeing your house burn down is traumatic. But we felt that something important was missing.

As we pressed Marion for more details, she told us that her mother had died in the blaze. In her first draft, she didn't realize she had omitted this important detail from her story.

Writing this narrative was excruciatingly painful for Marion. She had to revisit this difficult moment of her life, examine buried feelings of rage about her mother, and tenderness, too. Every time Marion found her narrative becoming incoherent, she reentered her past, discovered something she had missed. In time, as her work became understandable to her audience, she, too, began to understand her story. For as Mary Beth Caschetta, author of *Lucy on the West Coast and Other Lesbian Short Fiction,* has observed, "There's really nothing like a crystal clear *plot* to bring back all the meaning in life."

From Pain to Acceptance and Grace

In Nobel laureate Kenzaburō Ōe's memoir, *A Healing Family,* Ōe writes of his son Hikari, an established composer, who is, according to Ōe, mentally still a child. He was born with a growth on his brain that, his parents were told, would prevent him from being anything but a "human vegetable."

This was one of the most painful and significant moments in Ōe's life. Fictionalizing this agonizing time, first in his novel *A Personal Matter* (about a young father's feelings and experiences after the birth of a severely brain damaged child), and in numerous other works (*Rouze Up O Young Men of the New Age!* and *Teach Us to Outgrow Our Madness,* among them), helped him "synthesize" his feelings about these events and "make some kind of sense out of a senseless situation." He wrote to understand his pain. As he wrote, his attitude toward his pain and toward Hikari (whose name means "radiance" in Japanese) changed dramatically.

In the novel, Ōe is excruciatingly frank about his murderous intentions toward his son. Bird, the boy's father, believes he has the right to judge whether his son should live or die. He makes several abortive attempts to kill his son. But the infant survives. By writing, Ōe confronted his murderous fantasies toward Hikari without acting upon them. Ōe shows, too, how debauched and amoral a vision the father has toward the world—how he believes that the pursuit of pleasure and self-interest is the only thing that matters and that anything that stands in its way must be avoided at all costs. Still, the birth of this child provides Bird with an opportunity to grow as a human being, to change his ways, to achieve an integrity he never before possessed.

In *A Healing Family,* Ōe says that, like Bird, he first reacted to Hikari's birth by trying "to flee from the deformed child." This changed, in part, because of his writing. He decided, finally, to accept responsibility for his child's care and to make him a central "part of his life, though he will almost certainly be retarded, and to take the word 'patience' as his motto, the basis for his existence." Throughout, the family has done the best it could. "Sometimes we were angry, and sometimes forgiving, and sometimes ashamed of ourselves."

An important milestone in Hikari's life came when he was operated on to "remove the lump in his head and cover the hole with a plastic plate," a traumatic event for the family to which Ōe has often returned in his writing. Without the surgery, Hikari would not have survived. Yet Ōe and his wife almost refused permission for this operation.

Though Ōe had been writing for years, he says he matured as a writer and, consequently, as a human being only when he began dealing with this, the most painful experience in his life, in his work. "The central theme of my work," he has written, "has been the way my family has managed to live with this handicapped child." Before his son's birth, Ōe believed his work was trivial. And he believed himself to be an amoral, insensitive young man, unaware, even, of the suffering of the Japanese people who had lived through the bombing of Hiroshima. His early work conveyed a postwar world lacking in meaning and ethical values.

Then, his "son's birth burst like a bombshell" into his life. After, it was "through the pain of this experience," and through writing about it, that he regained his equilibrium, that he matured personally and in his writing. After Hikari's birth, Ōe's work describes how the acceptance of difficult burdens enables us to achieve grace and salvation. Central to his work, according to the critic John Nathan, is the symbiotic bond between father and son, "at once an oppressive burden and source of personal redemption."

Before he and his wife agreed to permit the operation that would save Hikari's life, while they were still contemplating letting him die, Ōe traveled to Hiroshima as a reporter to cover an international rally to banish nuclear weapons. He did this as much to escape the burden of this decision as to learn about those who had lived through the bombing. According to David L. Swain, "his encounters with the *dignity* of the A-bomb survivors in Hiroshima and with the *authenticity* of those who steadfastly cared for them" became the theme of the series of articles later published as *Hiroshima Notes.* By writing them, Ōe discovered his "commitment to his afflicted son." He was deeply moved, not only by learning of the excruciating human suffering people can endure, but also by how they can repair themselves even after experiencing what Ōe calls "the greatest misery suffered by human beings in the twentieth century."

In visiting the Atomic Bomb Hospital, Ōe met Dr. Fumio Shigeto, a bomb victim himself who treated others. In the days immediately following Hiroshima, in response to a colleague's hopelessness about treating survivors, Dr. Shigeto countered that he believed he had no choice but to try to help as many people as he could, "one patient at a time."

The attitude of this remarkable man was "Neither too much hope nor too much despair," a motto that Ōe has adopted for his life and his work. This stance neither cripples us in our attempt to overcome suffering nor renders us unrealistic in our expectations. It gives us a modest, pragmatic way of allowing ourselves to retain our humanism in the face of profound suffering; it gives us, too, a map for describing human sorrow.

In his response to Hikari's birth and to his pain, and in trying to write about it, Ōe says that he passed through several stages. Shock, characterized by apathy and withdrawal. Denial. Confusion, during which he felt anger, resentment, grief, and depression as he realized that this was a permanent condition. Then, an "effort phase" in which he sought solutions and enacted them. And finally, "acceptance." He passed through these phases often in his life with Hikari. For arriving at acceptance is a lifelong process.

Passing through these phases was facilitated by his writing, for it allowed him to explore these feelings and to observe them and reflect upon them as well. First, he entered the emotional terrain of these complicated and painful feelings. Then, as he made the effort of turning his experience into an autobiographical narrative that closely paralleled the events of his life, he found he could make an effort to care for Hikari. Finally, by seeing his experience transformed into art, Ōe achieved, if only for a time, acceptance.

In trying to pen a fictional portrait of his life with Hikari, Ōe enabled himself to face the pain in his life, which, in turn, enabled him to change the way he behaved and the way he interpreted his experience. As he grew personally through his writing and through his actions, his work became deeper, richer, more complex and profound.

Twenty-four years after Hikari's birth, Ōe wrote a novel called *Letter to the Nostalgic Years* to mark his thirtieth anniversary as a writer. In it he undertook, again, to understand the impact of Hikari's birth. And he contended that his acclaimed lifework grew from a single desire: to explore the shock of Hikari's birth and his pain and grief.

"This accident that happened to my son," he wrote. "How can I assimilate it as if it were part of my own fate? . . . I am devoting myself to literature only to understand why my son was born brain-damaged. My son is an essential part of myself."

Through writing of Hikari, Ōe developed the ethical stance that acceptance is the most critical and crucial value in life. It is necessary for us to "trust and acknowledge and coexist with other people despite difficult circumstances." For we can accept ourselves only if we have learned to accept others, we can empathize with others and treat them well only if we confront our anguish. This, then, is the foundation of living an ethical life. In Ōe's case, it has been made possible by writing.

Like Alice Walker, Ōe, too, believes in the transformative, redemptive power of writing. Through his work, in his work, he shows us how we can use the process of writing as a way of attaining grace, hope, and renewal.

Writing about our losses and about our pain in a healing narrative can greatly enrich our lives. For Kenzaburō Ōe, the "miracle of art" is that through its creation, "we come to know despair—that dark night of the soul through which we have to pass." Yet "we find that by actually giving it expression we can be healed and know the joy of recovering; and as these linked experiences of pain and recovery are added to one another, layer upon layer, not only is the artist's work enriched but its benefits are shared with others."

WHAT YOU CAN DO NOW   Are you writing? Is there something you'd like to write but that you've been afraid to touch because it involves emotional pain? Try starting. If you're not ready, write about what you're afraid will happen if you write about that subject.

Is there a writer's life or work that fascinates you? Can you read letters, diaries, journals, interviews, biographies to understand whether their writing was inspired by grief or loss? Can you understand how they transformed their experiences into works of art? Can you apply what you've learned to your process?

Are you ready to begin writing a short healing narrative? If so, try, through successive revisions, to incorporate the qualities of a healing narrative described here. As you work, reflect on how deepening your work affects your feelings and your understanding.

Part Two

The Process/
The Program

Chapter Five

The Healing Power
of the Writing Process

*One can't be an expert in process. By its very
nature process can't be mastered. Because it's not
finished. And who knows what will happen next?*

NANCY MAIRS, *Ordinary Time*

How you do anything is how you do everything.

ZEN PROVERB

In the year before I started writing my first book,
I became interested in Japanese Zen *ensō*, or circle
paintings, and, through this, in Japanese ideas about
the creative process. It was a significant turning point
in my life, for I began to think about creativity and
about the writing process in a new, enabling way.

Ink Marks, Ink Traces

One day, when haunting the Strand in Greenwich
Village, my favorite secondhand bookstore (with seven
miles of shelves, as the ads proudly proclaim), I

stumbled upon a book about Zen painting on a discount table. Flipping through it, I came upon some Zen circle paintings. I had never seen one before. From my training as a painter, I knew that the fewer elements a painting contained, the more difficult it was to pull the work off.

Each *ensō* was painted directly on silk or rice paper, without opportunity for change. It consisted of a single circle in black ink, accompanied by a calligraphic inscription. Japanese Zen practitioners consider the *ensō* one of Zen's deepest symbols and works depicting them, one of its most revealing and difficult art forms.

An *ensō* by Bankei impressed me particularly because of its strength and energy. Still, there was a calmness and order in the work. Looking at it, I felt the artist's spirituality and wisdom, his tremendous life force, too.

I wanted to learn how it was painted. But I also wanted to learn how artists and writers in Japan conceptualized the artist's role. For I felt instinctively that such an ancient aesthetic tradition had much to teach me.

In time, I learned how Zen artists and writers devote themselves to an orderly, contemplative way of life that prepares them for their work. But how doing their work, too, becomes a form of meditation. Work and life are deeply integrated. According to Japanese literary theorists like Zeami Motokiyo, writing cleanses the mind, enables the writer to achieve serenity, for it purges us of "tangled emotions." The writer, then, inevitably is changed by the act of writing. I wanted to adopt much of this: emotional, physical, and psychological preparation; orderliness; integrating life and work; using writing for contemplation, for spiritual and emotional growth.

By studying Japanese aesthetics I learned three simple, essential notions. First, we can approach writing as a normal, natural, even joyful part of life rather than as something difficult, esoteric, and painful. Second, we can approach writing as an act that is an integral part of our lives, that we engage in regularly and with commitment rather than as something that removes us from life or that we must be inspired to undertake. Third, if we write regularly, and watch ourselves writing, the process of witnessing ourselves doing our work is transforming. May Sarton, also a student of non-Western ideas of creativity, says this in *Journal of a Solitude:* "the discipline of work provides an exercise bar, so that the wild, irrational motions of the soul become formal and creative."

I had been wanting to write for some time when I discovered *ensō* and Japanese aesthetic theories. But my work then consisted of little fragments of writing about my life, which I stuffed into various manila folders labeled "Scraps" or "Fragments." I really wanted to write poetry, fiction, biography, even. But I knew I didn't want my life to be a struggle. I had assumed it would be if I became a writer. I had children to raise, a husband to partner, pets to tend, laundry to wash, meals to cook, an ordinary life to live. I couldn't afford to engage in a chaotic and risky life. I knew that I couldn't write if doing so would endanger a life I valued.

That was when Harold Bloom's view of literary creativity as a painful battle was popular. To Bloom, the writing process was a titanic struggle. Often, though the work might be important and deeply meaningful, doing it could hold catastrophic consequences for the writer. And, too, that was when Anne Sexton's suicide deeply affected many women I knew who wanted to become writers. If we wrote, we asked ourselves, would we end our lives as she had?

Writing as Practice

Studying Japanese ideas about writing taught me another vision of creativity, one more helpful to me than current Western views. Though one never masters the process, even in a lifetime of work, essentially, it is quite simple.

We devote some time regularly to the process of writing. We do this just as we would devote ourselves to any other practice, like yoga, meditation, the martial arts. As Susan Gordon Lydon, author of *The*

Knitting Sutra, puts it, we write, not to create works of art, but to build character, develop integrity, discipline, judgment, balance, order, restraint, and other valued inner attributes. Through writing, we develop self-mastery, which contributes to our emotional and spiritual growth. Writing, then, becomes the teacher.

Engaging in the process of writing is far easier than we think. To begin, we take some time—a half hour or an hour a day, a few hours a few days a week—to write. But a few minutes each day, too, will suffice.

We can start with short forms, which can be worked in small amounts of time. Journal entries. Letters to ourselves or to others that we don't necessarily share. Poems. Reflections upon our life, upon our reading. Snippets of essays. Recollections of significant moments in our lives. Miniportraits of the people we've known. Many published works have begun in just this way—diaries and journals by Anne Truitt, Doris Grumbach, May Sarton, Audre Lorde, for example.

After we begin, if we want to deepen our practice, we can try to write for an hour or two or three a few days each week or every day. However long we write, if, say, we can write five pages a week, we can write 250 pages a year—which is the draft for a short book.

We can take on longer forms, which may or may not require that we do some reading or research in preparation. Chapters that will eventually become books. Longer poems. Prose poems. Reflective essays. Memoir. Biography.

Some writers—Charles Dickens was one—write seven or eight hours a day. I've done this a few times in my life but haven't liked it at all. For me, there's too much else I need and want to do. Knitting sweaters. Reading cookbooks. Baking biscotti and bread. Walking. Taking long, hot baths. Sitting and staring at the trees, sky, and clouds. (But not cleaning out closets. Or organizing my drawers. Or ironing.) For me, writing is an important, essential part of my life, but it is not my whole life. Most everything we do finds its way into our work somehow. And even makes better writers of us.

Whatever we choose to do in the way of writing, I believe that it shouldn't be haphazard—that we should write according to a self-directed plan, though our plans may, of course, change as we work. I believe, too, that we work to bring pieces of work to completion. I believe that the more direction we give ourselves, the more healing our writing will be. When James W. Pennebaker conducted his experiments on the beneficial aspects of writing, he gave his subjects *explicit* directions about the length of time they should write, the form their writing might take, the subject matter they might explore, the qualities (detailed descriptions, for example) they should aim for in their work. The structure, he theorized, may have created a sense of safety that was itself healing.

Developing Resilience Through Writing

The writing process, no matter how much time we devote to it, contains a tremendous potential for healing. In part, this is because writing distracts us from our problems. Through writing, we cultivate the quality of absorption—becoming deeply immersed in our work. This quiets us and calms us while, paradoxically, engaging us, whether we are writing about pleasant moments or continuing psychic pain.

Writing regularly fosters resilience—a quality that enables people subjected to difficulties to thrive despite them. According to Tim O'Brien, Vietnam veteran and prizewinning author of *Going After Cacciato* and *The Things They Carried,* beginning to write about a difficult experience signals that we have chosen hope rather than despair. Conversely, when we're in despair, if we write we become more hopeful.

This is because as we write we become observers—an important component of developing resilience. We regard our lives with a certain detachment and distance when we view it as a subject to describe and interpret. We reframe the problems in our life as challenges as we ask ourselves how to articulate what is on our mind in a way that will make sense.

It is not what you write or what you produce as you write that is important. It is what happens to you while you are writing that is important. It is who you become while you are writing that is important.

Making Time for Writing

When I teach writing, my first requirement is for students to set up a writing schedule that will permit them to write five revised pages of work a week. If they can write five pages a week, I tell them, they can write the draft of a short book in a year.

This moment is always an eye-opener, for my students suddenly realize that, despite their harried lives and busy schedules, they can manage this. This is important, too, since many people hamstring their efforts at entering the writing life because they imagine that writing cannot coexist with what I call a "life in the world." It's important to know that Toni Morrison wrote her first novels while working full-time as an editor, that Carole Maso began her distinguished career as a novelist while she was a waitress at Bloomingdales in New York City, that William Faulkner wrote while he was a postman (though a bad one—he threw away letters he didn't feel like delivering).

Five pages a week. Sounds simple, doesn't it?

There are only two catches. You have to do it. And you have to do it regularly.

To simply make sufficient time to write, to simply do this for ourselves regularly, has tremendous healing potential. Nonetheless, for many it seems a nearly insurmountable challenge. To take some quiet, uninterrupted, private moments in our days to write signals that we have chosen to put our well-being ahead of other compelling demands. This seems especially difficult for women.

Through the years, in talking with my students about why it is so hard for them to keep a writing schedule, I have learned that this involves understanding that what we do now affects who we are now and who we will become. It involves taking responsibility for our actions and how we spend our time. It involves planning. It involves learning that we must defer immediate gratification for the sake of our long-term well-being. It involves learning that sometimes we must put our needs first.

One of my students, Carla, had several important insights about her difficulties in getting to her writing.

"I'm just an anxiety junkie, I guess," she told our class. "It only takes me two hours a week to do the required writing. When I make a schedule and keep it, I feel great. My work focuses me; I do better in my other classes; I feel powerful because I'm doing something to help myself understand my life. When I stop writing, I feel awful—anxious, unsettled, miserable. I guess I'm just hooked on feeling bad."

It was Carla, too, who told us that whenever she felt unsettled, she knew that she could take care of herself through engaging in a creative act. But she rarely did this. Instead, she shopped, flipped through TV channels, talked on the telephone. None of this helped as simply writing for a few moments did. "In a consumerist culture like ours," she speculated, "I guess it's important for us to feel miserable. If we felt centered, we'd be creating and making, which means we wouldn't be buying. To write, I've learned I have to resist the screwed-up norms of our culture."

To write my first book, I stopped watching television. To write my second, I stopped having needless telephone conversations. To write my third, I stopped reading the newspaper. To make time to write, we often have to choose to stop doing something else. Often, we must assert our right to take this uninterrupted time for ourselves. We must continually fight for it, even with the people we love.

When my mother was alive, she often called me about fifteen minutes after I'd started writing, just after I'd settled down, just as the first meaningful sentence began to emerge. Because she knew that I wrote from ten to twelve each day, I could never understand why she called then, not before or after.

"Mom," I would say, "I can't talk now. I'm writing. I'll call you back when I'm finished." She thought me a heartless, selfish daughter when I stopped her in midsentence.

I don't know if she didn't consider writing working. Or if she felt writing took me away from her. She died without our ever resolving this issue between us.

Writing as Ritual

It is a clear November morning. A morning made for a long, long walk. Most of the leaves have washed from the trees in the tremendous downpour we had a few days ago. But some are tenacious, and I seem to appreciate their beauty more—the rust of the oak, the scarlet of the Japanese maple—when there are fewer of them. I know that I must cherish the sight of them because they will soon fall, that I must wait a long year before I see them again.

This early walk I take precedes my writing. It is part of my writing ritual. It is why, on my walk, I'm alert in a way I wouldn't be if I weren't writing. Knowing that I'll be writing makes me receptive. Makes me see everything differently. Makes me feel alive. And centered.

Awaken. Breakfast. Knit some. Straighten up quickly. Walk (same three-mile route). Home. Snack: decaf coffee, homemade biscotti (chocolate orange hazelnut, these days). By now it's nine. Get special notebook (purchased in Venice). Special pen (Pilot Precise V5 Extra Fine Rolling Ball). Sit by the window (on the sofa with the shredding slipcover that needs replacing) where I always sit. Write about what I intend to write. Move to the computer. Write. Move back to the sofa. Write about what I've been writing and how I feel about it.

The predictability of this daily ritual comforts me. Writing, approached as ritual, is centering and healing as all rituals are. No matter what else goes on, this helps me. Which is why I wrote each day during the months my mother was dying, whether I wanted to or not. For I know that if I am writing, I can take care of everything else.

One key, I have learned, is not to keep from writing when you're feeling down. Another is not to stop writing when you're feeling well. (Our challenge is not to stop doing what makes us feel well when we start feeling well.) But we must write regularly, ritualistically, no matter what we're feeling.

Some Misconceptions About the Writing Process

In working with beginning writers I have discovered that certain misconceptions about the writing process have prevented many of them from starting or continuing their work. Many have begun significant projects in the past—a novel, a poem cycle, a memoir—only to abandon them when they stopped feeling inspired or when they became confused about the work's direction or when they became anxious about the material that was emerging. Here are some false assumptions I've encountered:

> To begin a work, we must be inspired. If we aren't inspired, we shouldn't waste our time writing. (In truth: Inspiration comes as we write.)

> To be a writer, we must have inborn talent. (In truth: Writing is something we can learn.)

> To begin a work, we should know what we're going to say before we start. (In truth: Most writers write to learn; many begin with only a vague sense of what they want to do; many begin in ignorance.)

> We write only when we want to write; we continue writing when our ideas are flowing freely; we stop when we feel we no longer have anything to say or when the work makes us feel uncomfortable. (In truth: Most writers write regularly; the regularity is comforting; writing through difficult times often yields what writers consider to be their most mature work.)

> We expect ourselves to get a sentence more or less right the first time. (In truth: Even writers who claim to write directly revise.)

> We can't write until we have huge blocks of time in our life to write. If we're leading "normal" lives, we'll never have the time to

write anything. (In truth: Small, regular blocks of time devoted to writing are sufficient for us to use writing as a way of healing.)

If we're working at something valuable, the work will proceed quite easily from the start. If a work presents us with problems, we should abandon it and start another, until we find something that comes easily. (In truth: Writing seems to go through distinct, predictable stages for almost everyone. And not every stage is pleasurable.)

How We Can Help Ourselves

Studies of people who have continued to be creative throughout their lives, like Howard Gardner's *Creating Minds,* can help us learn how to conduct our lives in a way that will nurture our writing.

Creative people, Gardner tells us, focus on a particular field that they spend much time learning. They trust their impulses to, say, spend a year reading Marcel Proust's *Remembrance of Things Past* (as the writer Phyllis Rose describes in *The Year of Reading Proust*) or to read everything about coach travel, stage makeup, gas lighting, river barges, and the Civil War (as my friend, the writer Vincent Virga did for a novel he's writing about a troupe of traveling players).

Creative people engage in creative activities regularly. They organize their lives to enable them to practice their art or craft or skill. They safeguard their solitary time. They don't wait for the "right" time— when the children are grown, when they have enough money. Waiting depletes creative energy; creating increases creative energy.

Creative people find emotional support to do their work. They cultivate creative friends.

Creative people give up something (often something inconsequential that contributes nothing to the quality of their lives or perhaps even detracts from it, but sometimes something significant) to enable their work to proceed.

Creative people travel frequently, or, if they can't afford to travel, they routinely experience their familiar environment in an unusual, enriching way. (Henry Miller sometimes lived on the streets of Paris because he was so destitute, but he walked the city according to an organized plan.)

Learning what the creative process entails, learning how "real" writers work through reading about writers' lives and their work, will help us immeasurably.

When she completed a brilliant memoir about her grandmother's life in Venezuela, my student Trina wrote about her experience as a writer before and after she began to understand some essential features of the writing process.

"Before," she writes, "I had no idea how to even begin to work at creating a written piece. I kept on thinking that one day this brilliant story was just going to pop into my head and WHAM! I would spill out a work of art smoothly onto the page.

"When I had tried to write before, I was too overwhelmed with trying to write 'the book' from the beginning as if it would just all come out in a flow like when you are reading one. No wonder I kept getting disillusioned. . . .

"It's funny, because I know from dancing that you can't just start leaping through the air at once. You need to warm up to it. You need discipline. Endurance.

"I know now a way in which I can actually write a whole book if I continue. I am thinking about it. Realistically. I am beginning to grasp how to organize my life so that I can write."

When we begin to write regularly, letting the process be our guide, everything will take care of itself. Show up at the desk regularly and with commitment. That's really all you have to do.

The Yoga of Writing

Committing to the practice of simply writing is as transformative as is telling our stories, as is linking our feelings to the events in our lives.

Though we will never completely master the writing process in a life-time of working, simply put, what I have come to call the yoga of writing goes something like this.

We make time to write.

We plan to write. We prepare ourselves to write. We care for ourselves so that we can write. We prepare a place to write. We prepare our materials. We think and write about what we intend to write.

We write. We work in a disciplined, orderly, ritualistic way. We concentrate on the work at hand, on the moment-by-moment act of writing. We honor the rituals we choose. We tell ourselves that all we need to do is show up at the desk to do our work and, when we're there, to work with commitment. We "do" our work.

We try to write regularly. We set aside specific times for writing. We safeguard our writing time. We do our work whether we're joyous or disgruntled or annoyed or tired or angry or bored. Whether or not we believe we're inspired. We stop work at the appointed time. We take time, too, for dreaming, playing, outings, hobbies, nurturing our relationships. Our work is intimately connected to our life, but it is not our whole life.

We try to work intuitively, spontaneously. We listen to an inner voice that tells us what to do, what to write, where to go with the work. But we also step back from our work to see where it's headed, to let it tell us about what we can do now. We make order, organize, and plan.

We witness ourselves writing, and we witness our writing without judgment. We allow ourselves complex and difficult feelings about our writing, but we don't question why we're having them. We take time to become aware of what we feel and think about what we're writing and about ourselves as writers.

We learn what we need emotionally to do our work; we provide ourselves with what we need. We protect ourselves from those who would harm us or curtail our ability to work.

We make changes in our lives, in the way we work, and in what we're writing based upon what we learn about our work and about ourselves through witnessing our work and ourselves. We safeguard ourselves so we can take risks in our work without compromising our stability.

We work without expectation. We work to work, not to produce a work of genius. Or to get a six-figure advance. Or to make the best-seller list. In time, if we write regularly, we eventually will produce a piece of writing. But we don't write simply to produce this piece. We write to engage in the process of writing. We write without attachment to the end of the act of writing, insofar as we can.

We engage in lifelong learning about creative work—its stages, its methods, its process. We do this so that our own process is grounded in knowing what we can expect as we work. We understand that though each of us is unique, all writers nonetheless encounter similar difficulties and similar triumphs.

We see ourselves as belonging to a nurturing writing (and artistic) tradition. We respect and learn about the work of our literary and artistic forebears. We know that we are not alone in our work, that others who have come before us have much to teach us about this practice. We find ourselves good companions and mentors and guides to help us along the way.

We see ourselves as belonging to a nurturing community of writers; we join such a community or establish one. We eschew competition and rivalry if we are writing to heal. We celebrate the achievements of others: their work enriches and enables ours.

We finish what we begin. (Or we decide to abandon a work.) When we're finished, we reflect on our process. We congratulate ourselves on the effort it took to do our work. We're grateful for the help we've received. We reflect upon how we're feeling now, upon what this work has given us, upon how this work has changed us. We engage in a completion ceremony. We pack away the early drafts of our work, we collect notes we've scribbled as we've worked for future reference, we tidy our work space. We reward ourselves in some spiritually significant way.

We share our work or we share what we've learned in a way we choose. We might choose to make our work public or to teach others what we've learned. We prepare ourselves for what this sharing entails.

WHAT YOU CAN DO NOW Can you make a writing plan that includes an event you'd like to explore, a moment where you'll begin, significant feelings and images you associate with the event?

Can you discover what you must do to write two, three, four, or more pages a week? What must you give up? Can you try making a writing schedule? Sticking to it? Seeing what happens in your writing? Seeing how you feel?

If you could construct a writing ritual, what would it be like? Can you enact it?

If you aren't already doing it, can you start behaving like a creative person? What happens when you do?

Can you approach your writing in a yogic way?

Can you start a writer's diary in which you write about your writing—its progress, the ideas you have, the images that come to you, your "grand ambition"? Can you use it to explore the feelings you have about your current project?

Some Self-Defeating Creative Scenarios

Some writers seem to use their work to disappoint themselves, to retraumatize themselves, to flagellate themselves, to murder their souls. You'll recognize the following creative scenarios as self-defeating. Working in this way will inevitably derail the healing potential of creative work.

———————

We have an essay we want to write about an important event in our lives. Someone we know is editing a collection of essays on our subject—single-parent adoption. We tell her about our idea; she likes it. We send her a short proposal. She accepts it, telling us she'll publish whatever we write. She wants the twenty-page piece three months from now; it's a firm deadline.

This is our first opportunity for publication, and we're excited but also afraid to start. The enormity of the project scares us. We tell ourselves we have plenty of time. We don't stop to make a schedule or to calculate that we need only write seven pages a month to be finished in time.

We mark the due date on our calendar. We think about the piece often. Ideas come, but we don't write them down. We're too busy. We wait to be "really" inspired to begin.

A week before our deadline, we're frantic. We haven't written a word. We decide we'll work long hours. We feel anxious and fearful, short-tempered and irritable. We work, but nothing seems compelling.

We're exhausted, and we have scores of pages but no essay. We feel like a failure.

I meet a writer friend for lunch. He's started work on a novel. He's imagined some wonderful characters—a minister, a backwoodsman, and his hardworking blind wife—and an interesting, complex, adulterous affair between the minister and the woman that raises issues about commitment and fidelity. The first twenty pages have come directly. "This is my magnum opus," he tells me. "This book will make or break me. I know I'll pound it out in a month, maybe two at the most."

Later, he tells me what he's going to do with the money he makes from this book—move to the country, start a magazine—and how he'll handle his wife's jealousy when he becomes famous.

He gives me some pages to read. There's an urgency in the prose I haven't seen in his work before. I suggest he take the work one step at a time. I think he's expecting too much from himself, he's giving himself too little time, staking too much on this project. He's confusing pulling off this book with his sense of self-worth, which is dangerous. I tell him the creative process can't be rushed.

A few months later, I hear from a mutual friend that he's not feeling well about his work, that he's frustrated and angry because he's run into a major snag. And that he's considering abandoning his project.

I pick up a writer's published journal. In it, she describes her phenomenal early successes—that she has published her work while young and won prizes. She says that publishing in places like the *New Yorker* is essential to her belief in her poetic ability. She changes her style, even her subject matter, to make it more likely that her work will be accepted. When it gets rejected, though, she becomes dispirited and often seriously depressed.

Meantime, she follows the emerging career of another woman poet. She sees this woman as arch-rival. She wants, more than anything, to "beat" this woman to a major prize. Every time her rival's work is praised, she berates herself and feels worthless.

This poet knows that to do her finest work she shouldn't marry (especially another poet) or have children. Still, she does both. She tries to be the perfect wife and mother, often under difficult circumstances. She never seems to have time for her work; she squeezes her attempts at writing into the corners of the day. Yet she bakes bread and pies and, for a time, even grows fruit and keeps bees—time-consuming, exhausting occupations.

She types up her husband's work, sends it around; she wants him to become famous before she does. Still, she resents her incapacity to work. She feels she never has time to do her work. Often, she waits until she's inspired to write, then she works feverishly. She believes that the creative process is filled with strife and that it's dangerous. She studies the lives of women writers who have killed themselves; they become her models.

This is Sylvia Plath. And understanding how she herself derailed the healing possibilities of creative work is instructive. She often worked more for the sake of fame than to do her work. She then felt herself a fraud because she believed she was untrue to her desire (and she often was). She had grandiose aims. And whatever she achieved didn't satisfy her. She worked for external goals rather than for internal growth: besting an opponent, making her husband or her mother proud, getting prizes, publishing in prestigious journals. She didn't create the life she needed to do her work. She became overinvolved in her husband's work, often neglecting hers. She worked irregularly, then feverishly. She patterned her life on a self-destructive model of the creative process.

Some Essentials in Using Writing as a Way of Healing

Some simple guidelines can keep us from enacting these self-defeating scenarios. These are essentials we can follow to support us in using writing in a healing way.

First, it is essential that we write regularly in a relaxed way. That we don't fight our process or try to force or control it.

Second, it is essential that we watch with a relaxed awareness what occurs as we write.

Third, it is essential that we don't judge ourselves or our work. That we write to create or, in time, to finish a piece of work but without expectation of the wealth or fame that such writing may bring.

Fourth, it is essential that we be patient. That we write routinely. But that we don't hurry our work.

If we show up at our writing, with commitment, and if we respect ourselves and the writing process, we trust that in time something worthwhile will emerge. We trust, too, that engaging in the writing process, by itself, is valuable.

How Keeping a Process Journal Helps Us Heal

As so many creative people discover, keeping a process journal is an extraordinarily useful tool in nurturing creativity. But apart from using it as a way of capturing our insights and planning our projects, I've found that keeping a process journal is an important way for us to understand our relationship to our writing and to the act of creativity. And, I believe, it is in understanding ourselves as writers that we optimize the healing potential of our writing.

When my students start writing, I encourage them to begin a process journal where they comment upon their writing—how it's going, how they feel about it, ideas they may want to examine, what they're excited about, proud of, looking forward to, what they've learned. In this way, we can reframe problems in our writing as creative challenges. Anthony Robbins suggests we explore these issues daily, and that this practice will alter our feelings about our lives. It will change, too, our relationship to our creative work.

Process journals are an excellent resource to use to learn about ourselves. Because our journal acts as a record of our writing, it shows us our patterns of work and feeling, our responses to ourselves and our writing, our strategies for dealing with difficulties and challenges. It helps us through difficult times; it helps guide our writing; it helps bolster our spirits.

Well into the process of writing a piece about how she was raped as a child, my student Alice paused to reflect upon her work and to make an entry into her process journal. I reproduce part of it below.

Her willingness to share her work and her process with our class inspired us all. That year, because of her evenhanded discussion about her childhood, many of us were urged into writing difficult material we'd avoided. Alice's courage helped me write about how painful it had been for me to live with a depressed mother, yet how strong my mother was in trying, each day, to do the best she could for me.

Through Alice's work, we were reminded what it means to have pluck and courage. She showed us how keeping a process journal (in addition to the writing of our stories) is immensely healing.

One day, Alice took her journal to a Laundromat and, as her laundry washed and dried, she wrote an entry showing how writing about our writing can engage us in a process that's as helpful—and healing—as the act of creation itself.

Alice's Journal

I made my way to the laundry Saturday evening. I needed to think about this stage of writing that I am in right now.

I thought of the millions of ideas I had in my head about how I should begin writing about my abuse. My abuse. It seems as if it is something that I now own. At times I'll admit that I hide behind it to avoid situations I can't or don't know how to handle. But this will only make me afraid to do the things I want to do. It is something too important for me to think I can wish away or pretend never happened. Yes, he abused me, but in my head I own the experience because I witnessed it and experienced it. . . .

I write about what I witness, sometimes I write about what I feel.

It would be easier to write about the bullshit things that happen in life. But I don't want to because they seem trite and inconsequential, though at times I wonder why I put myself through this every day by writing about the bad memories.

The writing I do is more than a release and it's more than a statement of rebellion that I have against people who abuse children. . . . I am full of doubts about my own sanity. This is where writing comes into the picture. My sanity is at stake. . . . How else can I cope with a past I oftentimes don't remember? That is the scariest thing about this process. You're putting yourself out there so that you can write about things you haven't even wanted to think about for years.

Now that I'm in the process I see that . . . some memories are not clear and there are some memories that I'm blocking out. It is scary to think that there is more to this than what I've already written about. It's as if a piece of the image has been cut or erased. Should I be happy that I don't remember or glad that I do? I'm glad that I do remember what I do because I can deal with what I know.

While I take each piece of clothing and drop it into the clothes basket, I think of the themes I could use to write my memoir: incidents where I remember the actual rape; happy times in my childhood as well as bad; the adults—where were they?; physical aspects; threats; how I'd hide; where I'd hide; fighting back.

I list these possible topics and am amazed at all the aspects of this story I could tell. One of the dilemmas I have is how I'd be able to tell this story with the details being very sketchy and unclear. I want to be true to this art, true to myself, and true to the audience. But how can I when I don't even remember most of the attacks?

After dumping all the clothes into the dryer I sit down and take out a notebook and record all of these ideas. This is one of my favorite parts of the writing process. It's the feeling you get when you can't stop writing and ideas are popping into your head left and right and your hand cannot write fast enough for these thoughts. At this point the process is all about getting the information down so that I can begin the work that I need to do. So immersing myself in the memories of terror and fear is actually pointless and unproductive. At this stage, it's a matter of divorcing yourself from the situation and looking at it objectively. It's very difficult to explain the emotional contradiction of writing any traumatic experience. This is how I am able to go on because I have to tell the story no matter how uncomfortable or how unsettled it makes me. When I'm in this mindset nothing is as important as conveying a truth and an emotional response so that the reader or audience can understand where I'm coming from despite their own inexperience or personal knowledge of sexual abuse.

My only fear in writing this is that my audience will be turned off. . . . The things that I know about through my experience of rape are unsettling and shocking. I guess that is one of the reasons why I've never attempted to address this issue before. I've always been afraid that people wouldn't understand me or worse not believe the words that I write.

The most important thing for me to do is to tell the truth.

In writing her process journal, Alice discovers she has many ideas for her work; that she can't repress or ignore what happened. She learns that her reluctance to do certain (unnamed) things in her life is linked to her rape but that she uses it as an excuse and that this probably isn't helping her.

She understands the value of her undertaking this difficult writing task. She learns that she is courageous, and she discovers how her sense of self-worth is buttressed. She knows, too, that writing is necessary for her, that keeping her feelings locked up would be damaging.

Examining what she can remember, she finds that her memories are fragmentary, blocked, or repressed. She understands that this is, perhaps, the way one remembers trauma. She knows that writing helps her feel productive and energetic. It's better than brooding. Writing helps her "go on." She knows, though, that there will be uncomfortable times ahead.

Alice gathers strength from knowing that sharing her story will be useful. Ultimately, although her experience has forced her into isolation, her writing will begin to help her connect with others. In anticipating the needs of her audience, she thinks about her writing in a more public context. She begins to think about giving her experiences a shape and form that will make them comprehensible to readers.

How Using the Process Journal Can Help Us Understand and Accept Ourselves and Our Writing

As Alice's process journal entry shows, reflecting upon what we feel and think as we write helps us heal. We ask ourselves what our writing has taught us and what we can now bring to our writing because of what we've learned. We keep in mind the question: "What am I feeling right now about my work?" In writing about her feelings about writing, Alice achieved a level of acceptance, wisdom, and insight that simply writing about her abuse couldn't have accomplished.

After reading Alice's work, I went back to the journals of Sylvia Plath. Though she kept a journal for years, she didn't reflect upon how writing her courageous work made her feel. Nor did she connect the effect of her writing upon her feelings and her life.

On March 28, 1958, for example, she describes how she wrote eight poems in eight days: "long poems, lyrical poems, and thunderous poems: poems breaking open my real experience of life in the last five years: life which has been shut up, untouchable, in a rococo crystal cage, not to be touched. I feel these are the best poems I have ever done."

By the end of the week, though, she was gobbling aspirins. She was completely exhausted and suicidal, "wishing to test my eye and fiber on tragedy. . . . I walk the razor's edge of jeopardy." Neither working nor writing about her work seemed to help her manage her feelings. Instead, Plath seemed to feel worse, perhaps because she didn't reflect upon the link between her feelings and the events in her life. Nor did she write about how doing her work made her feel. Nor did she understand how to care for herself as she wrote. Because Plath didn't witness herself working—didn't record her feelings about her creative process—she didn't connect what she was experiencing with her work.

Nonjudgmental, self-reflective witnessing of ourselves as writers helps us not to ruminate about our feelings (a destructive practice) or to engage in accusation or self-blame. Instead, keeping a process journal as Alice kept hers invites us to focus upon defining ourselves as active and engaged, not as passive, helpless, and hopeless.

Writing and reflecting about writing can enhance self-acceptance and self-love. Whatever we're experiencing, we tell ourselves, is what we're experiencing right now.

Writing as Gift

Recently, my writing partner, Edvige Giunta, called to check in with me after a particularly meaningful writing session. She was exploring how much she missed her family's garden in Sicily and the impact of the garden upon her sensibility. She told me she was prompted to write by recognizing how much she hated to shop for vegetables in our sterile, dehumanizing supermarkets, for it inevitably unleashed her sense of loss of the garden of her childhood.

"Write about the garden in Sicily," a voice suggested as she shopped. And she did.

When the piece was finished, she felt she had given herself something important; she had regained something of the garden she'd lost. But the process began with her accepting what the voice of inspiration that each of us possesses had suggested. And now she was on the phone, reading the piece, giving the gift of her writing to me.

In *The Gift: Imagination and the Erotic Life of Property,* Lewis Hyde writes that engaging in the creative process can unleash gratitude, self-nurturance, openness, and fertility within us. Artistic practice can be understood best as a present. While we engage in it, it will continue to give us benefits, acting as "an agent of transformation."

Wouldn't it be inspiriting to think of writing in this way? As a gift we give ourselves and others? Wouldn't it make the act of writing seem more joyful?

It isn't that we have to think we are "gifted" in the traditional sense to write. We all have something to give ourselves and others, says Hyde, and so we are all gifted. For many years now, I have believed that if we think only "special" people can write, we are depriving ourselves of a way we can nurture ourselves even in difficult situations.

In her memoir, *To the Is-land,* Janet Frame describes how her working-class mother made sure she devoted time to writing and reading poetry. For Frame's mother believed that despite her heavily burdened life, creativity wasn't a luxury: it was a necessity. Without reading poetry, without writing it, she knew she couldn't survive. "Only the poets know, only the poets know," her mother would often murmur.

Living in isolated railway outposts in New Zealand, Frame's mother received from poetry a needed sense of connection with others. She knew that without writing she would have complained about her life, focusing upon its difficulties, and that she would have taken her dissatisfaction out on her children. Through writing, though, she examined her life and valued it. Caring for herself by writing, she believed, enabled her to care for her children. Without it, she would have been dissatisfied and unloving.

Often she wrote poems in praise of the writers she revered. Or about the natural environment she loved. She shared her work with her children and published it. She encouraged her children to write and share their work, too. She was the reason Janet Frame grew up thinking that writing was a fundamental form of self-care, one that Janet Frame herself used to write her way out of a mental institution.

The Romans, Lewis Hyde tells us, believed we each are born with an internal guiding spirit, called our "genius," the source of sexual potency, artistic creativity, and spirituality. Though it was given to us at birth, we have a responsibility to cultivate it. "The spirit that brings us our gifts," Hyde reminds us, "finds its eventual freedom only through our sacrifice." If you care for your "genius," you become a god. If you don't, you become a "larva," a restless spook that preys on the living—which is how I behave when I'm not writing.

If we leave ourselves open, if we follow the voice of our genius that tells us what to write about, we will find that we inevitably continue to receive "gifts"—moments of inspiration that guide us, a sense of joy and abundance and plenty—and we will feel gifted. We can deny ourselves this and become restless spooks. Or we can engage in the act of creation that energizes and enlarges us.

Writing. A gift that comes to us. A gift we give ourselves. A gift we give to others.

Chapter Six

Caring for Ourselves as We Write

*You have a soul in you of rare quality,
an artist's nature; never let it starve for
lack of what it needs.*

MARCEL PROUST

Writing about traumatic or troubling life experiences initially unleashes difficult, conflicting emotions. In the long run, though, we feel better emotionally and are healthier and achieve a level of understanding of our lives that only writing can provide. Safe writing—writing what we already know or understand, writing that is superficial—won't help us grow, either as people or as writers. For our writing to be healing, we must encounter something that puzzles, confuses, troubles, or pains us.

An outgrowth of the kind of writing that digs deep, that takes risks, that arises from our desire to explore the unresolved emotional puzzles or ongoing pain in our lives is that we "gain greater psychological freedom" (as Albert M. Rothenberg, M.D., has observed) and greater range and depth in our artistic expression than we had before.

Managing Difficult Emotions as We Write

The emotional territory that we must learn to live with and manage, if we want to write powerful, authentic pieces of work, is complex. As a teacher and mentor of beginning writers, I have learned that when students begin to write "real," it is as essential for me to discuss how we can handle the difficult emotions that surface as it is for me to discuss, say, how to write good dialogue or to use imagery to deepen our work. It is necessary for us to learn how to care for ourselves as we embark upon complex but significant writing so that we can benefit from the healing potential of telling our stories.

The students James W. Pennebaker describes in *Opening Up* experienced unpleasant feelings while they were journal writing. But they participated in the study for just three days, so they had to tolerate their complicated emotions for only a short time. Usually when we write, though, we are not finished with a work in a few days. We are often working on projects that are long-term, that can take us weeks, months, even years to complete.

Our challenge, then, is to learn how to allow our feelings to emerge as we work, to let ourselves experience them and use them to deepen our work but not to let them disable us. We must enact principles of self-care as we write, like those articulated in Daniel Goleman's *Emotional Intelligence,* so that we use our writing to heal ourselves rather than to retraumatize ourselves. We can also discover what we must do for ourselves by reading works describing what writers determined to maintain their emotional equilibrium have discovered about managing their lives—such as Donald Hall's *Life Work,* Doris Grumbach's *Life in a Day,* bell hooks's *Sisters of the Yam.*

I believe that many people who would like to write about certain thorny subjects choose not to because they are afraid they can't handle the feelings that they foresee will emerge as they work. "I don't want to write about my father's death," a writer friend once said, "because I'm afraid of how bad I'll feel; I'm afraid writing about it will hurt me. Still, it's the only thing I want to write about."

It is surely true that sometimes writing uncovers emotions that temporarily make us feel uncomfortable. And because projects can continue for weeks, months, even years, the risk exists that unless we learn how to manage discomfort, it might continue unabated for a long time. Or that, unable to tolerate our feelings, we abandon our work.

How then, can we meet this challenge? And keep meeting it all our writing lives?

Once Karen, a student writing about a difficult childhood, told our class how she centered herself by using meditation and a self-designed religious ritual before writing. Then, whenever she felt she might become overwhelmed by her feelings about her work, she stopped, went out for a short walk in her neighborhood, and bought herself an inexpensive but special treat—a scented soap, a pair of colorful socks, a small bouquet of flowers. Or she did something special—sat on a bench in Central Park where she could see children playing or retreated to the interior of a serene neighborhood church and watched the sun filter through the stained-glass windows. These moments calmed and quieted her. When she returned to her desk, she found she could write another difficult detail.

Karen had taught herself how to write about the past without having it overtake her and poison her present—an extremely valuable and potentially life-saving strategy for writers dealing with knotty material. Karen learned, too, how resilient she was if she acted in her own best interests. Somehow, she said, taking care of herself as she worked helped her recover important positive (and healing) memories from her childhood that she knew she needed to examine in writing in order to present a well-rounded portrait of her life—the loving concern of a teacher who discussed books with her, a gift of a paint set from an uncle, which unleashed a passion for painting.

How Not to Crack Up While Writing

At thirty-nine, F. Scott Fitzgerald experienced a breakdown, which he subsequently described in *The Crack-Up*. In that work, Fitzgerald said that he now understood that writers must carefully nurture and care for themselves and their work or they will soon lose their gifts and their sanity. He had been, he admitted, "only a mediocre caretaker of . . . my talent."

True, a major part of his problem was his heavy drinking and his rambunctious and dissipated lifestyle—"a burning of the candle at both ends; a call upon physical resources that I did not command, like a man over-drawing at his bank." He hadn't learned how to live his life to protect his ability to write. But Fitzgerald wanted his readers to know, too, that other factors also had contributed to the decline of his mental health, self-esteem, and talent.

Fitzgerald realized he'd led an inauthentic life, a nonreflective, reactive life. He had done "very little thinking," he knew, except for matters of craft. Rather than looking within to determine what he needed to satisfy himself, Fitzgerald had assumed other people's values. Rather than determining for himself how he might most fulfillingly interact with people to suit his needs, he allowed someone else to dictate the fabric of his relationships: "how to do, what to say." This, he admitted, "always confused me and made me want to go out and get drunk."

Nor had he cultivated a genuine writer's voice. He didn't have the patience to permit artistic solutions to emerge organically as he worked, trusting that he could solve the aesthetic challenges he faced. He had avoided responsibility for making decisions. Instead, he let someone else (whom he doesn't name) be his "artistic conscience" and decide for him.

For years, too, he had been self-absorbed. Consequently, he knew nothing about what was going on in the world. His political conscience "scarcely existed," so he found himself completely disconnected from the most important issues of his time.

Fitzgerald believed he had lost his identity and his soul: "there was not an 'I' any more—not a basis on which I could organize my self-respect." He hadn't taken the time or trouble to reflect upon what his authentic self desired. Instead, he modeled his behavior on external, inappropriate, and destructive models. Nor did he grapple long enough with the challenges his work presented. Instead, he took shortcuts, making another person responsible for making decisions about his work.

Though he became an enormous popular success, he thought it was meaningless because he had been untrue to himself. He had "no self" left. His "constant striving" for the external trappings of success rather than for genuine, self-defined standards greatly contributed to his "unhappiness."

When Virginia Woolf wrote *To the Lighthouse,* her work went "fast and fluently," and, though she dealt with complex emotions concerning her family, she was content and her work helped her immeasurably. During the writing, Woolf cared for herself. Yet later in her life, when she again used her family as the source for another novel, *The Years,* her work was a continuous struggle and almost relentlessly painful. She admitted that she was more discontent than she had been for years. Near its completion, Woolf nearly succumbed to suicidal despair, and she blamed her disintegration on her writing that book. Not surprisingly, while she was writing *The Years,* Woolf behaved in the same manner described by F. Scott Fitzgerald in *The Crack-Up.*

As she wrote *Lighthouse,* Woolf led a balanced life. She controlled her writing time so she didn't become engulfed by her work, so she had time to socialize. She wrote slowly and steadily, completing two pages a day. She was orderly, unhurried, unharried. She systematically studied Elizabethan literature, which distracted and challenged her. She wrote in her diary every day, recording what gave her joy—small pleasures, like taking a bus ride, making an ice, reading a letter—so she could pursue her pleasures more actively, becoming a "pool of content." She learned that the secret to her happiness was to "feast on the moment." She explored what irked her, understanding that often the source of her misery was the way she had been mistreated by her friends. She wrote about what she felt—rage, fury, love, disappointment, unworthiness—and why she felt it. She tried to understand her difficult feelings as she wrote so they wouldn't endanger her or compromise her writing.

While writing *The Years,* Woolf overworked, producing about ten pages a day. She also started a biography of Roger Fry, which made her feel overwhelmed. "I am so oppressed by the thought of all the books I have to write that my head is bristling like a bursting boiler," she complained. She felt herself stressed, and her work and her physical and mental health suffered. All her reading was related to her work, so it provided no relief. She did little that centered her. She became overinvolved with the success or failure of her work. She had little to distract her from the pressure of writing, so if her work wasn't going well, it seemed that her life wasn't going well either. She kept her journal erratically, carelessly. Often, her entries were simple accounts of daily events rather than reflective insights into her life and work. She now wanted to control her feelings rather than express them: she tried to "suppress one self," for she thought it would bring her serenity. Instead, it brought emotional breakdown.

While writing *Lighthouse,* Woolf focused on finding a way of working that suited this project, on writing a work that was, as she put it, "my own expression." She didn't concern herself with her reputation. "I want," she wrote, "to dig deep down into my new stories, without having a looking glass flashed in my eyes." As she worked, she set herself challenges, "to learn greater quiet, & force," to learn how to use feelings in her work. She could truly say, "I am now writing as fast and freely as I have written in the whole of my life."

While writing *The Years,* though, Woolf tried to force her book into a predetermined concept. As she wrote, a character named Elvira became "too dominant." Instead of letting the evolving work guide her, Woolf battled her intuitive process. And instead of simply doing her work, Woolf thought continually about how it would be reviewed. She was too aware of her reputation, and this inhibited her. The writing was a constant strain. "Writing is effort: writing is despair," she wrote.

While writing *Lighthouse*, Woolf was emotionally intelligent (to paraphrase Daniel Goleman's term). While writing *The Years*, Woolf was emotionally stupid.

Fitzgerald's analysis of how he lost his emotional and psychic center and Woolf's contrasting experiences in writing *Lighthouse* and *The Years* can be transformed easily into a program for how writers can become self-caring, authentic, emotionally intelligent, and truly successful.

- Don't overextend yourself in your work or burn yourself out by leading a dissipated life.
- Renew yourself by study and reflection. Become knowledgeable and thoughtful.
- Live an introspective life, and determine what authentic success means to you and what kind of life and interpersonal and social relationships best suit your temperament and your talent. Change your behavior if you recognize you are working in a damaging way.
- Patiently strive for artistic authenticity. Though using examples and models of other people and their work is an important part of the creative process, use them as ways of learning how to solve problems and how to cultivate a singular artistic voice. For, ultimately, we must look within for solutions to creative challenges.
- And remain politically aware and involved so that you and your work stay connected to something beyond your own self-interest.

What the Research Says About Caring for Ourselves as We Write

Andrew Brink and Anthony Storr, who have studied intensively the creative process of many writers, have reached conclusions similar to

Fitzgerald's. Brink believes that writing alone won't help us heal. For creative work to be genuinely reparative and transformational, Brink says, "contemplation, discipline and ritual" seem necessary.

By *contemplation,* Brink means that we must think about the world, ourselves and others, and the subject of our work. We must relate what we are learning in our work to our lives. We must be willing to use these insights to change our behavior if necessary. For example, if my student Alice, whose process journal I quoted in the last chapter, learned in working that she used the history of her abuse to prevent herself from interacting with people, and she didn't act upon that insight, her writing couldn't help her heal. For we must use what we learn as we work to enrich our lives.

By *discipline,* Brink means that we must attend to our work and our lives in a carefully planned and regulated way. Bringing order into our lives is crucial. If we know that we must organize our workspace, we must respect that need and act upon it. We must not use our creativity to create chaos in our lives by working in a frantic, undisciplined way. Nor should we use it to separate ourselves from the people we love. Rather, we use our writing in the interests of our stability, which often means balancing our responsibilities to ourselves and to others. It sometimes also means making compromises. It never means giving up our writing or the people we love.

By *ritual,* Brink means enacting patterns of behavior that cultivate the concentration necessary to do deeply creative work. Each of us must learn what these are and must adhere to them. If we know we need a long, uninterrupted stretch of time to be alone to write, for this helps us immeasurably, we do what we must to find that time and, for example, we don't answer the telephone while we're working.

Similarly, Anthony Storr believes that for writers to work in a way that will permit them to achieve relief from emotional tension, they cannot just blindly write about whatever compels them or mindlessly act in any way they desire. By nature, people drawn to writing, Storr believes, seem to have a tenuous sense of self. They tend to prefer complexity, incompleteness, individuality, impulsiveness, and expansiveness—all potential sources of strength, to be sure, but also challenges to emotional well-being. To be successful and content, then, writers must cultivate their strengths and modify their weaknesses, which doesn't happen automatically. They must nurture "a strongly functioning ego, capable of judgment, inhibition of immediate impulses, persistence, and control."

To do creative work that enables us to come to terms with the difficult realities of our personal lives, we must control our potentially self-destructive impulses. We must refine our ability to make careful and considered judgments about our lives and our relationships, our work habits and our writing. Then and only then will we profit from the enormous potential for change that our writing can bring us in helping us accept and understand the painful reality of our lives.

Enacting a Program of Self-Care

I was not always a writer who knew how to care for myself as I worked. For years, when I was in college and graduate school, writing papers was accompanied by anxiety and stress. I always focused upon wanting a good grade rather than on the work; I started my writing too late, then worked myself into panic and frenzy. And after every major paper I wrote, I became ill.

When I began to write professionally, though I loved writing, and though I gradually learned many important ways of avoiding the difficulties, which I describe here, there were certain times in my writing life when I didn't attend to my needs. Once, when writing about the difficult beginning of Virginia Woolf's marriage, I worked in an unwise way. My mother had recently died. I was using my writing to *control* my feelings of loss. Nowhere in my process journals are there any references to my emotions. They stayed buried and harmed me. I offhandedly remarked to a friend that because my mother was often so seriously depressed, I felt I never had a mother and now that she was dead I was experiencing a dual loss. Yet when she died, honestly, I was relieved, too. Though I felt guilty at the time about these feelings, I now understand that they were reasonable given the circumstances.

Often, during that time, I awakened at five in the morning and wrote for several hours before driving into New York City to teach. I was working very long hours, not taking time to decompress, to exercise, to cook nutritious meals. I was doing little else but working. I had nothing to distract me or to enrich my life.

The unrelenting stress, the unexamined feelings undermined my health. And I believe that I paid for not tending to my needs with a year-long serious illness that was finally diagnosed as asthma.

When I reentered therapy, at first to deal with my feelings about having asthma, I began to learn that there were some issues in my life—my sister's death, primarily—that I'd never written about, never addressed. Though intellectually I understood what loss meant, I hadn't yet reflected upon what her death meant to me, nor allowed myself to grieve. This I began to do over the next several years in the more personal form of memoir writing. And in my therapy, which was ongoing.

I had resisted writing about my sister's suicide for years. Not understanding that writing about her would be healing and helpful if I did the work in a self-caring way, I feared that writing about her would harm me. For ten years, I occasionally wrote about Jill in my journal. Even then, though, I didn't examine my feelings about her or her death in any significant way. Mostly, I recalled incidents from our past—how we shared a bed, how I resented her when my mother made me take care of her—and I described it in vague and general terms. Nothing too specific. Nothing that I feared would stir up a messy grief I had buried with her. Yet because for years my feelings remained unexamined, unexpressed, unexplored, the quality of my life, and my health, too, was seriously compromised.

When I finally began to write about my sister's death, I started my work with an event I thought about frequently—the moment my husband came into our bedroom to tell me he'd received a call that my sister had killed herself. I described it in detail. Next I turned to the moment I went downstairs into my messy basement to do the laundry one day but decided, instead, to sort through the boxes of my mother's personal effects stored there after her death and my father's remarriage.

I came upon many cartons containing mementos of my sister's that my mother had saved and cherished—Girl Scout badges, souvenirs from her dates, her dolls and handmade dolls' clothes, autograph books, letters from me and from her boyfriends, prom pictures.

When I discovered them, I found myself grieving for my sister, but also for my mother. Why, I asked myself, did my mother choose to keep these few remnants of what I thought of as my sister's pathetic and foreshortened life? And why had my sister, near forty, saved her dolls? Was it that she had never really grown up?

"My basement is a complete mess, and has been for years" was the line that unlocked the deadbolt of my feelings about my sister, about my sister's suicide, and that enabled me to write and begin to understand the impact of her death upon my life. "At last," I wrote in my journal, "after ten years, I am writing about Jill."

In writing about my sister, I uncovered many unexpected, complex feelings—rage, loss, a terrifying sense of loneliness, betrayal, guilt, terror, my fear of death, my occasional suicidal fantasies. Often, I cried as I wrote. But writing was life enhancing, for I had learned to care for myself as I worked.

It would do me no good, I knew, to dwell upon the past in a way that would provoke unbearable pain and sorrow. As I worked, I heeded the instructions of a yoga teacher.

Concentrate on what your body is saying. Ask yourself if you can relax though you might initially feel some discomfort. See if you can extend yourself somewhat beyond your limits. But don't force it. If you must, back off if it becomes too uncomfortable for you. Eventually, if you come to this practice each day, you can do what you formerly could not. Listen to the wisdom of your body.

This, I realized, was as useful for the process of writing as it was for doing yoga. Here was a sure guide for my work, for my self-care, and for avoiding emotional injury as I wrote.

Concentrate on what your body is saying. Ask yourself if you can relax into the writing though you might initially feel some discomfort. See if you can extend yourself somewhat beyond your limits. But don't force it. If you must, back off from the writing if it becomes too uncomfortable for you. Eventually, if you come to this practice each day, you will find that you can do what you formerly could not. Listen to the wisdom of your body.

Before I began writing, I had learned what I needed to do to write without precipitating an emotional crisis. I knew now that to take risks on the page without endangering ourselves, we must do so from a position of relative emotional safety. I prepared to do the work, and as I worked I continued caring for myself. I asked myself, "What must I do to write this essay and enjoy the process of doing it, though I'll be working with difficult emotional material?"

Before writing, I read about how other writers had described the death of a loved one. I read general works about grief, loss, and dying so I could remind myself that others, too, had shared my experience. I made sure I didn't focus exclusively on my loss; I wanted to learn how others rebuilt their lives.

Doing this helped my work, too, for as I read I noticed style, imagery, form, structure. I learned how best to describe feelings, how to use dialogue, how to depict people, events, and places. Focusing on aesthetics provided a welcome distraction.

I continued to learn about creativity by reading books and articles so I could better understand my own process. From an interview with Peter Høeg, the author of *Smilla's Sense of Snow,* I learned that while he worked on a major project, he routinely led a quiet and orderly life, which reinforced my desire to do the same.

I organized my life so that I could have the time and emotional space to do this demanding creative work. I set aside a realistic amount of time for it. With calendar in hand, I drew up a schedule for the work. I set limits on my social life throughout this period, for I knew the work would be demanding. But I made sure I engaged in exchanges with my network of supportive writer friends and went on periodic excursions. And I took evenings and weekends off to relax and enjoy my family. In my writing journal, I wrote, "I would like to work on understanding that I know what I need to do to nourish my writing life."

I withdrew from unnecessary obligations and declined several opportunities to speak and write because I knew it was important for me not to feel overwhelmed as I worked. In my journal I wrote, "I am developing a sense of when to say no—I want to say no to just about everything right now. I need to put so very much effort and energy into keeping myself stable while I do this work that I can't allow anything or anyone into my life that might endanger my work or stability." I also paid attention to my health. And I meditated. Meditation, besides helping me manage stress, permitted me to be more alert to the world, to my body, to my feelings. To reduce stress, I worked in a systematic way; I kept my workspace organized. "The more harrowing the subject," I wrote, "the neater your desk must be."

I always had emotional support available. I checked in with my writer friends weekly, sometimes daily. And I was in therapy while writing, which helped integrate the difficult and shameful feelings my writing was unearthing. I wrote in my journal, too, about the positive aspects of my life to maintain my perspective while I worked.

At the time I was reading Anthony Robbins, *Awaken the Giant Within,* and was greatly influenced by this work. Robbins made many valuable suggestions I embraced about managing difficult feelings. Adapting one of Robbins's practices, I began to write about what I was happy about in my work, what I was excited by, proud of, grateful for, enjoying most, committed to, learning, and giving/sharing. So, though I was writing about pain, my journal acted as a welcome respite and necessary balance. These insights eventually found their way into my memoir.

Writing about my sister's death helped me begin to mourn her loss and to understand much about our family history of depression and its consequences. Though I had lost Jill, I felt I had regained something of her by writing.

The most difficult challenges we face as we write are not technical but emotional. Of working while we feel pain. Of working through our pain to acceptance, insight, and emotional repose.

The process of writing can be healing only if we learn how to examine and express our feelings in our work without dwelling upon them while we are away from the work, for that might forestall our progress. Or, more dangerously, it might lead us to overidentifying with our work so that we relive our traumas or ruminate about our losses and dissatisfactions rather than represent them on the page.

As writers, we all pass through many emotional way stations—loss, exhilaration, despair, sorrow, rage, happiness, grief—as we work. We learn, too, that letting ourselves have our emotions without becoming overwhelmed by them as we work is an important (and all-too-often ignored) skill for us to develop. We discover that we must learn to manage our difficult feelings, to distract ourselves, to find relief from the work's intensity if we are to develop a wholesome relationship to our work. This is surely as important as learning to write well.

As we hear how other writers successfully faced their difficult feelings and worked through them and how they wrote despite them (or, perhaps, because of them), we learn strategies that we, too, might find useful.

We learn how to write deeply and authentically, without risking our well-being.

And, if we are to use writing as a way of healing our emotional pain, we must learn that the life we're presently living is (or can be) different from what we're describing. For we are not merely the selves we describe on paper.

WHAT YOU CAN DO NOW   Can you identify and write about the feelings you're having as you work? Can you be explicit about them? Are they, perhaps, feelings of sorrow, grief, excitement, elation, despair, helplessness, euphoria, accomplishment, resentment? What does each feel like? How does each make you feel about the writing process?

Can you describe, as Anthony Robbins suggests, what in your work makes you happy, excited, proud, or grateful? What you're enjoying most, what you're committed to, what you've learned, what you've accomplished, what your work offers others, and how your work has added to your quality of life?

What does *overwhelmed* mean to you? How do you become overwhelmed? Does it interfere with your writing? With your life? Can you ascertain how to avoid this state? Or how to extricate yourself from it once you're in it? (Anthony Robbins in *Awaken the Giant Within* shows how.)

Can you reflect upon any factors that enable you to write well or that complicate your process? Can you list the elements of self-care you must initiate or continue?

Chapter Seven

Stages of the Process, Stages of Growth I

Preparing, Planning, Germinating

*The novel is finished at last. It has been a lifeline.
I do not have to win in order to know my dreams
are valid, I only have to believe in a process of
which I am a part. My work kept me alive this
past year, my work and the love of women.
They are inseparable from each other. In the
recognition of the existence of love lies the answer
to despair. Work is that recognition given voice
and name.*

AUDRE LORDE, *The Cancer Journals*

For our writing to be healing, it's important for us to
understand that there are different stages of the writing process, and different challenges at each stage.
Working against the process rather than accepting
what is possible and likely at each stage can drive us to
despair. But learning what we can reasonably expect
from ourselves at each step of the way, how it's most
advantageous for us to work, and what we'll most
likely feel will ensure that writing will be a beneficial

experience for us. It will also enable us to understand the extraordinary opportunities for growth available to us.

For years I've been reading books about creativity, reading about the writing process of famous writers, and observing my and my students' processes. And I've come to understand that the most healing way of approaching the writing process is to focus upon the potential and possibilities for growth rather than upon its problems and pitfalls. Knowing what each stage of the process affords us and making explicit our intention for using the process as a healing experience assure us that we will pass through each stage in the most enriching way possible.

Engaging in creative work, perhaps more than any other human endeavor, allows us to be autonomous while also providing us with opportunities for establishing a sense of our interconnectedness with others. This healing effect is especially important for those of us whose sense of ourselves has been compromised. Our creative work is one arena into which no one can penetrate without our explicit consent, yet we can offer our work to others if we choose.

Though hundreds of valuable books and articles have been written about the creative process, one is so outstanding that I reread it regularly. It is a piece by Eugene Raudsepp, called "A New Look at the Creative Process," about creativity in engineers, that my husband clipped for me many years ago from a copy of *Creative Computing*. What I learned from it changed my work. It enabled me to write without undue anxiety, to work in a healing way, and to undertake, create, and finish long, complex writing projects. I understood what I could and couldn't expect from myself at various stages of the process. And what I could do to help myself minimize stress and anxiety and maximize the healing benefits of my writing.

What I learned about the stages of the creative process from Raudsepp and others, like Albert Rothenberg, M.D., Howard Gardner, and Anthony Storr, I've shared with my students. I make them responsible for reflecting upon their process and for understanding what stage they're passing through, whether they are working appropriately for that stage, and what healing benefits they would like to strive for. Invariably, they tell me that working in this way enables them to write better—more authentically and more powerfully—than they've ever dreamed possible. It also enriches their lives.

Though each creative project is surely different, each seems to require that we pass through a series of stages in a predictable order. These stages overlap; nonetheless, they are definable. With just a bit of reflection, we can easily identify each and so know what to expect from this stage, how we can best help ourselves and our projects, and how we can exploit the growth potential of doing our work.

Here, then, are the stages we can expect to pass through as we work.

There is a *preparation stage,* which seems partially conscious, partially instinctive. For a time, ideas and images drift into our consciousness and we pay them some attention. At some point we stop musing and begin to actively plan our work and articulate our preliminary intentions. We read, we learn about literary forms, we search for and find models and mentors for our work. I've discovered that beginning writers often spend far too little or far too much time at this stage; some avoid it altogether and plunge right into working, which can derail our process.

There is a *germination stage,* during which we gather and work on fragments of ideas, images, phrases, scenes, moments, lines, possibilities for plots, characters, settings. Sometimes we don't quite know what we're doing or where all this is leading. Sometimes we feel like we're working haphazardly. Sometimes, though, we have a clearer conception.

There is a *working stage,* during which we begin, build, and elaborate our project. Sometimes we seem to know precisely what we're doing. Sometimes what we're doing eludes us. Sometimes writers mistakenly assume the work is finished when the working stage is over. But for us to do our finest, most authentic work, we must proceed further.

There is a *deepening stage,* during which we revisit, rethink, reimagine, and revise what we've been doing. Often during this stage we learn what our project is *really* about, even if we've been working on it for years.

There is a *shaping stage,* during which we find the work's order and form.

There is a *completion stage,* during which we again revise, revisit, re-think, and refashion. During this stage we sometimes seem to know more easily whether an element belongs or doesn't, whether a solution will work or won't. Often the drive to finish a work takes precedence over other needs and obligations—like being social or taking showers or eating well. When my sons lived at home, they called it "the de-mented stage" because I was so completely involved in my work. Jason tells friends he would come to me at my desk when I was finishing a book and say, "Mom, I'm bleeding to death." According to him, I would respond, "That's nice dear, get yourself a snack, I'll be with you in a minute." I don't think it ever happened. Still, it has the ring of truth to it.

Finally, there is a *going-public stage,* during which we make the work, and ourselves, ready for others and, perhaps, ready for publication.

At the beginning stages—as we prepare and germinate our work—we can derail our process if we don't follow our urges to read; if we don't honor our desire to begin thinking about a work; if we consider our fleeting thoughts too trivial; if we imagine that we should know pre-cisely what we're doing; if we adopt an all-too-serious attitude toward our work; if we expect too much of ourselves too soon.

At the working stage, we can derail our process if we expect our work to have shape and form; if we don't follow our impulses and instincts; if we don't let the work teach us how it wants to be done, what it wants to be about; if we work feverishly; if we don't take time for relaxation; if we give up when we get confused; if we think about the product rather than the process; if we judge and criticize our work and ourselves.

At the deepening and shaping stages, we can derail our process if we can't maintain our interest in the work through periods when our enthusiasm wanes; if we abandon our work.

At the completion stage, we can derail our process if we work needlessly; if we refuse to let go of it; if we lose interest; if we become careless; if we don't follow through and finish well.

Some writers work on one creative project at a time. This kind of writer seems to need one deep, all-consuming preoccupation. Others, like me, find that we do our best work, and that we are more challenged and satisfied, when we are involved in two or more projects simultaneously. ("Flighty" or "easily distracted," my mother used to call this trait, which I now see as an advantage.)

This kind of writer probably needs much stimulation; needs, too, the advantages that come from being involved with several stages of the process simultaneously. Stephen King, for example, writes one book in the morning and plays with a second one in the afternoon. Virginia Woolf realized she worked best if she alternated writing fiction with nonfiction; she exercised different parts of her brain. Mozart, too, worked this way: he often scored one piece while composing a second while germinating ideas for a third, fourth, and fifth.

Of course, we alone can determine our best way of working. Still, I've discovered that many students restrain themselves from working on two pieces simultaneously because they think they're supposed to focus on one. Holding back from germinating a second work when we feel inspired, though, can frustrate our process. Often working on more than one project helps both.

Preparing

It seems paradoxical to think about organizing the stages of our writing because creativity is such an unpredictable affair and there's no telling what will happen as we do creative work. But I've found that planning and writing down intentions helps my students' work (and mine) immeasurably.

Formulating a Writing Plan: Some Practical Suggestions

First, I invite students to think about lifelong writing goals and to write them down. And I ask them to formulate a five-year writing plan. My lifelong writing goal (which may change) is exploring how and why works of art are created. Everything I've written contributes to this larger ongoing project.

Knowing this gives us a larger perspective on ourselves and our writing; it enables us to see the grand design in our life's work. Focusing on short-term goals alone can be self-limiting: after we realize them, we can feel empty.

Just as undertaking a yoga session according to a predetermined plan helps us focus on the moment-by-moment experience of each posture, so, too, having a writing plan helps us focus on the moment-by-moment experience of writing. We decide the length of our project, the time it will take and our completion date, the time we'll devote to each stage, our preliminary intentions. Then each time we write we can enter fully into our work without the anxiety and worry that often emerge when we have no long-range goals.

Although we can't predict what will happen as we write—sometimes a biography becomes a soulful exploration of our relationship with our subject; sometimes essays become books—it's useful to decide the scope of our undertaking. A short story or essay—about ten pages or 2,500 words? A twenty-page or 5,000-word piece? A thirty-page or 7,500-word piece? A 120-page or 30,000-word book? A 360-page or 90,000-word book? I always imagine that once I decide upon the length of a project my unconscious mind goes about the work of setting aside so many blank pages in some part of my brain and then filling them with words without my even being aware of it. For at some point in my process it seems as if the words are coming without my even having to write them. And my books are usually roughly the length I imagined.

My computer is set for a 250-word, double-spaced page. It takes typing some sample pages and fiddling with margins to do this because each computer is different. The font I use is ten characters to the inch. This produces an easy-to-read page with ample borders for rewrites. A too-dense page is difficult to read, nearly impossible to revise. With a 250-word page, too, I can easily determine how many words I've written—essential information for publishing.

I'm often asked how long a particular work or each stage of the process should take. Although it's tempting to say "It'll take as long as it takes," I am a writer who very much needs to know how much time I will devote to any given project and its stages. I need a due date so I can organize my work life. It makes me feel somewhat in control of an essentially unpredictable process. Many other professional writers state they must do this, too. Alice Walker, for example, sets aside two years to write a novel.

My students tell me that they write well while attending my classes because they know I am firm about deadlines; I permit no late work. They confide that when the course is over, unless they themselves set completion dates, they find their work founders. Choosing a completion date forces them to organize their days. Without it, they are tempted to tinker with a work longer than necessary or, worse, never to finish it.

For me and for most writers, completing works is important because of the sense of closure and accomplishment that attends finishing. Without setting a due date, I suspect I'd work on a project until the end of time.

What I do is simply this. I determine how long a project will take—three months, say, for a thirty-page essay; two years, say, for a 360-typescript-page book. (Even for beginning writers, this is feasible.)

Then I divide the time into thirds. I spend a third of the time on preparing and germinating; a third on working; a third deepening, finishing, and preparing for publication. For a three-month, thirty-page project, then, I allow a month for each stage. During the month-long working stage, I must write thirty typescript pages. I know I can usually write two pages in three hours, so I know how many writing hours I must schedule during the month: forty-five hours—eleven or twelve hours a week; two and a half hours a day. I tell my students knowing how long it takes to write a page is as important for a writer as knowing how long it takes to paint a room is for a painter.

I write down my schedule in a planner, mark off the hours I'll be writing. Writing down plans and having completion dates, studies show, mean we stand a good chance of finishing what we hope to accomplish. It means, too, that we're more likely to be satisfied with ourselves and our work. An important study of Harvard graduates discovered that the people who considered themselves most successful and content (despite difficulties encountered in their lives) differed from those who didn't consider themselves accomplished or satisfied in one major way: they wrote down their goals and plans.

Before I begin a long project, I plan in great detail. An emotional challenge of planning is being realistic. If we aren't realistic, we'll needlessly feel like failures. If we *are* realistic we will feel instead satisfied, powerful, and able.

Planning, then, affords us the opportunity to learn, realistically, what we can accomplish in a given time. It teaches us also that we can always accomplish something, that small steps taken regularly will yield results. It shows us that we can act upon our desires and fulfill them. Planning, too, helps prevent us from feeling engulfed, anxious, and overwhelmed. It helps us feel effective. It changes our relationship to time, enabling us to learn patience. It helps us see that we can control some aspects of our work and our lives. Working with a plan makes me feel as if the world is a much safer, more predictable place.

If you've never worked in this way, try it. My students find it helps them work joyfully, for then they needn't worry about what they're supposed to be doing. They know because they've planned.

Considering Our Intentions

Capturing our earliest ideas about our work is essential, for these are usually the most fruitful. This early "intimation of the whole," as the researcher of creativity Eugene Raudsepp calls it, guides our later work through the elaboration and formulation of our ideas and the "shifting chaos" of the creative process.

Years ago I discovered that when an editor forced me into writing a proposal for an article or a book, though I always protested, I would suddenly, intuitively, know what the work should be like. I had a vision of the whole and a felt sense, too, of the way I might organize the work. Writing my proposal captured all the latent knowledge I already possessed. Later, as I worked, it provided me with a sturdy guide that I constantly consulted. Sometimes I changed it as I worked. Often, though, it accurately predicted the shape and substance of the work.

What I do is this: I set aside a quiet time to sit at my computer, and I write as quickly and freely as I can about what I imagine I will be writing about during this project. I continue writing until I finish. (Sometimes, later, I draft a tiny piece of the project to help me develop its voice.) I write, too, about how I expect the writing to enrich my life and what the work will contribute to readers. I try to accomplish this in an hour or so, even for a long project, though I might later need to expand it.

I write a letter to a friendly editor, to an imaginary editor (if I don't yet have a publisher), or to myself. This seems to free me, for I know I am writing for a sympathetic reader, yet it makes me serious about my intentions, too.

When I wrote my proposal for my memoir *Vertigo,* I was astonished that in a single hour I discovered everything I wanted to cover in that book, though I'd never thought about it before. I learned that I wanted to use the work to examine my life as a working-class Italian American woman; to discuss my formative years during World War II in Hoboken, New Jersey; to discover why I was drawn to the healing power of reading and writing; to discuss how my life was enriched by my chosen work.

I knew I wanted to "image" scenes from my life as if they were happening; that I wanted to interrupt those scenes with reflections from my grown woman's perspective; that I wanted to show what the ever-changing process of reflecting upon our lives entails, how coming into knowledge about who we are and why we have become who we are is a messy, ongoing, shape-shifting process. I hoped I'd reframe my life as a survival story. I wanted to contribute an account of how I used reading and writing to heal myself and how others might do this too. I knew nothing of this until I wrote it down.

Henry Miller and scores of other writers clarify their intentions before they begin work. In notes Miller made between 1932 and 1933, published in *Henry Miller on Writing*, he wrote of how he wanted to describe a "new type of man. Kill history, culture, cyclical development. . . . The individual as against the collectivity."

Once we write down our intentions, we give our unconscious an instruction sheet, as it were. We invite it to help us make this work. We anticipate, too, how our work will change us. Through writing, Henry Miller became the kind of man he imagined.

At some point we may feel impelled to clear out some old books, clean our desks, buy some office supplies. I know that I'm truly preparing, truly committed to my project, when I find I'm engaging in these tasks.

WHAT YOU CAN DO NOW Can you write a proposal for a writing project? Include a list of subjects you'll cover; some organizing themes; the form you think your work will take; what it will contribute to you and others. Can you articulate your intentions for this project? How long do you think it will take? What is your completion date?

Reading

Lewis Hyde, in *The Gift*, tells us that most writers decide to write because they have been deeply moved by their reading. When Janet Frame recalled why she had become a writer, she credited her reading. "Literature streamed through [my life] like an array of beautiful ribbons through the branches of a green, growing tree, touching the leaves with unexpected light." Before Sylvia Plath wrote *The Bell Jar*, she read Virginia Woolf. Woolf's *Mrs. Dalloway*, including the madness of Septimus Warren Smith, greatly influenced Plath's work. According to Plath scholar Steven Gould Axelrod, many details in *The Bell Jar*—Esther Greenwood's recuperation from mental illness, her living through dangerous historical times, her negative attitude to marriage—are patterned upon Woolf's novel.

Jamaica Kincaid wanted to write so badly that each New Year's Eve she'd make another abortive resolution to start a novel. One year, though, someone gave her a collection of Elizabeth Bishop's poetry. Reading "In the Waiting Room," Kincaid said, was "a tremendous gift for me." After reading it she said, "I felt as if someone opened the door and showed me my own tools, the things that I needed. I just knew how to write after that." Toni Morrison, after finishing her sixth novel, *Jazz,* prepared for her next work by reading. She discovered that during the 1870s, after the Civil War, former slaves settled in Oklahoma and beyond, lured by the hope of a new life and the challenge of living in the near wilderness. This reading led to her novel *Paradise.*

Sometimes writers read with a plan. Henry Miller, when preparing for *Tropic of Cancer* between 1932 and 1933, decided to read scores of works that would give his work intellectual depth and substance. Among them were Freud's *Pleasure Principle,* Jane Harrison's *The Orphic Myths,* books on medieval culture, works of Japanese chess (Sho-Go), and tracts on the writings and paintings of idiots savants. Few of Miller's readers are aware of the intense reading that preceded the writing of his anarchic novels. Virginia Woolf, when planning *Three Guineas,* her critical work about the condition of women and British imperialism, kept a notebook into which she pasted scores of articles that she clipped from *The Times* and *Daily Herald* and notes from books she'd read for the project, like Frances Clark's *The Position of Women in Contemporary France.*

Preparing to write, then, involves reading. Although we might not be consciously aware of what we're doing, this is an essential first stage of the writing process. For years before I wrote my memoir *Vertigo,* before I knew I'd write my life, I read one memoir after another, trusting there was a reason. The first I read that made an indelible impression upon me was Maya Angelou's *I Know Why the Caged Bird Sings.* Others, too, like Susanna Kaysen's *Girl, Interrupted,* I reread often, copying important passages into a notebook, just as Henry Miller had done while doing *his* reading.

Sometimes, writers read without a plan. They read what grabs their attention, taking something off a shelf they wouldn't ordinarily choose, and it turns out to be a profoundly influential work. This happened to Henry Miller when he stumbled upon Rider Haggard's *She,* whose "mysterious creature Ayesha," the archetypal "femme fatale," in time served as a model for Miller's numerous portraits of his wife, June. Sometimes something important finds a writer, and, because the writer is receptive, it strikes a deep chord. When Nobel laureate Toni Morrison was editing *The Black Book* for Random House, she discovered a newspaper clip that told the true story of a woman who killed her daughter rather than allow her to be taken back into slavery. This Morrison transformed into her highly acclaimed novel *Beloved.*

When reading, we often fantasize what someday we, too, might write; we long to find a way to share our experiences in such a sublime way with others. Preparing to write, then, often involves fantasy, wishing, yearning, longing. We may also feel a sense of incompleteness and unfulfillment, hoping that one day we'll write. These are all appropriate feelings for this stage of the process, for if we harness them they can, one day, urge us to act.

The ways we can derail our creativity during this period are to engage in our reading haphazardly rather than with attention; to use it as a way of avoiding writing, of procrastinating, rather than as a way of actively preparing.

Two major emotional challenges confront us at the preparation stage. One is the challenge not to remain here endlessly, for then all our hopefulness and promise will fossilize into deep and abiding regret that we haven't written, haven't fulfilled our desire to write. The other is the challenge to encourage our hopeful fantasy rather than blunting it by imagining that no one as ordinary as we are could possibly write something meaningful. We can encourage ourselves most easily by learning what we can about writers' lives. Knowing, say, that Janet Frame grew up poor in railroad outposts in New Zealand with no special advantages except a mother who believed it was natural and life giving to write can help us understand that we, too, can write.

In "They Were Alive and They Spoke to Me," Henry Miller's wonderful essay about the place of reading in a writer's life, he describes how reading made him feel like an adventurer and an explorer. Miller speaks of his joy at finally having money to buy books and of his struggle, during years of poverty, to acquire them. But because they were so hard to come by, Miller learned to revere them.

Reading, Miller says, connects us to others; we learn we're not alone in our experiences or suffering. And because we tell others about our reading, we forge links with other people. "A book is not only a friend," he says; "it makes friends for you." Reading offers us opportunities to connect to others, to engage in deeply meaningful conversations. This breaks down our sense of isolation; it gives us meaning and purpose.

Through our reading we can travel to other times and other places, into other people's minds and hearts and souls: it is a transcendent experience. A writer "takes possession of you and leaves you thoroughly altered," says Miller. Through reading, our imaginative faculties are nourished, enriched, expanded. This is why, for writers and would-be writers, reading is not a luxury but a necessity.

Through reading, we enjoy the product of someone else's effort, of someone else's creative work. Their creativity is not only inspirational, it's catching: for Miller, the writer "breath[es] spirit" into readers. We connect with a creative power beyond ourselves—the writer's, and our "Maker's," too. We learn that we can partake of the universe's creative spirit, for we are composed of the same "substance" as the writer. Reading, then, is "the key to paradise."

In the reading part of the preparation period, we have many opportunities for emotional growth. We can experience appreciation, humility, gratitude, and a sense of community. We understand that it has taken creativity and effort to accomplish the work we're reading. We permit ourselves a sense of reverence and awe at the capabilities of creative human beings. The heart and soul of the creative process, for Bertrand Russell, is reverence—"a wondering sense of the infinity in everything. The beauty created by the artist rouses this feeling."

We're grateful to the writer for providing us with this enriching experience. And we express our thanks, says Miller, by writing letters to the writer and to the publisher, when possible, and by telling others about the work.

If we read as Miller does, lovingly, we will learn to read our own work in this way and we will work well. If, instead, we read competitively and derisively, we will learn to read our own work in this way.

I have an acquaintance who has started writing many books but who has finished none. Each time I speak to him he tells me about all the faults of a book he's reading, how it never should have been published, how he could do better. When I ask him about his work, he tells me he's frustrated. He can't be generous to himself and grateful for his ability to work, since he can't be generous and grateful to another writer. Hypercritical of another writer, he is hypercritical of himself as well. Adopting Miller's attitude would help him immeasurably.

Through reading gratefully, thankfully, reverentially, we practice attitudes of mind and spirit that will be essential when we turn to our own work. We can use our reading in a fecundating kind of way, to paraphrase Miller.

For Henry Miller, the acts of reading and writing are intricately intertwined. Reading is so necessary a part of the writer's life that Miller says we should take our reading as we take food or exercise. Reading is where the act of literary creation begins, where we begin to imagine the kind of literary creators we'll be. "Reading," he says, "may not at first blush seem like an act of creation, [but] in a deep sense it is."

WHAT YOU CAN DO NOW Can you observe the pattern in your reading? What might it tell you about what you must write? What emotional advantages might you gain from the reading you're doing now?

Finding Models and Mentors

Alice Walker, in her essay "Saving the Life That Is Your Own: The Importance of Models in the Artist's Life," describes how finding models and mentors to guide our work is an *essential* stage of the writing process. If we ignore this need, our work cannot proceed, for we will not have a firm foundation upon which to build. But we must become, too, our own mentor, our own model—we must attend, create, learn from, and realize ourselves.

External models, she argues, even if rejected, "enrich and enlarge one's view of existence." They provide us with a deeper perspective about our work: "Connections made, or at least attempted where none existed before, the straining to encompass in one's glance at the varied world the common thread, the unifying theme through immense diversity, a fearlessness of growth, of search, of looking, that enlarges the private and the public world."

Walker has felt "a desperate need to know and assimilate the experiences of earlier black women writers, most of them unheard of by you and by me, until quite recently." She discovered the work of the relatively unknown Zora Neale Hurston while auditing a class taught by the poet Margaret Walker. Then she began reading. First, *Mules and Men*—a "perfect book" depicting African Americans as "complete, complex, *undiminished* human beings." Next, she read *Their Eyes Were Watching God,* the story of Janie Crawford, a strong heroine with whom Walker identified. She learned that Hurston, though a literary sensation in her lifetime, died a pauper. Her remains were buried in an "unmarked grave in a segregated cemetery in Fort Pierce, Florida."

In time, Walker learned what she could about Hurston's life (from a biography and Hurston's autobiography), went to visit her home in Florida and her burial site, and erected a tombstone on her unmarked grave. *"A people,"* Walker argues, *"do not throw their geniuses away."* It is our duty, she believes, to find our geniuses, to learn from them, to remember them.

When Kenzaburō Ōe (whose work I've discussed earlier) realized he wanted to write about his relationship with his son, Hikari, he, too, looked for models to inspire him. He wanted to find works of literature describing "honestly and accurately . . . the feelings that develop between a sick or handicapped person and the family taking care of him" in a way that had "universal" meaning.

Ōe felt compelled to read works written by people with grave illnesses. Through them, he learned what his son might be experiencing. He read Flannery O'Connor's works; she had lupus erythematosus. O'Connor described illness as "a place, more instructive than a long trip to Europe, and it is always a place where there's no company, where nobody can follow." Nevertheless, even as she was dying, O'Connor composed. "My my I do like to work," she wrote, after a rare hour of renewed energy that allowed her to write. "I et up that one hour like it was filet mignon."

Ōe discovered, too, the work of the poet Shiki Masoka, who for years was confined to a sickbed with tuberculosis. Yet Shiki wrote much of his important work while he was an invalid. His work described how hard it was for his caregivers to feel compassion for him, to understand what it was like to be dependent upon others and unable to care for himself.

Ōe ascertained much from O'Connor and from Shiki about his son's experience. He found ways to describe illness and to articulate difficult feelings. But he saw, too, that illness can spur creativity and that creativity can help us when we're ill. He encouraged his son to pursue his interest in music. And in time Hikari began to compose his own work.

When I discovered I had asthma, I searched for writers who had asthma. Finding many such mentors—Dylan Thomas, Edith Wharton, among them—helped me discover I wasn't alone. Understanding that some writers' important work and changes in style grew directly out of their having asthma was surprising. I found out that Marcel Proust wrote *Remembrance of Things Past* because he was bedridden with asthma, that his sentence structure mirrored an asthmatic's breathing. I saw how Elizabeth Bishop used the rhythms of asthmatic breathing in her verse. In reading their letters, I learned how severely they suffered and how asthma was treated before the use of inhaled steroids and bronchodilators. I discovered that they nevertheless did their work, often coughing so severely they couldn't speak.

I also use mentors and models to find out what the writing life entails, having had no models for this in my family. I read writers' private diaries and letters describing their methods of working. From Virginia Woolf's works, I first learned what living a writer's life was like. I also read interviews with writers, and I watch films about them.

A film about one of my mentors has been an important continuing guide: *World of Light: A Portrait of May Sarton,* by filmmakers Marita Simpson and Martha Wheelock. Through it, I discovered Sarton's work, especially her journals, which are so helpful for anyone wanting to lead a writer's life.

The film taught me that paying careful and loving attention to who we are right now, to what we're feeling and thinking and seeing, to the ordinary routines of our life and our pastimes and pleasures, is healing and will help us write healing works. Sarton is seen contemplating the rich and lush color of the flowers she grows, the light that plays luminously across the ordinary objects in her home—a teapot, a bedspread, a dark wood antique bureau—endowing them with a mystical, transformative quality. Sarton's work grew from the simple fabric of her life—her walks along the seacoast in Maine and in the woods, her gardening, her love affairs, her love/hate relationship with solitude, the process of aging (which became perhaps the most significant object of her contemplation). As she said, "one regards oneself, if one is a serious writer, as an instrument for experience. Life—all of it—flows through this instrument and is distilled through it into works of art. How one lives as a private person is intimately bound into the work."

For it is in learning this kind of focus upon the present that we come to experience a particular kind of awe and reverence for the miracle of the world we inhabit and of our connection to it. Sarton wanted her work to say, "Look through me and find everyman, yourself." Through her wisdom, I learned that we can transform the simplest of lives into art.

Finding mentors and models, as Walker teaches, as I've discovered, provides a "historical underpinning" for our experience. By finding them, we ensure our connection with the past, we provide ourselves with self-chosen forebears, and we see our lives as a continuation of their experience. If we ourselves feel unparented, if we feel we are outsiders or adrift in the world, if we are experiencing special challenges in our life, finding appropriate mentors and models can be a comforting emotional experience. As Walker remarks, it can enable us to save our lives.

Finding mentors and models, then, is an important part of the preparatory stage of our work and an important healing phase of it. We come to see ourselves as members of a self-chosen community of writers with whom we share struggles, challenges, and triumphs in life and in our work. We learn that we are not alone.

WHAT YOU CAN DO NOW   Have you found a model or a mentor for your work? If not, it might be profitable for you now to engage in a search for a writer who speaks to the heart of what you'd like to accomplish in your work.

Germinating

If we have prepared well, when we move on to the germination stage of the writing process, fragments of ideas, images, plot lines, and structure begin to come to us, often unbidden. They seem to come out of nowhere, to just pop into our heads.

The hallmark of this stage is that our creative notions may seem murky, problematical, fleeting, puzzling. They may appear tiny, trivial, meaningless, formless, fragmentary, or insignificant. But they are not. And we cannot treat them as if they are.

Some writers actively initiate the germination phase, as Henry Miller did when he created his "June" notebook, into which he gathered photos, memories, phrases, names of people for the magnum opus on his relationship with her that took him the rest of his life to complete. Some writers, though, wait for this stage to come upon them; they hear a line in their head (not necessarily the first line of the finished piece); they imagine a situation that strikes them as compelling; they suddenly "see" what their work is about; they visualize a character. Then they know their work has begun in earnest.

The stories of writers valuing simple early images and fashioning important works from them are legion.

Anne Tyler began *Searching for Caleb* when a character wandered into her mind. He was "wearing a beard and a broad-brimmed leather hat." Soon after, she took a month to block out the novel. But because of her complicated family life—children home from school during spring vacation, a sick dog, housework, her daughter's illness, visits from her husband's relatives—the novel proceeded in what she calls "a choppy life of writing" punctuated by other events, such as "plastering the dining room ceiling, and presiding at slumber parties."

Joan Didion began *Play It as It Lays* "with no notion of 'character' or 'plot' or even 'incident,'" she said. "I had only two pictures in my mind . . . and a technical intention, which was to write a novel so elliptical and fast that it would be over before you noticed it. . . . About the pictures. The first was of white space. Empty space. . . . The second picture was of something actually witnessed. A young woman with long hair and a short white halter dress walks through the casino at the Riviera in Las Vegas at one in the morning. She crosses the casino alone and picks up the house telephone. . . . Who is paging her? . . . How exactly did she come to this? It was precisely this moment in Las Vegas that made *Play It as It Lays* tell itself to me, but the moment appears in the novel only obliquely."

Virginia Woolf, when germinating *To the Lighthouse,* drew a picture of two squares connected by a small rectangle. This suggested that she write two large chunks of narrative connected by something that seemed like a tunnel. The tunnel in the drawing evolved into the evocative and poetic "Time Passes" section of the novel. It connects two narrative chunks, each of which describes a single day in the life of the Ramsay family, separated by much time. During the intervening years, there have been many changes—World War I, the death of three family members. But that little tunnel was the tiny seed from which Woolf's philosophic discourse on the ravages of time, on the significance of life, evolved.

An early image I had for a novel I'll soon be revising was that of a woman wearing deep red lipstick, and having two black eyes—she seemed to have been beaten up—who came over the crest of a hill, walking over hot black pavement. She was carrying a wicker basket, which served as a suitcase. Out of the suitcase fluttered the end of a chiffon scarf. Accompanying her were two small boys. I wrote the novel to find out who she was, what had happened to her—I knew she was trying to escape from something, someone—and how she had made her way to that street.

Alice Walker began her first novel, *The Third Life of Grange Copeland,* with a few simple, unforgettable images from a childhood experience. At the funeral parlor where her sister worked as a cosmetologist, she saw the body of a poor woman murdered by her husband, who "shot her face off" as she came home on Christmas day bearing a bag of groceries. On one foot was a shoe with an enormous hole in the bottom, its inside padded with newspaper. "This shoe, this foot, this face, this woman," Walker said, "just lived with me."

Once we begin capturing these moments and working from them, we will notice that many more come our way, sometimes so quickly that we can feel as if we're being deluged with ideas. Everything we read, everything we experience, everything we see suddenly elicits another glimmer of inspiration for our project. Sometimes it seems we're being helped by an outside force that guides our work.

At this stage, my students often tell me they have found special talismans or charms they know will help their process, which begins to seem magical—a blue jay feather found in Central Park, a piece of worn glass found by the seashore. For this project, I myself have two: a ballpoint pen with an angel on its cap for making manuscript corrections; a used brick I bought (yes, bought) at Hemingway's house in Key West, Florida, ostensibly from a building that had fallen into disrepair, which I use as a paperweight.

At this stage, too, serendipitous moments seem to happen. After my student Julie started to honor her tiny seeds of inspiration for a memoir she wanted to write about her life as a musician, she once came to class all excited. Someone she wanted to talk to for her project, a singer and former collaborator she'd lost touch with, had called her. "It's spooky," she said, "but I'm sure I got that call because I was 'plugged in.'"

When the work is still indefinite, just beginning, writers usually experience certain feelings. We might feel a sense of eager anticipation. We might also feel impatience or frustration. We want the "real" work to begin. We want to know what all this means. We want to know where it all is leading.

We can grow as writers and as people during the germinating stage by learning to value the first stirrings of excitement we feel. We can also learn patience—that this stage, which seems so fraught with questions, will pass and that one day we will more completely understand what our project entails.

The idea that a work of art presents itself fully formed to our consciousness is a highly exaggerated, romanticized notion of how creativity works. The notion that an idea must be big to yield a great work is simply untrue.

When I tell beginning writers that Henry Miller began the work of his lifetime because he simply wanted to write about how miserable he felt when his wife, June, left him, they often seem surprised. They, too, have wanted to begin work on similar topics, but, as one woman said, "I told myself, hey, that's been done before, no one would want to hear about it."

If we begin to value our creative urges, we begin to value ourselves. If we deny our creative urges, we deny that our lives have meaning and significance. During this stage, we have a splendid opportunity to learn to trust ourselves, to believe in our self-worth. We can develop, too, a sense of faith in a higher creative power, as Henry Miller did, one that will generously provide everything we need to do this project.

During the germinating stage of "Combat Zones," a chapter of my memoir *Vertigo,* I remembered that my sons had given me a copy of the *New York Times* from my birth date. I followed my impulse to find it and read it. Images and ideas started coming quickly—the clothes my mother wore when I was little; my father in his Navy uniform; the three-room tenement apartment we lived in (with no bathroom, no heat); the drugstore on the corner; the clothes my mother sewed for me. A few days after, I knew I wanted to write about that time, and about how the women spent time together when the men were away at war, and about what happened to our lives when the men came home.

Thereafter, ideas and images came piecemeal—my mother singing and reading to me; my sailor suit; my father's homecoming; a furious fight he and I had when I wouldn't submit to him; how enraged I was that I was displaced by him; my sister's birth; my mother's depression after.

Recalling that I had a family photograph album, I found it and searched for pictures from that time—my father on a ship; me in a sailor suit; my mother and me on Halloween while my father was away (I was dressed as an old woman)—which prompted other moments I wanted to explore.

Though I often wasn't actually at my desk while I was germinating the piece, I religiously wrote in my diary about the moments that were emerging, and I scrupulously took notes to preserve my ideas that I kept in a file until I began working.

I was exhilarated but confused because initially I didn't know where this piece was going. But one day, while I was doing laundry, the title "Combat Zone" came to mind. Immediately thereafter, I knew that, instead, "Combat Zones" had to be the name of the piece. I recognized that the title provided an armature that could support the details of my work, that I would write about the war, but also about the fights my father and I had after he came home.

I knew I'd soon be ready to begin the working stage of the piece. I knew I *was* ready when a line—"On Sunday, September 27, 1942, the rainy day that I am born at the Margaret Hague Maternity Hospital in Jersey City, New Jersey, toughened, sunburned Marines cling tenaciously to a beachhead on Guadalcanal"—came into my head while I was doing dishes. I always know I'm ready to begin work when the words start coming when I'm away from my desk—at the sink, in the shower, on my walk.

Seasoned writers train themselves to value and capture their tiny moments of inspiration; beginning writers often devalue theirs and do not pay attention to them. One sure way to help our creative work is to train ourselves to pay attention to these gifts when they come to us. In doing creative work, we can learn a particular kind of alertness and sensitivity to the way our creative spirit works and to what we're experiencing. We will quickly learn that we truly possess a creative spirit.

I once had a student whose work wasn't going well. I bumped into her in the cafeteria and asked her to join me for a quick lunch. We discussed her problem. I asked her whether she had any images that consistently came to her that didn't seem important. She blushed and told me that she kept seeing herself having sex on a fire escape in New York City with a close male friend—this had once happened—but, she said, "I couldn't write about that; I wouldn't know what to make of it."

"Write about it," I said. "In time, you'll figure out what it means." And she did. In her memoir, called "Flash," which was stunning, she wrote about how for years men had exposed themselves to her on the subway. She talked about the evolution of her sexuality in a culture that seemed obsessed with women revealing themselves, how she had reacted to pictures of seminaked women on posters. Once she started valuing her creative impulses, she began to work effortlessly and meaningfully. Her attitude toward herself changed, too. She realized that her experience was significant and that her writing it down could help others. It marked her coming of age as a writer.

Preventing ourselves from writing when such images intrude upon us is harmful. It subverts our process by setting up something like a creative logjam. If we don't honor such an image, explore it, value it, we'll never learn what lies behind it. But if we do, we will discover, as my student did, that there is ever so much more to this seemingly simple moment than we ever imagined.

As writers, we must learn to value tiny creative gifts. We must learn that many mighty works have developed from the simplest of images. At this stage, we can help our writing process by not censoring whatever comes into our imagination and by writing down these ideas and capturing them in some way so that we can elaborate upon them and develop them and see where they will take us. The way we can derail our process at this stage is to consider these specks of illumination worthless, to trivialize them when they come to us, to ignore them or deny them. Or we can derail our process by censoring ourselves. Or by forcing our work to be more complete or structured than it can be at this time. Or by stopping because we believe the work should come more quickly, more fully formed, than this. Or by staying at this stage past the moment when our creative impulse tells us to begin actually writing.

We can acknowledge that we don't yet know where the work is headed and that we don't yet know the form it will take. We can admit to ourselves that we don't know what we're doing and that we don't know how we'll use these pieces. We can understand that the anxiety often accompanying this stage is the fuel that drives the creative process. We can learn to tolerate ambiguity and uncertainty (a hallmark of maturity). We can trust that in time it will all become clear.

WHAT YOU CAN DO NOW Can you capture tiny moments of inspiration? Can you value them? Can you imagine where they might lead?

Chapter Eight

Stages of the Process, Stages of Growth II

Working, Deepening, Shaping, Ordering, Completing

*Creative energy tends to be self-renewing,
and to produce its own chain reaction
of health and further effort.*

COLIN WILSON

Since reading Naomi Epel's wonderful *Writers Dreaming*, I have become especially aware of the dreams I have as I write. For me, often, just before the working phase, I have a helpful dream that indicates I've reached a pivotal point in my work. For this project, I had a wonderful one. I dreamed that there was a huge, powerful, black-and-white speckled stallion that I had to ride. It was beautiful and had strong, muscular flanks and would take me far, I knew. But I was having a hard time getting on top to ride. My husband, Ernie, was helping me. I kept trying, but the saddle kept falling off. Finally, I said, or he said, we have to tighten the saddle. Which we did. Ernie gave me a boost. And up I went. And I thought, it's a little scary up here. But I roared off to see where this beautiful, powerful horse would take me.

Working

I have described the working stage of the process in chapter 5, "The Healing Power of the Writing Process." Here, though, I will focus on the emotional challenges and the benefits we garner at this stage of our work, and the special challenges and benefits of writing long autobiographical pieces.

Our major emotional challenges now are tolerating difficult feelings as they emerge and keeping our promises to work and to persist.

Rollo May, in his landmark work, *The Courage to Create,* speaks of the many benefits of creative work. We develop an appreciation of solitude. We cultivate our openness and receptivity to experience. We develop a sense of loving attentiveness to ourselves and to the world. We accept our vulnerability and past suffering. Yet we learn, too, of our power to change our point of view, hence, to change our lives. As we articulate what we'd never expected ourselves to describe or understand, we experience a sense of release and unburdening, perhaps joy, even ecstasy.

Through our work, we can profoundly change our relationship to ourselves and to the world. Through writing we indicate that we have made a decision to be hopeful and to eschew despair, to become active and to cease being passive.

These, then, are the major emotional and psychic benefits we can derive from the working phase of our projects.

Poet and essayist Nancy Mairs, in *Remembering the Bone House,* observed that though writing poetry helped her, writing lengthy narratives based on her life healed her. "A narrative," Mairs says in *Ordinary Time,* is "a mechanism for making something comprehensible/bearable/pleasurable out of a welter of data so raw that even time doesn't exist there. Its function is precisely this: to make time happen." I believe, too, that writing an autobiographical narrative that's, say, thirty type-written pages and that takes three months or so from preparation to completion enables us to participate in a healing process that is deeper than if we write only journal, short works, or poetry or only works about others, never about ourselves.

Longer pieces require that we change our relationship to time. We can't accomplish what we'd like in a few hours or even a few days of working. But if we write regularly, we will finish. Thus, we practice patience—an important trait to develop, especially in our current cultural climate, which expects instant results, immediate gratification. Learning to defer gratification, to act today in a way that will later benefit us, Daniel Goleman writes in *Emotional Intelligence,* is the single most valuable character trait we can cultivate. Writing longer works helps us mature. We learn persistence. We recognize that profound understanding takes time. In elaborating our first impressions, we discover there's more to our stories than we'd thought. We identify patterns in how we work, in our work, and in our lives.

All this takes time, which is important. As Isabel Allende observed in an interview published in *Contemporary Literature,* "You need a lot of time to exorcise the demons and take enough distance to be able to write with ambiguity and irony—two elements that are very important in literature."

Each day, I divide my writing time into three distinct phases—preparing, working, concluding. Before I begin working, I prepare to work, often by reviewing yesterday's writing, by browsing through books and notes, by carefully planning my work for the day, by scribbling some phrases and ideas.

Each day, I write a set of goals. Often they are as simple as "Sketch what life was like during the war when Mom and I lived alone in the apartment in Hoboken. Try to write two pages. Try to remember specific details, and feelings, and to relate feelings to happenings." I try to make sure these are clear and attainable. This keeps me feeling good about my work.

Henry Miller, too, planned carefully. In writing *Tropic of Cancer,* he describes one small part of his grand plan: "Hereditary picture—the ancestral swarm, blood, race, prejudices, taints. Insanity and deaths . . . death as dominant philosophic theme."

After my day's work, I review what I've done. Sometimes I sketch a plan for the next day; write some ideas into an ongoing list that I generate as I work. Then I print my work, back it up on a disc I take with me everywhere, clear my desk, file and store my material. I take a break, have a snack. Then I read. After my day's work, I need a physical activity—a walk, say—to clear my head and help me move on to the other parts of my life.

One way we can foreclose our process during the working phase is not to pay attention to our intuitive sense of what we need to write. I continually remind my students to be open and receptive, to let their work surprise them. Successive stages—deepening and ordering—will enable us to make sense of our bits and pieces. Now, though, is the time to stay free, to write what commands our attention. We *sense, feel, intuit* what we should be doing rather than telling ourselves what we must do.

One day a former student, now an acclaimed novelist, came to my office. She was distraught that her work wasn't up to the high standards she'd set for herself. She was writing about her young female character's summers in the Catskill Mountains. She had established that the girl was the daughter of an Orthodox Jewish rabbi. But the work was wooden. She couldn't manage to make it come alive.

"What happens while you're working?" I asked her.

"Well, I work on what I think I should be working on, and then something pops into my head, and I get distracted, but I force myself to keep at what I'm doing."

"Why?" I asked.

"Because I'm afraid of using whatever comes to mind."

At this stage, though, it is "whatever comes to mind" that will unlock our work most successfully. I suspected she was censoring herself. The "real" story, or the moment that would inform the rest of her story, was in what was surfacing but she was unwilling to use.

"Tell me one image," I said.

"Yesterday," she said, "a picture of my heroine in the basement of her father's temple with a group of her friends came to me. They were smearing her menstrual blood on the walls."

I was stunned and thrilled by the transgressive power of this original image, yet I could see why she initially chose not to welcome it. It would take her into complex emotional terrain.

"You *have* to use it," I said. "It'll unlock your story."

She did and, in time, wrote a brilliant, acclaimed novel. Emotionally, her difficult work lay in dealing with her feelings about this image—her shame, her guilt, her fear. But using it taught her to take risks that made her work mature.

Working on "Combat Zones" was joyful and enriching. The major surprise in my writing was how accurately I remembered what our street and our apartment looked like, what my mother wore, how I behaved when my father came home, what our fights were like.

As I wrote, my sense of myself broadened. I felt I was regaining something I hadn't even realized I'd lost—my and my family's history. I recognized the richness of my past. I started to feel rooted in a way I hadn't before.

I took a few trips to Hoboken. I saw the old apartment where I grew up. I remembered what the streets looked like in wartime with only women, girls, boys, and old men—virtually no men my father's age. I remembered the blackout curtains, the druggist Mr. Albini, who helped us when we kids got hurt. I visited the school I went to. Doing this unleashed many more memories that became "Finding My Way," the next piece I worked on.

At times, as I worked, I felt the piece was writing itself. I had a treasure trove of jottings and journal entries from the germinating stage. A great surprise was recallng and describing details about my father I had forgotten—how he stayed with me for a year after I was born to ensure I was getting good care, for he suspected my mother's depression might compromise my well-being. I had known that my mother's depression and inability to care for me was a significant piece of my personal history, but I realized that it was linked, in part, to the war. I saw that it must have been horrifying for her to have a husband in a combat zone while she tried to care for me singlehandedly. I was beginning to realize that my parents' lives, and mine, were profoundly affected by the times in which we lived. This was something I'd never before understood.

At some point we will probably wake up and notice, suddenly, that we know what we must do to finish our work. We have a felt sense that our work no longer poses any major challenges to us, that all we need do is put in our time and the work will surely someday be finished. With every project I've undertaken, I've eventually had this feeling. For me, it's signaled by an urge to organize, clean, and polish my desk. With one book, I had to wait until almost the very end, though sometimes this feeling comes early. Whenever it comes, though, enjoy it: it is a generous gift the process gives us in return for our commitment to it.

Deepening

After I completed the working stage of my memoir "Combat Zones," I had about twenty or so pages of bits and pieces, each of which I had revised often, none of which was complete. There was no comprehensible narrative, no development, no clear beginning, middle, or end, no pattern to the work. The portraits of my parents weren't fully realized. Though some of the writing was clear, detailed, even powerful, it wasn't yet complete. Nor was there much depth to the story. Events ranged over time—my father going to war, my being born, his coming back, my beginning to feel enraged at him for imposing rules—with no real plot, no causation.

These are common features of our writing before we deepen and order it.

During the deepening of our work, we ask ourselves many, many questions:

What else can I say about this?

What else was I feeling?

What else might have been happening?

Why did this happen?

Why else did this happen?

Is this really how it happened?

Is this really how I was feeling?

Is this really how they were?

Can I say even more here?

Would someone who didn't know me or what I experienced understand this?

Is this as clear as I can make it?

What connections can I make here?

I love the deepening stage more than any other. For by revisiting what we've written, by revising what's there, by adding what's missing, by eliminating what's extraneous, by clarifying what's murky, we can come to an even richer, fuller understanding of ourselves and our stories, and we mature in ways we hadn't imagined were possible.

During this stage of writing "Combat Zones," I realized I had to write much more about my parents' personal histories. Their portraits were too skimpy. I wrote more about my father—that he had to work from when he was seven; that his father routinely abandoned his family, leaving my father, just a boy, in charge; that he had witnessed much violence during the war; that he had a spectacular tenor singing voice and had wanted to study opera but couldn't. I wrote what I knew about my mother—that her mother had died, leaving my mother to be cared for by abusive and neglectful caregivers; that she detested her stepmother who, she felt, never loved her; that she had won an important award for her writing in high school; that she couldn't go to college but instead had to work to help support the family.

Doing this made me begin to understand cause and effect in my history. I saw that my parents' behaviors had roots in how they had been treated, just as mine did. This made me see them as people with histories and problems, too. Isabel Allende has observed that during this phase we write "to understand," to "find the motivation to people's actions."

Through writing about my parents' pasts, for the first time, I could understand their points of view and could feel empathy toward them. This occurred because I was deepening my writing. As I learned more about my parents' characters, I was forced to go beyond my solipsistic point of view and to enlarge my perspective. I became sensitive to the contexts of their lives as I became more aware of mine.

Because I'd formulated a new story about them and me, my behavior changed. My mother was dead, but now I could love her as never before. And when my father was eighty and I was fifty, we started to become friends and to enjoy each other. I wrote these feelings into my work.

During this stage, I reexamined family photos I had looked at earlier. Some, of my parents on their honeymoon, captivated my attention. In them my father looks dapper, handsome, happy. By looking at them, I remembered what he was like before the war, and I felt an upsurge of love for him—something that if I hadn't been deepening my work, I would have missed.

My mother, though, looks disconnected, sad, and unhappy, and I realized that her depression predated my birth. Somehow I'd always felt responsible for her sadness. Now I saw it was something she'd suffered for years. This unlocked a memory that she'd been institutionalized as a child. The pattern of my life was becoming clearer.

As I revisited my work, revising and deepening it, I learned about ambivalence. I learned that my parents weren't the cardboard cutouts I'd held in memory. I learned they'd had problems, that there were reasons for their behavior. I started again to feel the love for them I'd felt years before, while also still harboring feelings of sorrow and resentment against them for how I'd been treated.

I also learned to tolerate ambiguity. I understood that there were mysteries about the past that I could perhaps never resolve. My mother's childhood, for instance. Why and when was she institutionalized? I might never know.

One day, as I was driving home from Hunter, I heard a report on National Public Radio about post-traumatic stress syndrome in veterans of World War II caused by their untold stories from their wartime experiences. I suddenly realized that I wasn't the only child in the world who had a father who came back changed from the war. It had happened to the children of an entire generation whose history and mine were connected. I learned that my father's rages were no doubt caused by the war. I learned to contextualize my story. This is healing, for it teaches us that many others share our experiences.

Another way of deepening our work is by using figurative language. Sometimes, as we're searching for a way to represent our feelings during a particular moment or to describe what someone looked like or how they acted, we stumble onto an image, simile, metaphor, or symbol that enlarges the meaning of our work. It also more completely defines our experience by exposing the set of connections we make. Sometimes it shifts the meaning of our work onto another plane entirely by bringing seemingly unrelated material together.

This technique is central to Marcel Proust's genius and to his great wisdom as well. (Can it be that writing figurative language makes us wise?) Early in *Swann's Way,* Proust is trying to describe precisely his pleasure when allowed to be with members of his family and his supreme anguish when forced to spend time alone in his room away from them, most especially, from his mother. When separated from her, he expresses that thinking of the future when he'll rejoin her serves, for him, as "a bridge, across the terrifying abyss that yawned at my feet." To distract himself from his pain, he repeats some favorite lines to himself, but he compares the effort to that of how "a surgical patient, thanks to a local anaesthetic, can look on fully conscious while an operation is being performed upon him and yet feel nothing." Both images—the bridge across the abyss and the surgery performed on the conscious patient—show us the intensity of the child's suffering—his sense that leaving his mother was unbearably painful, even potentially lethal—in a way that prosaic language never could.

In deepening "Combat Zones," I suddenly realized that for their honeymoon trip in 1941, on their way to Maine, my father took my mother on a tour of the Revolutionary War battlefields of Massachusetts! I hadn't understood the importance of this enormously important symbolic detail while writing my early version: I hadn't even included it. Now, though, I could see how deeply unsettling this must have been for my mother. Knowing she might lose her husband to war, she was walking across fields where scores of men had died.

Suddenly I realized I could unify the piece by using war imagery wherever it seemed appropriate. As an infant, my parents stuck to a rigid feeding schedule, which meant I cried constantly; I compared my crying to "the blaring of the air raid sirens." I describe myself in pictures after my father goes away as looking "shell-shocked." And so on. As I wrote these images, which seemed to come naturally, I understood that I was another kind of war casualty. Finding this symbolism, then, introduced another layer of meaning into my story.

The poet Susan Kolodny, in "Writing and the Psyche's Assessment of Danger," has described the challenges facing us as we revise and deepen our work. This process, she says, requires "time and patience." It confronts us with "charged emotional material and so often mobilize[s] anxiety."

She advises us to revisit our experiences, to "re-vision" them. If we do, we might find that thus far we have been distorting and misrepresenting ourselves and our story—for instance "turning negative feelings into positive ones, selfish feelings into generous ones." Or omitting positive moments from our narratives.

This happened to me in writing "Combat Zones." What I left out of an extremely early draft was the happiness I experienced during the war years in having my mother all to myself. This I initially refused to write about, though the moments had presented themselves during the germinating stage, because I was so intent upon writing a narrative about my grievances against my parents. I hadn't written about my mother singing to me, her reading to me, her teaching me to read, the pampering I received, the jubilant parties we had with other women and their children, the free and easy rhythm of a life lived without men and without too rigid a daily structure. But, at first, I also couldn't write about the intensity of my father's rages.

Once I re-visioned the war years, I wrote many scenes about how close my mother and I were. This enriched me; I regained my former happiness and joy. As Yeats wrote, "When ever I remake a song, . . . / It is myself that I remake."

Ordering, Shaping

As with other stages, in the ordering and shaping stage it's important to follow our intuition about how our work should be organized— what scene should come first, what should follow, what should be juxtaposed with what, and how it should end. This involves an openness to our creation, to the form it has started to take almost without our realizing it.

For some projects, we will find that our work is now nearly complete. We reshuffle some paragraphs; write transitions and a new opening or closing, say; trim, expand, reword, sharpen.

For other projects, the form might become apparent only very late in the process, and we may still have some major work to do. Usually, though, we will proceed with the work with a degree of confidence we may not have had before.

However much we must do, it is at the shaping stage that we take a piece of writing and turn it into a work of art. For it is at this stage that we can finally give our full attention to form, and we can reap the emotional benefits of having turned the seeming chaos of our experience into the order of a fully realized, carefully crafted, highly original work. The shape of our work will contribute much to its meaning, and paying attention to its form can teach us much, too, about how we've come to understand our experience. For Andrew Brink, the emotional advantage of this phase of our work is "making whole what was sundered or incomplete."

Perhaps now, for the first time, we think of a reader, someone completely unfamiliar with our experience, to whom our work must be completely intelligible. We begin to realize that we *will* finish.

Our major emotional challenge now is to prepare ourselves to complete the work and to let ourselves finish it. For we must not prolong our work on this project indefinitely, shaping it and reshaping it endlessly, if we want to garner the benefits—senses of worth, accomplishment and closure, primarily—that come when the work is done.

Still, many of us (perhaps unconsciously) fear the loss of our work, which often reawakens other losses we've endured. What will we do with ourselves when we're finished? What feelings have we kept at bay that will return once we're done? Sometimes we subvert our process, shaping our work haphazardly, undoing what we've done, giving ourselves even more work to do so we can hang onto our work indefinitely. Somehow, for some reason, it took Goethe sixty years to complete his *Faust.*

To help ourselves finish, we can write about these feelings in our process journals. Or write about how we've felt before upon completing our projects. Perhaps reading entries made at this stage during another project will help. Now, too, we can plan some special reward. Or take some time to plan a new creative venture we can look forward to beginning.

When one of my students was finishing her memoir about her child-hood, the title "Snapshots" came to her suddenly, very late in the pro-cess. She realized its appropriateness when she remembered that someone who'd harmed her had taken photographs of her. She hadn't yet described the photos. Her title gave her an idea about how to orga-nize her work. She realized that because her memories were disjointed, she could organize her piece as snapshots of her experiences. She could also play with the word—the "snapping" noise of the elastic band of her garments, how this person "shot" glances at her during family parties.

Now she clearly understood the final work she had to do. Break up her narrative. Order the moments. Write some images and metaphors. She remembered, too, that once this person had taken photographs of other children, too. Describing her response to this moment added greater depth to what was already a potent work.

When another of my students came to this stage, as she was writ-ing a work about her father's suicide, she realized that the only part of her project she thought worthwhile was when she used the form of an imaginary letter to tell him how his act had affected her life. She de-cided to rewrite her entire work as a series of letters. Though this meant rewriting thirty pages, she intuitively sensed this was necessary. But her work went quickly and directly, and she discovered that con-verting what she'd written into this new form wasn't difficult.

I have found that at this stage reshaping our work intuitively is advan-tageous. This I learned from Eudora Welty.

At this stage Welty took a typescript of her work, cut it into sec-tions, and shuffled the sections around until they made narrative, artistic, and emotional sense. Then she used straight pins to fasten the pieces she thought belonged together, as one pins the pieces of a dress before sewing. This artful, homespun, carefully crafted process suited her and her work.

It is a method I've borrowed (without the dressmaker pins) and one I've taught my students. There's something about taking the typescript of a nearly finished work—I use a copy of the original—cutting it to pieces, and moving them around that lets you alter your preconceptions and see new organizational possibilities in your work. This method lets you play with the form of a work that's not necessarily logical, one that might instead be a new synthesis of thought and feeling.

When I shaped "Combat Zones," I knew that I wanted the work to be organized according to how I had developed emotionally in writing the work. I wanted to contrast my life with my mother during the war with my life with my parents upon my father's return. I wanted to highlight the "big battle" my father and I had when he came home— to use it to represent all those early fights. I wanted to interrupt descriptions of my childhood with present-day reflections. I wanted to begin with strife and battles—in the world, in our home—but end with peace and contentment.

It was a complex design, but I accomplished it in less time than I imagined. Very late, I decided I would sometimes use present tense for immediacy, sometimes past tense for reflection. Two distinctive voices emerged—a narrative voice and a reflective voice. Without being entirely conscious of what I'd done, I'd described how events and feelings are connected in an elaborate formal design.

The work begins with a long litany of what had happened the day of my birth—battles on Guadalcanal and New Guinea, wartime blackout regulations—to give a sense of the historical context that shaped my life. But I end it with an idyllic memory of my mother, during the war years, framed in the kitchen window of our apartment, singing as she takes washing off the line and I play in the yard below. Though this has been a war story, the last words of "Combat Zones" are "I have never been, will never be, happier." Writing the piece let me remember that moment and return to it emotionally, an enriching, healing experience.

Completing

The literary critic Mitchell A. Leaska once said that every word in a finished work is there by choice, not by chance. As we finish our work, we must revisit it again, sometimes with a writing partner's or editor's help. We don't make major changes (unless they're warranted). But we fine-tune what's already there. We learn to pay attention to detail.

This is a slow, meticulous, often plodding process—something many of my students prefer not doing. Yet it's necessary, though sometimes unpleasant, work. Like heaving bricks over a wall, Virginia Woolf said. Finishing strong is something great athletes learn, a champion sprint swimmer student of mine once told a class. Finishing strong is something writers also must learn.

In taking care of details, in polishing and finishing, in making sure that we produce a beautiful, clean manuscript, we show that we respect ourselves, our work, and our readers. It makes no sense to spend weeks, months, or years writing and then, when finishing, to produce a slovenly, careless effort.

As we revisit our work, when we come to the realization that we are finally completing it, we might sense that though we've said much, there is so much more to say. If we want to finish this work, though, we must understand that each effort will be incomplete and imperfect. Each time we write, we can tell only a small piece of our story. We must realize, too, that our sense of these events might change with time as we ourselves change and grow and that what we have written is inevitably only a partial rendering. Many writers—Nancy Mairs, Virginia Woolf, Tim O'Brien, Isabel Allende, Tennessee Williams among them—continually rewrite their lives.

Completing our work, then, can help us learn to live with change and impermanence but to find, too, a solid center beneath the flux.

Through our work we come to respect our limitations—that at a given time we can understand only a small fragment of a very big picture. This, then, helps us become humble and wise.

When we finish, we find a way to let go. This is important, for life is a series of partings. Ted Hughes, husband of Sylvia Plath, felt compelled to write poems about her and her death for thirty-five years. It wasn't until he collected his *Birthday Letters,* though, that he felt this chapter in his life was complete. Frank McCourt, Pulitzer Prize–winning author of *Angela's Ashes,* said that though he had *told* stories about his childhood, if he hadn't *written* his about growing up Irish and poor he "would have died howling": completion brought him peace. "It's captured," he said.

Our challenge now is to take care of ourselves, since finishing perhaps reactivates former painful experiences of loss. It helps to have something to anticipate—a holiday, a treat, a new piece of work, a new skill to learn.

Perhaps the most eloquent expression of what we accomplish by writing, particularly by writing narrative, is provided by Daniel Taylor in *The Healing Power of Stories.* Our work, he tells us, helps us take "ourselves and our lives seriously." It links "past, present, and future in a way that tells us where we have been (even before we were born), where we are, and where we could be going." We realize how "choices and events are tied together, why things are and how things could be." Through writing, we can see ourselves "as something more and better than we are presently," and so we can chart a course that can help us grow beyond the profound changes we've accomplished in doing our work.

Finishing my memoir was a complex experience—exhilarating yet wrenching. To ease the loss I knew I would feel upon finishing, I decided to learn, really learn, everything about biscotti and how to make them. Standing in my messy kitchen, trying out one new recipe after another, deluging the family with tins of cranberry pistachio biscotti, chocolate orange hazelnut biscotti, double almond biscotti, visiting coffee houses in New York to sample their wares—all eased the transition to life beyond the memoir. Of course, given the kind of person I am, I now wanted to write a biscotti cookbook. But I discovered, too, that I wanted to write *this* book.

Here's the best biscotti recipe I devised from that complicated time.

THE WRITER'S BLUES CHOCOLATE HAZELNUT
ORANGE BISCOTTI PICK-ME-UP

Ingredients:

> 3 large eggs
> 1 cup sugar
> Diced rind of one orange (blanched for a minute
>   in boiling water)
> 2¼ cups flour
> 1 teaspoon baking powder
> ½ teaspoon salt
> 1 cup chocolate pieces
> 1 cup shelled, hulled hazelnuts, toasted

Method:

> Preheat oven to 350 degrees.
>   Beat eggs, sugar, and orange rind together for three minutes. In a separate bowl, mix flour, baking powder, and salt. Mix egg mixture into flour mixture with a wooden spoon only until incorporated. Add chocolate pieces and toasted hazelnuts. Mix only until incorporated into the dough.
>   Using wet hands, shape dough into two rounded, long loafs. Bake for about 30 minutes, or until very well browned. Remove from baking sheet and cool on rack for ten minutes.
>   Slice on a diagonal. Place biscotti upright on pan. Return to oven and bake until dry—about 10 minutes.

Having one with a cup of latte, I guarantee, will be a sublime experience.

When I finished my memoir, I felt that a phase of my life was over. That some of what had pained me and overwhelmed me I had put behind me. Yet I felt that my past was connected in many positive ways to my present life. I would not, I realized, be the person I am now without these experiences, no matter how painful. "We weave our memories into narrative," says Leonard Shengold, author of *Soul Murder,* "from which we construct our identities."

My writing, then, enabled me to have a more sympathetic yet paradoxically a more detached understanding of who I had been and who I now was. As Edvige Giunta observed, through writing we learn to read our lives.

Aaron L. Mishara, Ph.D., in "Narrative and Psychotherapy," says that writing changes our "*relationship* to [past events] and what they *mean* . . . in the present. This is not done by 'language' alone but by an 'opening up' to the experience . . . that involves the entire bodily self." As we write, we see ourselves as part of a larger story rather than continuing to see the story through our singular perspective.

Through writing my life, I became ready to move on. And I hoped that what I'd written might prove useful to others, just as what I had read had helped and sustained me. As Edmund Wilson observed in a letter to Louise Bogan, "The only thing that we can really make is our work. And deliberate work of the mind, imagination and hand, done, as Nietzsche said, 'notwithstanding,' in the long run remakes the world."

Now, at the completion of our work, is when we celebrate ourselves and our accomplishment; when we take pride in ourselves and our writing; when we fashion and engage in a completion ceremony to mark our work's end. As we pack and store our earlier drafts, as we clear our desks, we ready ourselves for the future. Now, too, is when we can reflect upon what our work has given us, and we can show our gratitude for having writing to turn to whenever we choose—to help us grow, to help us heal.

WHAT YOU CAN DO NOW As you work, can you pay respectful attention to what emerges, letting the writing tell you where to go?

Can you, nonetheless, work in an orderly way?

Can you complete a draft of a lengthy work?

Can you deepen your work, using the suggestions provided?
Can you use metaphors, images, and symbols?
Can you revisit your experience as you revise?
What does your work tell you about its organization?
What form has it started to take?
Can you discover a method for shaping your work?
Can you accept the challenge of completing your work?
Can you discover how you've grown?
Can you celebrate your accomplishment?
Can you imagine what might come next?

Part Three

From Woundedness

to Wholeness

Through Writing

Chapter Nine

Writing the Wounded Psyche

I have to write. If I avoid that mandate, I wind up
trying to kill myself. It's as simple as that. But I
don't have to be scared out of my wits every time I
pick up my pen. I don't have to be mad. It's a role
I've learned. . . . But it's a role I can't afford. . . . I
want to be thrown into the world, my pen and pad
flung after me, and to sit . . . scribbling until my
fingers are bone. I want to survive out there,
and maybe even have a good time.

NANCY MAIRS, *Plaintext*

The Pulitzer Prize–winning author Alice Walker has
often remarked that the deep personal pain she experienced as a girl prompted her to become a writer. All
her work originated with her need to fend off the
disabling effects of anguish and hopelessness, to
write her way out of suicidal depressions. "I have not
had an easy life," she said. "I started out writing to
save my life."

Walker doesn't often reveal the origin of her despair. But she once described how, as a child, she was
shot in the eye by her brother and was partially
blinded. After, her family refused to blame him or to

hold him accountable for what he'd done. Instead, somehow the incident became her fault. This forced her into an outsider position in her family.

As a child, Walker wrote to comfort herself. Or she told herself stories, which she kept in her head. She feared her brothers would find them and destroy them. Now she can fashion an entire novel in her head before putting pen to paper.

Walker compares her lifesaving habit of storytelling to the tradition of Native American sand painting. In Native American cultures, she reports, "when you feel sick at heart, sick in soul, you do sand paintings. Or you make a basket. The thing is that you are focused on creating something. And while you're doing that, there's a kind of spiritual alchemy that happens and you turn that bad feeling into something that becomes a golden light. It's all because you are intensely creating something that is beautiful. And in Native American cultures, by the time you've finished the sand painting, you're well. The point is to heal yourself."

Through Psychic Pain to Redemption and Salvation

Walker's first published story, "To Hell with Dying," was written when she was extremely depressed, feeling hopeless. She wrote it, she says, instead of killing herself, instead of slitting her wrists.

"To Hell with Dying" tells of an old guitar player, Mr. Sweet, who "continued to sing" though he felt deep, ineffable pain. Through his music, he "continued to share his troubles and insights" with his audience. He turned his suffering into art. When making music, he felt better. But his listeners felt better, too, because his work was redemptive. It freed them from their suffering because he showed them what pain felt like and how to journey from it through art.

Mr. Sweet's portrait was based upon countless musician/healer/survivors Walker had encountered in African American culture. Their work provided the model for hers.

The wisdom Mr. Sweet derived from his suffering made him a shaman. The paradox in Mr. Sweet's music—showing that we can be redeemed through pain and that we can become joyful through describing it—is central to Walker's work. She could describe it because she lived it.

In Walker's philosophy of art, "saving" means memorializing our experiences in permanent form through writing. "Saving" also means sharing our wisdom so our writing can save others.

Through writing Mr. Sweet's story, one of a man who saved himself through art, Alice Walker saved herself. She gave herself the courage to live, to "turn [her] back on the razor blade." And she has helped others by her work. She unflinchingly explores the pain she's experienced and shows how we can find our way out of it. Her courage is catching.

In "Saving the Life That Is Your Own," her essay about writing, she says, "It is, in the end, the saving of lives that we writers are about. . . . We do it because we care. . . . We care because we know this: *the life we save is our own.*"

Writing, for Walker was—is—redemption and salvation. Writing, literally, saved her life. Her obligation, then, is to help others save theirs by teaching them to reject self-destructive behavior. Walker rejected self-annihilation and embraced literary creativity. She understood that harming herself would reenact the harm that had been done to her.

Creative Psychic Illnesses

In *Creativity as Repair,* Andrew Brink describes what William James called "a creative psychic illness." It can last for years. Though it can involve enormous suffering, it precipitates a major, positive life change that probably wouldn't have occurred without it. The illness has a lesson, if we're willing to listen to it.

As with Walker, we can sometimes experience a long-lived journey into despair and an intense inner psychic struggle. Our old ways of thinking and behaving seem empty and self-defeating. We move, per-haps, to the brink of self-extinction. But, because of some sudden and profound insight, we turn back and reclaim the potential and possibil-ities of life. We are, in a sense, reborn into a new life. Our struggle and what we've learned become the subjects of our work.

Henri Ellenberger, author of *The Discovery of the Unconscious,* de-scribes how, when recovery occurs, it happens "spontaneously and rapidly. It is marked by feelings of euphoria, and is followed by a trans-formation of the personality." The person has "gained access to a new spiritual truth" that must now be revealed to the world.

After, profound behavioral and emotional changes take place in the writer's life. There is self-acceptance and expiation (of guilt, self-blame, self-hatred, and self-reproach). Fewer self-defeating and poten-tially self-destructive behaviors appear. These transformed writers now devote themselves, too, to lives including self-discipline and self-care, contemplation, and sacredness.

Jane Redmont, in "Praying in a Time of Depression," describes her creative psychic illness. After resigning from a high-pressured "killer job," Redmont became seriously depressed. She had severe panic at-tacks and compelling suicidal urges. She took antidepressants and was hospitalized in a psychiatric ward for a time. The love of friends and faith and prayer helped her, she knows.

When she was discharged, she feared a relapse. But she had learned some essential self-care skills that eased her passage to normal life. Make a small, workable plan, she told herself, and carry it out one step at a time.

Soon she found herself at the computer, writing poetry. Writing and reflecting upon it made her feel "alive and well." Most important, she says, "I was no longer silent."

Her next work was an essay on the harmful psychological effect on her family of the McCarthy era. Because her father refused to testify against an innocent man, he lost his job and was blacklisted for a decade. Subsequently, he worked wherever he could, committed to providing a good life for his young family. But the family lived with stress and un-certainty.

Redmont says her depression stemmed from her family's oppression. And from suppressing their untold story.

After her depression, through writing, she became increasingly politicized. She now wants to share what she learned: "the way oppression breeds depression." Through introspection and writing, Redmont learned an important truth about mental illness she must share. The causes of emotional distress, she believes, "go beyond the biochemical and the intrapsychic, even beyond the family system, to the larger structure and events that shape our lives."

A dramatic example of a creative psychic illness is Janet Frame's, described in volume two of her autobiography, *An Angel at My Table.* After Frame left her home in Oamaru, New Zealand, to attend college in Dunedin, she became increasingly withdrawn. It was the accumulated effect, she later realized, of years of suppressed grief, rage, and anguish about the events in her life—the drowning death of two sisters, the ongoing violence of her father toward her epileptic brother (who, her father believed, should control his attacks), her mother's self-sacrificing ways, her peers' ostracism and cruelty because of her appearance and the family's extreme poverty.

While training to be a teacher, Frame suddenly felt unable to teach and walked out of a classroom. Because she buried her feelings, because she felt so completely isolated, she says she saw no way out of her dilemma except suicide. She tried to kill herself by taking an overdose of aspirin. But she hadn't taken a lethal dose.

When she awakened, she was overjoyed, ready to embrace the future. Most important, she knew she would never try to kill herself again.

When, during a psychology class, she was asked to write an autobiography, Frame described her suicide attempt. She revealed that afterward she was put in the psychiatric ward of the local hospital. When she was released, the prospect of life at home seemed hellish to her. When her mother came to fetch her, she refused to leave. She didn't realize that the alternative to going home was being committed to an institution.

Frame was misdiagnosed as schizophrenic. During her eight-year incarceration, she received over two hundred unmodified electroshock treatments. Each, she said, was equivalent "to an execution."

Through the years, she'd had less than eighty minutes of therapy. The experts administered no tests to see if their initial diagnosis was correct. Still, they persuaded Frame's mother that the only hope for her daughter's recovery was a leucotomy, or lobotomy. And she gave permission for this procedure. Then in vogue in New Zealand, Frame says, it was a " 'convenience' treatment" to control people in mental institutions.

Throughout, though, Frame had been writing. She even managed to send her work off to publishers. And it is because of her writing that Frame was spared the lobotomy for which she was scheduled.

"I repeat that my writing saved me," Frame said.

She had seen the list of those scheduled for operations. Her name was on it. She knew her turn was coming soon. But she didn't know how to stop it.

One evening, the superintendent of the hospital visited her, asking her whether she'd seen the newspaper. Did she know she'd won a major award for her book *The Lagoon*? Of course she didn't know. On the back ward, there was "no reading matter."

Because of the prize, the superintendent canceled her operation. He moved her to a less restricted ward, gave her occupational therapy, preparing her for discharge. Suddenly, she says, "I was treated as a person of some worth, a human being, in spite of the misgivings and unwillingness of some members of the staff." Seeing friends who had the operation being "silent, docile" showed her what her fate would have been.

After her release, Frame kept in touch with one friend, Nola, who had the operation. Seeing her "was like living in a fairytale where conscience, and what might have been, and what was, not only speak but spring to life and become a living companion, a reminder." Frame says she carries the image of Nola and "her dehumanising change" with her.

Nola's fate, and that of other people in mental hospitals, became a major subject of her fiction. In works like *Intensive Care*, she has explored the consequences of living in violent and destructive families and the mistreatment of people deemed to be inferior by those with political power.

In her autobiographical novel *Owls Do Cry,* she merges Nola's history with hers. She tells how her character Daphne, who undergoes electroshock therapy and a lobotomy, is ultimately deprived of her ability to sing.

A common theme in Frame's work is the dual nature of language. If we use it ill, it can victimize others and persecute them. But if we use it well, it can provide us with an imaginative distraction from our problems.

Challenges in Writing About Trauma

Writing about the traumatic events that we've experienced is an extremely helpful way of integrating them into our lives, of helping us feel happier, of improving our psychic and physical well-being. Still, writing about events severe enough to have caused deep and abiding pain, serious enough to have caused us post-traumatic stress disorder, poses special challenges.

For Cathy Caruth, editor of *Trauma: Explorations in Memory,* post-traumatic stress disorder is a "response, sometimes delayed, to an overwhelming event or events." It "takes the form of repeated, intrusive hallucinations, dreams, thoughts or behaviors stemming from the event." It is characterized by psychic numbing, begun during or after the experience, and possibly also hyperarousal. A potential aftereffect is our engaging in dangerous behaviors (alcohol abuse, drug abuse, self-mutilation). All are attempts to alleviate profound psychic pain.

There are two major challenges in writing about extreme trauma caused by natural disasters, sexual and physical abuse, rape, torture, or wartime experiences. The first, and most important, surely, is emotional. We must not use our work to retraumatize ourselves or put ourselves in danger. The second is artistic and, ultimately, moral. We must find a way to convey an experience that essentially seems beyond language and form.

Some psychiatrists, like Judith Lewis Herman, M.D., believe that revisiting trauma for people with post-traumatic stress disorder *should never be done* without the assistance of highly skilled, highly trained professional help. For healing to be accomplished, an explicit narrative about our experiences must be recovered, but safely. Herman reports in *Trauma and Recovery* that revisiting traumatic moments with a trained therapist who ensures that we are safe successfully forestalls the most damaging effects of trauma.

bell hooks, in *Daughters of the Yam,* reminds us, though, that not everyone who is severely traumatized can afford to pay for therapy. Writing often provides the only available healing outlet for poor people. James W. Pennebaker and Amina Memon, in "Recovered Memories in Context," say writing about extreme trauma has proved so helpful precisely because it is self-directed and unmediated by another person. Stephanie Mines, in *Sexual Abuse, Sacred Wound,* says that if therapy for abuse survivors "involves the creative arts, the intervention or supervision of a therapist may not be necessary."

All my writing about abuse has been done while I've had psychotherapy. I personally believe that a strong, highly qualified support system is essential for writers with histories of extreme trauma and writers with post-traumatic stress disorder. It is what I suggest to my students.

Some Necessary Precautions

If we are writing from a position of extreme psychic woundedness, it is essential that we don't retraumatize ourselves, take on subjects before we're ready, or work in a way that is too distressing or too stimulating. Tim O'Brien, in *The Things They Carried,* recounts the emotional challenge of writing about his time in Vietnam. "I'm forty-three years old, and a writer now, and the war has been over for a long while," he says. "Much of it is hard to remember. I sit at this typewriter and stare through my words . . . and as I write about these things, the remembering is turned into a kind of rehappening. . . . The bad stuff never stops happening: it lives in its own dimension, replaying itself over and over." Through writing, though, it is possible, as Tim O'Brien recognizes, to change the *reliving* of events into a creative and healing *retelling*. This sometimes requires help. O'Brien discloses his need for therapy and drug treatment in "The Vietnam in Me."

Why trauma survivors tend to retraumatize themselves is brilliantly analyzed in Anna C. Salter's *Transforming Trauma*. Salter relates that deliberately putting ourselves in danger triggers the production of endorphins. These successfully self-medicate pain. When they dissipate, the level of pain increases. We then require even more pain relief, in an ever-increasing, ever-more-dangerous cycle. Still, the original impulse behind this behavior is to help ourselves.

If we are trauma survivors, before we start writing we must make a firm plan (preferably, with qualified help). It should detail specifically what we will do if we find we are at extreme risk. Writing can help us heal only if we ensure we're safe while we write. As we work, we must proceed slowly and cautiously, continually monitoring our responses to our work. If we find that we are at risk—if we feel suicidal or violent or out of control or unable to carry out life's ordinary tasks—we must implement our plan and seek professional and qualified help *immediately*. We must not use our work, as A. Alvarez (in *The Savage God*) says Sylvia Plath did at the end of her life, as a call for help. Nor should we write about our suicidal and murderous feelings at this time. We must ask for help directly and discuss these feelings with someone professionally qualified to help us understand them, protect ourselves, and integrate them into our lives.

We can later explore this time and these feelings (if we choose) in our work when the crisis has abated. In time, we can write about any subject, no matter how distressing. But only when we are in a position of relative safety.

If we are not presently at risk, we must become conscious nonetheless of the impact of our writing upon our lives. If we want our writing to help us heal, we must not glamorize or glorify dangerous lifestyles, as A. Alvarez said many poets (including Plath and Anne Sexton) did.

We must think about whether we are currently using our work to express our feelings or, instead, to control them. Whether we are dealing in a constructive way with the anxiety that might arise from working or whether we are not. Whether we are linking our feelings to events in our life or just venting them. Whether we are working in a way that keeps us safe or one that overwhelms us or floods us. Whether our sadness, grief, or rage about the subjects we describe is bearable or too difficult to bear. Whether we feel safe working or feel in danger working. Whether we are integrating what we learn in our work into our lives or ignoring the messages our work is trying to teach us. Whether our work helps our lives or whether we are shunning interpersonal relationships to focus obsessively or compulsively on our work. Whether we are using our work to enhance a sense of self that exists separate from our work or whether we are using it to gain recognition and approval.

We might find that creating a support group of writers and other artists or getting a writing partner might help us explore these ongoing questions and challenges. Surely, we must examine them in our process journals. But if we find we're working self-destructively, we must seek help.

Finding Forms to Convey Extreme Experiences

Some thinkers, like Elie Wiesel, believe it's necessary for all Holocaust survivors to write their stories. Still others, like Linda Alcoff and Laura Gray, authors of "Survivor Discourse: Transgression or Recuperation?," believe it is the right of each person to choose to remain silent. Surely no one should feel coerced into exposing what they choose not to reveal.

A study by James W. Pennebaker, Steven D. Barger, and John Tiebpit about the health effects of disclosure in Holocaust survivors merits our attention. It showed that the physical health of people who hadn't already discussed these events seemed to suffer if they suddenly started making their testimonies. They reported, though, that describing what they had endured was emotionally beneficial.

The negative aftereffects of extreme abuse are both physical and mental. But writers who choose to describe their experiences of extreme abuse, torture, or the Holocaust also face enormous moral and artistic challenges. They must find a language and a structure that will communicate something that seems fundamentally incomprehensible, beyond the power of words to describe. Yet finding the language to narrate what occurred, what was felt, what was done, what was imagined, what was remembered in order to survive helps integrate even the most extreme experiences into our lives.

It seems difficult, if not impossible, to find a language that can replicate the often fragmentary, surreal, hallucinatory, dissociated quality of what was experienced. Sometimes the experience was endured in a semiconscious, semidrugged, semiawake state. Sometimes the writer is unsure about precisely what happened because it happened so long ago or because she or he was in a state of shock or emotional numbness while it was happening. The most basic and important survival tactics often involve blunting the emotions, carefully watching, splitting the consciousness (watching the event as if it's happening to someone else), even splitting the self (into two or more personae). Finding words, finding literary forms to convey these self-preserving defensive tactics, these superlinguistic layers of meaning, often seems impossible.

The dilemma writers face is that though writing an organized, well-structured piece of work helps us integrate trauma into our lives, writing an organized, well-structured piece of work about extreme experiences seems (is) unethical and immoral. If we present such experiences as if they can be subsumed into coherent, orderly aesthetic objects, aren't we ourselves participating in the misapprehension of these experiences? in their misrepresentation? As Dori Laub, a psychoanalyst who has worked with Holocaust survivors and their children, has observed, we must somehow express the inaccessibility and incomprehensibility of these experiences to our readers. But we must also try to find order in seeming chaos and "seek out causes and consequences," as Tim O'Brien phrased it.

For Tim O'Brien, another moral issue is ensuring that stories about brutality do not mollify the reader. Fighting in Vietnam, O'Brien said, made him feel like a "conscripted Nazi." There is no way he could write an uplifting narrative about such a war. If we write uplifting war stories, O'Brien believes, we are perpetuating "a very old and terrible lie." Still, if we describe only the negative moments and omit the "pleasure" people can feel in extreme circumstances, we also misrepresent our experience.

There is also the ethical problem of unwittingly or knowingly falsifying truth to gain an audience. People who aren't survivors can't imagine the horrible events survivors have endured. Survivors often realize that a complete and complex record might be dismissed as fabrication. They often feel they can tell only part of their story lest their experiences be rejected as exaggerated or false. As one student, a survivor of political torture, told me, "I am forced to write a part to stand for the whole. No one could tolerate reading the entire story." Writing, too, that replicates the disorderly chaotic nature of these experiences might challenge the patience and credulity of even the most well intentioned reader.

Though writers often feel compelled to tell these stories, though some believe they *must* tell them for personal, ethical, or political reasons, they often also want an audience. So how to render extreme experiences while retaining the interest of readers is an important issue that every survivor faces. Fortunately, there are mentors and models who can help us find our way.

I always suggest to my students that reading other writers' works akin to the experiences we're trying to represent can help us discover our own solutions to the twin issues of finding a suitable language and finding an appropriate form. Before writing of my sexual abuse, I read memoirs and novels like Maya Angelou's *I Know Why the Caged Bird Sings;* Virginia Woolf's "A Sketch of the Past"; Toni Morrison's *The*

Bluest Eye; Susan Osborn's *Surviving the Wreck.* Memoirs, poems, and novels written about extreme experiences have much to teach every writer because they are often conscious and self-reflective about the power of form to convey meaning.

Here are some other narratives I've found useful:

Tim O'Brien's *The Things They Carried* provides an aesthetic form for his tale about Vietnam that brilliantly solves many problems inherent in writing about extreme trauma. In the novel he writes what is, ostensibly, a memoir. But then he tells the reader the only way to tell the truth about his life is to make it up, to use "story-truth." He does this, in part, he says, because all memory is fictive. But he says, too, that to tell truthfully what happened to him as a foot soldier in Quang Ngai Province in Vietnam, he has had to resort to invention. Throughout the work, as in sections called "How to Tell a True War Story" and "Notes," he steps outside the narrative to comment upon the moral and ethical challenges he has encountered in writing about the war. Any writer encountering a similar dilemma can learn much about potential solutions from reading O'Brien.

Others have found different aesthetic solutions to such writing. Janet Frame has used imagistic and figurative language and dislocations of time and place to convey the phantasmagoric quality of life in a mental institution. Toni Morrison has used a broken parody of the traditional narrative (including children's primers) in *The Bluest Eye* to represent the fractured experience of Pecola Breedlove, a survivor of incest and racism. Sapphire, in *Push,* has used a journal and poetry ostensibly written by her character Precious, an incest survivor who has borne two children by her father, to describe the healing power language has for her character.

Anne Michaels's first novel, *Fugitive Pieces,* depends largely upon metaphor to convey traumatic meaning. Her poet, Jakob Beer, orphaned and rescued during World War II, ponders many years later how language can be used destructively. But he also knows it can invoke and recover a past that must be preserved. Another character, a young professor, is himself helped by Beer's work. Throughout the novel, there are poetic meditations on the limits and possibilities of language: "Languages. The numb tongue attaches itself, orphan to any sound it can: it sticks, tongue to cold metal. Then, finally, many years later, tears painfully free." This stunning metaphor shows what finding language to describe painful experiences feels like. Such metaphors help Michaels solve the problem of how to convey the complex, elusive experience of her character.

Eliezer Witztum, M.D., Haim Dasberg, M.D., and Abraham Bleich, M.D., have used metaphoric language effectively in the treatment of combat veterans with post-traumatic stress disorder. The authors suggest that creating metaphors and deriving meanings from them are useful analytic tools in treating stress disorders. Metaphor seems especially useful with people who resist describing their experiences directly.

Because metaphors say one thing while meaning another, they are important vehicles for conveying information that seems beyond the limits of language. The metaphor compacts meaning, but it also evokes emotion, so it enables us to express nonliteral experiences in a highly individualized way. Its use presents one solution to the challenge of how to render extreme situations. Reading writers like O'Brien, Frame, and Michaels can help us understand the potency of metaphoric language for survivors of extreme trauma. Creating metaphors and examining them, the above researchers maintain, is healing because, by using these comparisons, writers are forced to link events and feelings.

Finding Feeling Through Writing Stories

One special problem faced by survivors is that often our feelings about these events are blunted. Ordinarily, writing helps us understand and manage our feelings. But writing helps victim/survivors of extreme trauma learn to feel again, even if the writing causes difficulty. We can write, not to express feelings we don't have, but to discover what we might have felt if we hadn't been terrified. This is best done, O'Brien believes, when we strive for "story-truth" rather than literal truth, when we describe semifictional stand-ins for ourselves.

By inventing what our fictional characters feel and how they think, we are understanding ourselves. O'Brien learned about feelings by imagining what he might have felt if he hadn't needed to shut off his feelings to survive. The function of storytelling moves the writer from a position of detachment—the consequence of profound stress—to that of feeling for ourselves and for others. If the emotional aftermath of our trauma is similar to O'Brien's, we, too, can use semifictional alter ego to tell our stories, to help us feel.

Moreover, storytelling teaches or reteaches us empathy. This trait is a prerequisite for treating others well. But it depends upon our ability to imagine what it feels like to be another person. We do this through storytelling. Because the capacity for empathy is often lost in extreme situations, restoring empathy in survivors is essential. Writing is one important way to accomplish this.

Using Writing as a Substitute for Self-Harm

A long time ago, when I myself was in the kind of deep despair that preceded Walker's writing "To Hell with Dying," I wrote in my journal that I was feeling so hopeless, so helpless, that I wanted to run my wrists over broken glass.

Later, the crisis past, on impulse I went back and reread that entry to see what I could learn. And was startled to discover that what I had *actually* written so hastily on that gloom-filled day was this:

"I feel like running my *writs* over broken glass."

This was a significant, informative slip. For I learned that instead of harming myself, I could, as Alice Walker had before me, run my *writs*—my *writings*—over broken glass. I could use my writing as a substitute for self-harm and as a way of healing.

Many researchers, psychiatrists, and psychotherapists, like Alice Miller, Anthony Storr, M.D., and Albert Rothenberg, M.D., believe that mental illness and suicidal despair are not caused by trauma itself. They occur because the survivor can't verbalize what has happened and what has been suffered; they are caused "by not being able to describe our feelings of rage, anger, humiliation, despair, helplessness, and sadness," says Miller. Feeling suicidal, then, means that there's a story that hasn't yet been told, that there are feelings linked to that story that haven't yet been expressed.

Kay Redfield Jamison, in *Touched with Fire,* cautions that writers with manic-depressive illness or writers with suicidal urges should not write without therapy. Manic-depression, she warns, requires a combination of drug therapy and psychotherapy. She has written this study of manic-depressive writers and an account of her own illness in *An Unquiet Mind,* she says, to try to save the lives of writers with this illness.

Manic-depression is ten to thirty times more frequent in writers than in the general population, she says. Rothenberg, though, disputes her claim. Risk factors, such as early trauma and abuse, stress, and alcohol or drug abuse, Jamison admits, also seem to contribute to its development. Jamison believes that writers must not romanticize this illness or believe that their creativity depends upon it or deny its lethal potential. Effective treatment, she says, with a new generation of effective drugs is now possible.

Using Writing to Help Transform Ourselves from Victims into Survivors

In *The Politics of Survivorship,* Rosaria Champagne has written that "the difference between a survivor of violence and a victim of violence is the political meaning made of the traumatic experience. . . . Victims become complicit with abuse and honor injunctions posed by perpetrators to dismiss the abuse's import or impact. Survivors, in contrast, move to a place where they reject the demand to remain politely silent."

Survivors remember. Survivors speak up. Survivors speak out. Survivors tell stories. Survivors write and exchange them, sharing their meaning with "an interpretive community." But survivors do this on their terms, with the help they need, and when they're ready. And they don't do this unless they're ready.

By sharing our stories under the safest conditions, we learn from one another that we need not engage in shame and self-hatred. They are the result of what happened to us, of what we survived. In time, we can learn to transform those feelings; we can learn to value ourselves and love ourselves. Linda Alcoff and Laura Gray report that survivors who have been silent "because they feared retaliation or increased humiliation . . . report that the experience of speaking out is transformative as well as a sheer relief."

But it is important, too, to understand that, as Alcoff and Gray write, "survival itself sometimes necessitates a refusal to recount or even a refusal to disclose and deal with the assault or abuse, given the emotional, financial, and physical difficulties that such disclosures can create." We should never be coerced into such writing; nor should we coerce ourselves. Instead, we will profit from writing about our choice *not* to write and from describing the feelings we have that are connected to that choice. One of my students wrote a powerful piece about why she refused to write about a particularly shameful moment in her life—when she helped victimize another woman. The piece began, "What I don't want to write about, what I never want to write about is . . ."

Writing as an Antidote to Depression

A study by Arnold Ludwig, M.D., established that many women who want to write report having emotional problems—suicidal urges, manic-depression, depression—possibly linked with early physical and sexual abuse and physical illnesses (chronic pain, asthma) also associated with abuse. Writing, though, can become a vital form of self-nurturance, as necessary as taking a daily medication, according to the essayist Nancy Mairs.

Mairs believes it is healing to "use your hardships to augment your understanding of the world you dwell in." Because a difficult emotional life is complex, "it offers opportunities for developing a greater range of response to experience: a true generosity of experience," she says.

In "Living Behind Bars," in *Plaintext,* Mairs describes her stay in a mental hospital after a serious suicide attempt. Through writing, she has learned about her illness and has found the reasons for her "dis-ease" in her life history.

By writing, Mairs understood she had a pattern of becoming adulterously involved with inappropriate men, losing them, and becoming suicidal to try to regain her father, who died when she was young—to reenact that early, traumatic loss and to reenact, too, perhaps, the pain of an adolescent rape. When each affair ended, her feelings of panic, grief, loss, and rage were revitalized and reexperienced. Inevitably, she became suicidal.

Initially, she didn't write because she was disgusted at the ineptness of her early work. She expected herself to be brilliant immediately. She was fearful, she now knows, of entering a world of writing where time, patience, and effort are necessary for growth. But she didn't write, too, because she was taught that her duty was to please others, not herself, to do what others wanted, not what she wanted. To make time to write meant making time to be alone and putting her needs first, which she couldn't do initially. But because she was not writing, she says, "I almost died of sorrow."

Not writing, if we must, Mairs believes, is potentially harmful, even lethal. Many people who want to write have had traumatic experiences (as Ludwig's study indicates), which *must* be described. Left unexpressed, the effects of trauma can become toxic. Mairs links her mental, even her physical illness—she has multiple sclerosis—to her silence.

Mairs has gained much from writing about her life's difficulties. A sense of perspective. A sense of humor. A "valuable attentiveness to the objects and people around me." A sense of delight in life's pleasures. A sense of connection with others, a greater tolerance of others' shortcomings. And, most important, gratitude. "Hardship," she contends, "can be terrifically humanizing."

Writers through the ages have often intuitively or knowingly used their work to try to self-heal from depression.

In 1819, during a summer of life-threatening crisis, Mary Shelley, author of *Frankenstein,* kept her suicidal urges in check by writing her novel *Mathilda.* Her young son, William, had just died. The year before, she had suffered the death of her daughter, Clara. Rather than allowing her to mourn, her husband, the poet Percy Bysshe Shelley, wanted her to contain her sorrow. Her father, the famous liberal philosopher William Godwin, castigated her for her grief; he told her "it is only persons of very ordinary sort, and of a pusillanimous disposition" who need to mourn. He warned her that unless she controlled herself, her family would "finally cease to love you, and scarcely learn to endure you."

With no place to turn to for comfort, Mary Shelley turned to her writing to explore the issues of love and loss and parental abuse. According to the literary historian Rosaria Champagne, she composed *Mathilda,* a novel describing a sexually abusive father, to fend off her suicidal urges caused in part by her mourning and in part by her father's behavior that, in her childhood, might have been incestuous or emotionally incestuous. Connecting her desire to die with this heretofore unexamined, unspoken experience in her life saved Mary Shelley's life.

In *Mathilda,* a young dying woman takes on the "last task" of writing the story of herself and her father. She tells how, after her mother's death, her father abandons her and how she has been raised by an aunt. After sixteen years her father returns and, jealous of another man's attentions to her, insists that she live with him as his wife, while he also emotionally abuses her.

Mathilda is remarkable, says Champagne, because it deals with the "somatic and psychological aftereffects [including suicide] of abuse" in anticipation of Freud. Though her character Mathilda dies, Mary Shelley writes her way into life, not death. The two major reasons are that Mary Shelley doesn't wonder whether she's made up her experience, as her character does—she knows her excessive involvement with her father is based upon his alternating between seductive and abusive behavior. And Mary Shelley connects her feelings with the events in her life while her character can't. These are essential for the incest survivor to thrive.

"Without the act of narrative," Champagne maintains, "the body of an incest survivor is forever trapped." If the survivor doesn't write her life, "her body will remain only a signifier of despair."

After she finished her book, Mary Shelley's despair lifted temporarily. She sent her only copy to her father. After reading it, Godwin declared it "disgusting and detestable." He "quietly put the manuscript in a drawer" and refused to return it. For years, Mary Shelley tried to recover it but never did, and it went unpublished until 1959.

In 1892, Charlotte Perkins Gilman, author of "The Yellow Wallpaper," published an article about why she had written that work. It describes a seriously depressed woman who wants to write but who, instead, is forced into a rest cure by her doctor-husband. The effect of his treatment is the serious worsening of her illness.

"For many years," Gilman writes, "I suffered from a severe and continuous nervous breakdown tending to melancholia—and beyond." Desperate, after three years, she consulted Dr. S. Weir Mitchell, the famous Philadelphia neurologist, who advised her to undertake a rest cure similar to the one described. Though she had written from childhood, she was told not to "touch pen, brush, or pencil again."

After three months, she believed she came "so near the borderline of utter mental ruin that I could see over." Going against Mitchell's regimen, she decided to begin to write again. "Work, the normal life of every human being; work, which is joy and growth and service, without which one is a pauper and a parasite." Through writing, she learned that her mental illness was caused in part by her childhood and in part by her "mismarriage"—she was, she believed, temperamentally ill suited for marriage and motherhood.

Through writing, Gilman's spirits revived. She shed her feelings of desperation and helplessness. She learned that she could be a purposeful human being. She left her marriage and changed her life.

For Gilman, hysteria and depression are caused by not telling your story. The self, filled with fury at having its desires impeded, at having no outlet, begins to attack itself. She believed there was much for others to learn from her experience, for she was "naturally moved to rejoicing by this narrow escape." Her message was that the "inevitable result" of not being allowed to write when we must is "progressive insanity." She wrote "The Yellow Wallpaper," she says, "to save people from being driven crazy, and it worked."

Gilman's biographer, Ann J. Lane, says that though Gilman says she wrote the work to save people from insanity, "perhaps one of the people she saved was herself, for in this story she seems to have let herself go, allowed her unconscious to help her creative art, and in so doing may have helped to purge the demons that terrified her. . . . [and] achieved some control over both her illness and her past."

After, Gilman continued to write. During her long career she published the landmark *Women and Economics* (1899) and the feminist utopian novel *Herland* (1915).

In William Styron's memoir of depression, *Darkness Visible*, he describes how throughout his career he created suicidal characters in his fiction without realizing they were a way for him to manage his suicidal impulses. Styron believes his long-standing depression was caused by his mother's death when he was young and that he never fully acknowledged or understood or worked through the meaning of that traumatic loss and its effect on his psyche until recently, though he used the subject in his work.

His depression worsened, he knows, because of his addiction to and abuse of alcohol and Halcion, a drug with dangerous side effects, prescribed for him by a physician who told him it was as safe as aspirin. He used these to manage his chronic anxiety. Hospitalization, he said, saved him when he became seriously suicidal. After, through therapy he began to understand his condition and how he'd used writing to manage it.

In the 1940s, Djuna Barnes deliberately wrote her play *The Antiphon* to help manage her long depression. As an adult, Barnes manifested many symptoms of post-traumatic stress disorder—anorexia, many stress-related illness, anxiety, alcoholism, and suicidal urges. "What do you want, Djuna?" her good friend Emily Coleman once asked her. "To die," Barnes replied.

Reworking the story of her life over the twenty-nine drafts of the play she completed in about seven years gave her some mastery over the effects of the multiple traumas she had endured as a child. She once told her friend T. S. Eliot that she couldn't "picture anyone['s] family quite as abominable as mine."

In her work, she described how her father sold her into sexual slavery and paid someone to rape her. How he had physically abused her. How her mother despised her and wanted her dead. How her grandmother sexually abused her.

The purpose of her work, she said, was not revenge, but justice—to right the wrongs done to her. She believed that unless we tell the stories of our traumas, we become members of the "living dead." This was another way of saying that unless we tell our stories, we become seriously depressed.

Exposing her family's secrets and the abuse she endured helped Djuna Barnes manage her suicidal depression for the remainder of her life. Through writing, she realized she wasn't responsible for what had happened to her. Her parents were. Her family's impact could destroy her, but only if she let it. Her writing was a deliberate act of exorcism, a way for her to rid herself of her parents' possession of her spirit.

Considering how horribly she was abused, Barnes's life is a triumph of the human spirit and the power of writing to heal the wounded psyche. The answer to why she survived is found in Barnes's writings. She never doubted the accuracy of her recollections. Though it took her many pain-filled years to write her life with appropriate compassion for herself and rage at her parents, she didn't keep her story secret or deny it. She found emotional support in carefully selected sustaining friendships. She used her abuse, not to withdraw into a lonely and terrifying isolation, but instead to connect with others who might profit from hearing her story, with others who might be similarly wounded. She hoped that what she suffered and how she endured could help others understand their pain, giving it value and meaning and perhaps even preventing abuse.

After years of leading a dangerous and potentially self-destructive life (much like Anne Sexton) and after almost dying, Barnes (unlike Sexton) learned that to survive she must care for herself as she'd never been cared for as a child. She created a safe space within which she could do the emotionally difficult work of writing her life. She got sober and stayed sober. She discovered that her self-worth didn't depend on whether others loved her or her work. She controlled her relationships and disentangled herself from those that were damaging. She lived frugally and carefully. She developed a fierce integrity by satisfying herself in her writing rather than worrying about satisfying publishers and critics.

Trauma and the Imagination

For Harry B. Lee (writing in the 1940s) and Andrew Brink (writing in the 1970s), any traumatic challenge to the psyche increases our vulnerability to depression. But trauma acts, too, as a "strong stimulus to the imagination," as the distressed person tries to replace what has been lost or to restore what has been damaged. Creativity, then, seems a basic human response to trauma and a natural "emergency defense against depression."

One important reason this is so is that writing conveys messages to the self about the inner state. Unfortunately, say Lee and Brink, this healing function of creativity isn't well known, even among therapists and literary critics, much less among writers, writers-to-be, and ordinary people, who all could profit enormously from knowing about this age-old means of psychic self-care and how it functions.

The psychic repair accomplished by writing may never be final or complete, especially in cases of extreme trauma or abuse. Still, the ongoing discipline of writing may help us ward off the most crippling aspects of depression. Because, for Brink, depression and obsession go hand in hand—we continuously revisit the traumatic event—writing serves as a distraction. It can provide a new and healthier obsession (especially if the writer pays attention to ritual and order). And, perhaps most important, it can provide an imaginative, healing antitoxin (to use the word that Anaïs Nin used to describe her writing) to our psychic pain.

But writing can do all this only if we use it, says Brink, to recoup the nurturing we lost or to give ourselves the nurturing we never had. We can't use our work to persecute ourselves or others, to cling to our ills. (This is what Sylvia Plath did in writing "Edge," near the end of her life, a poem about her suicidal intentions: "The woman is perfected. / Her dead / Body wears the smile of accomplishment.") Exploring traumatic material in writing if it's done under extremely threatening, unsafe conditions or if the depression has turned suicidal is extraordinarily risky. A writer can be driven even deeper into despair during such crises if feelings of helplessness, hopelessness, powerlessness, worthlessness, or self-blame are expressed.

When we most need to marshal whatever fragile psychic resources are available to us, we should be careful not to use our work to make ourselves even more desperate. We can use our writing, instead, to affirm our very significant strengths. For every survivor has them.

To create a work of art, Brink says, "may be to administer the best anti-depressant known to the [writer]," perhaps the only means the writer has "of mobilizing a natural healing capability of the psyche."

WHAT YOU CAN DO NOW   *A note to the reader:* I believe that writing about severe trauma for a writer with symptoms of post-traumatic stress disorder should be done with professional, qualified, empathic help. Before engaging in any such writing, please get help, get assistance. Make an emergency plan (with qualified assistance) about what you will do if you find you are at extreme risk.

Is there a healing narrative about your surviving extreme trauma that you feel ready to write?

Can you write it, enacting suggestions made here and in part 2 of this book, "The Process/The Program," especially heeding the cautions made in this chapter and in chapter 6, "Caring for Ourselves as We Write"?

Chapter Ten

Writing the Wounded Body

In the absence of any record of my illness,
I shall write it myself. Invent it out of whole
cloth. It is what a writer can do that a
doctor cannot.

RICHARD SELZER, *Raising the Dead*

Inside every patient there's
a poet trying to get out.

ANATOLE BROYARD, *Intoxicated by My Illness*

In 1997 I attend an exhibit called "Art That Heals: The Image as Medicine in Ethiopia." I stand in front of an Ethiopian healing scroll, an iconic drawing of geometric shapes and five sets of eyes and written prayers and invocations. It was made by a cleric for someone gravely ill in Ethiopia over a hundred years ago. Ethiopia has a thousand-year tradition of using words and images to cure illness or heal the spirit of the stricken person if a physical cure isn't possible.

If I were sick in Ethiopia, the process of making my scroll would involve me in a therapeutic journey or quest. A cleric would ask me questions about how and when I became afflicted, about why I think I became ill, about my present condition, about my life before my illness, about my relationships with others, about my feelings and thoughts—anything that could help unravel the mystery of my current ailment. For illness is viewed as a mystery to try to fathom (though it might not yield its secrets) rather than as a puzzle to be solved (as it tends to be viewed in North America).

I wouldn't be alone in dealing with my illness. The cleric and I would form a healing partnership. This is because my illness is understood in communal, mind-body, and interactive terms rather than in individual, physiological, and singular terms. It might be an outgrowth of social causes; it might be an outgrowth of my state of mind or soul or psyche; it might be an outgrowth of people who have wanted the worst for me.

I wouldn't be left alone to contemplate my illness, nor would I be told of its meaning by someone surer than I of what my body was experiencing. My healing journey, then, would constitute a collaboration. I would tell my story; the cleric would listen. Together, we would ponder the conundrum of what I was experiencing. Together we would try to understand its meaning. After hearing my story and assessing my circumstances, the cleric would devise a scroll for my personal use, drawing upon his knowledge about efficacious signs and symbols.

Reviewing my life in the context of my illness would constitute the single most significant part of my healing journey. For it would invite me to impose a kind of narrative order on what had happened, on the seeming chaos and destabilizing effect of my illness. It would invite me to think of possible cause and plausible effect. It would invite me to link my present with my past; to ponder how I might have come to harm; to imagine what my future might now hold. It would give me something to do now—a present-day task that I could effectively fulfill. Most important, it would involve me as an active participant in my journey to wellness. Being involved would make me feel less victimized, more efficacious. And thinking of myself as capable would require restoration of belief in myself, a belief that had been seriously undermined by my illness.

Rather than assuming that a specialist in the care of the body knew more than I ever could about the message my illness was conveying, I would be seen, instead, as an important repository of knowledge about myself and my illness. It would be assumed that I could "read" the text of my body and that I could help write the text that would heal me. In Ethiopia, then, it is believed that telling stories helps people heal.

Tapping into that deeply personal and singular wisdom about the self would be considered an essential part of my eventual cure. Reminding me that I knew much and that I could help myself, too, would be useful during a time when I might feel great despair. The scroll, too, would act as a permanent record of my journey.

In reading the text of my scroll, in contemplating its images, I would help myself heal. So potent is the power of the word that the scroll itself might be wrapped around me so that the meaning of its message could more effectively penetrate my body.

Illness as Quest

I have come to see "Art That Heals" because I have been studying how beginning and experienced writers have used writing to help themselves heal from bodily affliction. So far, I have read scores of works (Audre Lorde's *The Cancer Journals;* Kenny Fries's *Body, Remember;* Kat Duff's *The Alchemy of Illness;* Donald Hall's *Life Work;* Sandra M. Gilbert's *Wrongful Death;* Richard Selzer's *Raising the Dead;* May Sarton's *After the Stroke;* Gillian Rose's *Love's Work;* Lucy Grealy's *Autobiography of a Face;* Anatole Broyard's *Intoxicated by My Illness;* Barbara Lazear Ascher's *Landscape Without Gravity;* Harold Brodkey's *This Wild Darkness* among them).

The title of the exhibit has lured me. It presents work from a culture in which the power of the word to heal is a commonly held belief.

I find the five sets of eyes on the healing scroll I am studying arresting. They seem to invite me into a contemplative state. "Look within," they seem to command. "Examine yourself."

As I walk through the exhibit, I overhear two museum guards discussing the bad flu they've had (I've had it, too), the medicines they've taken to quell their symptoms, their anger at being sick, at wasting so much time in bed. How ironic, I think, to see the way we typically regard illness in the midst of this exhibit that shows a completely different perception of illness, of the sick person's role, and of the function of language.

The guards speak of illness and its symptoms as something to banish, not understand. They see themselves as passive victims of something that's invaded their body, not as active participants in their bodies' healing. And they see doctors as singularly possessing the power to cure them. They use language to complain about what's happened, not to describe what they've experienced, not to help themselves heal.

In Ethiopia, illness is an opportunity. It is something to contemplate. It invites the sick person to undertake an internal spiritual and healing journey. It provides a possibility for growth. The sick person is a seeker, a voyager, an explorer. And the word can cure. Illness can be experienced, expressed, and understood, but only in the way that one understands a mystery, for that, in part, is what illness is.

Why Write About Our Wounded Bodies?

Arthur W. Frank, in his remarkable book *The Wounded Storyteller*, reminds us that when we face serious or chronic illness, disability, or dying, we are plunged into a terrifying, chaotic place where nothing seems secure, where the very nature of time changes. We experience anguish and physical and mental suffering. Illness and disability, says John L. Coulehan in "The Word Is an Instrument of Healing," entail our sustaining gigantic losses: of meaning, of wholeness, of certainty, of relationships, of freedom, of control. They are a threat to the meaning we ascribe to our lives, to our integrity, to our very existence. We can write, Anatole Broyard says in *Intoxicated by My Illness*, "to confine the catastrophe." We can write, Frank says, "to *repair* the damage that illness has done," to restore a sense of meaning and coherence to our lives. We can write, as Audre Lorde did, "to sort out for myself who I was and was becoming throughout that time." Writing, then, as she attests, can be "a gateway, however cruelly won, into the tapping and expansion of [our] own power and knowing."

The guidelines and values by which we formerly lived our lives can no longer help us. "The body," says Frank, "sets in motion the need for new stories when its disease disrupts the old stories." For Anatole Broyard, though, "a critical illness is like a great permission." Because we have so little time, we can finally let ourselves see who we truly are, and we can quickly become what we might have been before. In "AIDS and the Poetry of Healing," Rafael Campo says "AIDS, in the process of rendering people almost unable to talk, filling lungs with secretions and opportunistic infections, has at the same time brought the same people to an opportunity for an unmatchable eloquence, to retell their lives, to write the poems that will last forever."

One reason, then, to write as we face these critical junctures in our lives is that illness and disability necessitate that we think differently about ourselves, about everything. We can write a new story for ourselves, to discover who we are now—what we're feeling and thinking and what we desire. We can learn, too, what our bodies are like now, and we can imagine what will become of us.

Though it's necessary for us to speak of these changes, often the people we love seem locked away from us in their own fear and loss, incapable of listening to the stories we must tell. As I wrote in *Breathless,* my asthma journal, "When I was at my worst, and could only talk about how sick I was (for my illness had become my only reality), I once calculated that the most that any listener—husband, child, relative, close friend, distant acquaintance—could endure without changing the subject, was about thirty-five seconds." Writing is often the only outlet we have.

Discovering what we're feeling and thinking, through writing, helps us negotiate and tolerate a new psychic space. It is one that is sometimes terrifying but sometimes exhilarating. It is one that is altogether unfamiliar and one into which no one else can accompany us. For, as Richard Selzer (who writes of his near death from Legionnaires' disease in *Raising the Dead*) describes, writing when we're critically ill helps us heal because healing "means a restoration to wholeness as perceived by the healed." Through writing, we adjust our perspective: we move into "an acceptance as whole of what remains."

Writing gives us back the voices we seem to lose when our bodies become ill or disabled. We want to speak for ourselves and our particular experience of illness and disability rather than have someone else speak for us. Writing helps us assert our individuality, our authority, our own particular style. All are seriously compromised by medical treatment and hospitalization, which deny us our complexity as human beings by seeing us as "a case," by reducing our wounded body stories into indecipherable markings on charts, graphs, and medical histories (that say nothing about our own personal histories).

When Audre Lorde learned that she had breast cancer, she started a diary that became *The Cancer Journals*. In it, she talked about her reasons for writing. She wanted to give her illness "voice, to share it for use, that the pain not be wasted." Lorde discovered she had to regard her body in a new way: "I must tend my body with at least as much care as I tend the compost," she said. When our bodies are failing us, Lorde discovered, is when we can learn what they mean to us. It's when we need to love our bodies the most because we risk loving them the least.

But we write about our wounded bodies, too, to guide others who will follow us into these uncharted places. As Nancy Mairs puts it, "Disability is the one minority group we will all belong to."

When he developed prostate cancer, Anatole Broyard discovered he needed to read what others had written about cancer so that he wouldn't feel so alone with his illness. He read Stewart Alsop's *Stay of Execution* and Natalie Spingarn's *Hanging in There*. Leo Tolstoy's *The Death of Ivan Ilyich* and Thomas Mann's *The Magic Mountain* are, Broyard believes, among the few great novels about illness. (Susan Kenney's *In Another Country* and *Sailing*, too, are great, complex novels about illness.) Sick people, Broyard rightly believed, "need a literature of their own" to describe the experience accurately and completely, without falsifying. "To be ill," Broyard says, "is an odd mixture of pathos and bathos, comedy and terror, with intervals of surprise.

To treat it too respectfully is to fall into the familiar, florid taps of the Romantic agony." Not to romanticize ourselves or our illness, Broyard believes, is essential. We can learn how to do this by reading others.

When I developed asthma, I wanted to find out about writers with asthma and to read their works: Elizabeth Bishop, Marcel Proust, Olive Schreiner, Djuna Barnes. I did, and they helped me immeasurably; I discovered that all, despite enormous changes in their lives, continued to write.

It's important, when we're sick, to write to leave a legacy or to help others, as the poet Jane Kenyon did as she was dying, as the diarist Alice James did as she was dying. By writing about our illness, about our experiences and feelings about our dying, we change the meaning of our life and our illness. Through our work, we can affect the lives and the dying of other people. "The ill person who turns illness into story," says Frank, "transforms fate into experience; the disease that sets the body apart from others becomes, in the story, the common bond of suffering that joins bodies in their shared vulnerability."

Why Wounded Body Narratives Are Comforting

Nancy Mairs calls memoirs about illness "the literature of personal disaster." Anatole Broyard called them "the literature of illness" and "the literature of death." I call them "wounded body narratives," though I recognize that there cannot be a wounded body in need of healing without a wounded psyche or spirit that is also in need of healing.

In 1930 Virginia Woolf, in "On Being Ill," observed that it was strange "that illness has not taken its place with love and battle and jealousy among the prime themes of literature." Literature, Woolf believed, concerned itself too much with the mind while pretending that the body was "negligible and non-existent." Woolf called for a new literature, one that would report on "this daily drama of the body" during illness. She believed that looking illness "squarely in the face" and writing about it would require "the courage of a lion tamer; a robust philosophy; a reason rooted in the bowels of the earth." For these works to be penned, Woolf remarked, writers would need to invent a new language—"more primitive, more sensual, more obscene." And people would have to reorder their hierarchies to include illness (along with jealousy, for example) among life's central experiences.

Woolf wanted to read such works (though many hadn't yet been written) because, given the many illnesses she suffered during her lifetime (a near-fatal whooping cough, depression, serious influenza, heart ailments, an extremely difficult menopause among them), she wanted the comfort and wisdom they might have given her. If such a literature had existed in her time, she suggests, she wouldn't have felt so alone in her suffering or so negatively marked by its effect on her life.

Such a literature now exists. In "When Bad Things Happen to Good Writers," Nancy Mairs has spoken of the important cultural work being done by people writing the literature of personal disaster— the work of helping to assuage suffering. For Mairs, these works are "singularly instructive" to other people with afflictions, to people who will one day, too, face disastrous circumstances in their lives. "What we can offer you, when the time comes," she says, "is companionship in a common venture. It's not a lot, I know, but it may come in handy. The narrator of personal disaster, I think, . . . wants to comfort."

Rather than bemoaning our condition, when we write, we report on it "in detail." Reporting on our wounded body experiences, she says, is like "taking up a severe and rather odd new discipline, spelunking, perhaps, something that draws one through the stink of bat guano toward an unfathomable abyss." This discipline serves to distract our attention from our suffering. Using language to capture the "welter of little incidents" that accompany an illness or a disability, Mairs believes, counteracts "disorientation and disintegration." Making sense of "a flood of random data" gives the writer a feeling, no matter how illusory, of control. Reading the literature of personal disaster gives the audience a sense that meaning can be found in life's most difficult moments.

For Mairs, an icy distance from our experiences should not be the aim of our work. Readers need a clear sense of what the experience looks like from the outside, but also what it feels like from the inside.

Shying away from describing the often messy and painful facts about what sick bodies suffer, refusing to talk about "piss, shit, vomit, blood, bedsores, hallucinations," as my student Geoffrey, writing about the death of his lover from AIDS remarked, contributes to our culture's refusal to reckon openly with illness, disability, disease, dying, and death. Hence our discomfort and fear. Writing, then, dispels ignorance.

If we want to "console and hearten" others, says Mairs, we must make ourselves and our anguish "wholly transparent, revealing not illness as metaphor but illness as illness." We do this to show others that, through the act of writing, "survival (at least till the last page) is possible."

Though I am outspoken, in the earliest drafts of my memoir *Breathless,* I didn't mention the word *mucus* in my account of what an asthma attack feels like, though managing a mucus so productive that it can stop my breath and kill me is the most salient feature of my life with asthma. Maybe it's that I was fed up with thinking about mucus—it's on my mind more than anything else, including my husband, grandbaby, and good cooking.

But though I certainly knew what asthma felt like on one level—I had, after all, been living with the disease for years—on another level I really didn't know how asthma felt. I hadn't really let myself pay careful attention to what was happening to my body until I started writing about it.

I suppose that I was initially afraid that describing what happens when I'm having an asthma attack would make me have an asthma attack. But as I composed (created) my description, I felt more composed (calmed, quieted, settled, soothed). In composing accounts of our illnesses, we not only compose ourselves, we compose others.

Writers of the literature of personal disaster, too, can shift our focus about three salient features of life, says Mairs: the necessary presence of often-grotesque humor in the most tragic circumstances; the appreciation of the mundane, commonplace, and everyday aspects of life often overlooked by the well; and the preciousness of time.

Mairs herself writes of the times she's tumbled to the ground as a result of multiple sclerosis as the riotous occasions she sometimes believes them to be. Anatole Broyard complained that, though all his friends were "wits," as he was dying, "instead of being ironical and making jokes," they were "terribly serious." Broyard says he needed their merriment, but they instead gave him "a grotesque lovingness" he didn't want. In *Breathless,* I reported how, after I needed to wear a face mask to go outside in cold weather, my sons started calling me "Darth Mother." Recognizing that these days, out at night, in winter, wearing my mask, *I'm* the person people cross the street to avoid always makes me laugh.

Witnessing how a writer like Audre Lorde in *The Cancer Journals* writes of the gardening that sustains her, how a writer like May Sarton in *After the Stroke* describes the changing appearance of the ocean ("dark clouds now over a dark gray ocean"), the antics of her beloved cat Pierrot ("rushing in and out where I'm working like a frenzied *Comedia del Arte* actor"), the sight of a "monarch butterfly floating over the last phlox" of the season, the deep satisfaction of having salmon for dinner, helps readers cherish what we often overlook. For illness often confers a wisdom about how to make ordinary life deeply and transcendentally meaningful.

Writers of wounded body narratives often share their insights, those that have taken them suffering and struggle to understand. Writers facing death have learned that the passage of time is an extremely subjective phenomenon—that, as Robert Grudin reminds us in *Time and the Art of Living,* a lifetime can be lived in a moment or that a lifetime can seem as if it's lasted but a moment. Often writers remark upon how time, when we face death, seems to become infinitely expandable.

Writing a Loved One's Dying

In the preface to Mark Doty's remarkable memoir, *Heaven's Coast,* about his lover Wally's death, Doty tells us that his aim in writing was simply "to make some record" of those many days that he spent "adrift in the sea-swirl of shock and loss." Doty knew that he would soon lose Wally; his death from AIDS was a certainty. Still, the process of Wally's dying forced upon Doty a "species of vision, an inwardness which was the gift of a terrible time." As the Lakota Sioux say, he tells us, "when nature gives one a burden, one's also given a gift." Doty's gift during that "terrible time" was a narrowing of focus, a "dizzy-making oxygen of an unfamiliar altitude," which enabled him to pay attention to the man he would soon lose in a way that we rarely regard the people we love in ordinary times. Losing his partner, Wally, necessitated that he turn to his other partner, writing, to describe his feelings of love, loss, anger, grief, guilt.

Making a record of Wally's life and death was a way for Doty to remember him, to hold onto him. Remembering, he says, "is the work of the living." It is what the living must do for the dead. Recalling faces and the way they look in all moods and weathers. Anecdotes that they tell and tell and tell again. Incidents that signify the shared life in all its variety—its ecstatic and banal moments. "Gestures, tics, nuances, those particular human attributes that distinguish us as individuals." Doty believes it is his duty to capture the singularity of Wally, to erect a monument of words to his partner. He does this so we can all understand that though the enormity of the AIDS epidemic can be gauged by ceremonies surrounding the Quilt, they can't remind us "of the particular loved body" the way a memoir can.

But *Heaven's Coast* is a testament, too, to Doty's love for Wally and to his loss and grief, too. Psychic pain like Doty's is enormously difficult to describe, difficult to share as we experience it. More than anything, Doty suggests, when we're faced with loss, we can take time to understand what we're feeling. We can develop a personal vocabulary to articulate our emotions.

On a walk by the Provincetown seashore on a foggy Sunday in early May, Doty examines his state of mind. What he feels, he says, is "perfectly clear." But the right word to describe it isn't "immediately available." Thinking like the poet he is, he discounts grief, for it is "too sharp and immediate" a word for his sensation, perhaps because of "the monosyllabic impact of the word." Sadness, though "is too ephemeral," for "it sounds like something that comes and goes." Mourning feels "a little archaic" with its associations of widows and "a closeting of self away from the world"; it suggests being preoccupied with grief and doesn't convey "the weird interpenetration of ongoingness and endings, of this spring's sproutings and my continuing sorrow."

Sorrow. *"Sorrow,"* says Doty, "feels right, for now." It seems "large and inhabitable, an interior season whose vaulted sky's a suitable match for the gray and white tumult arched over these headlands. . . . This sorrow is capacious; there's room inside it for the everyday, for going about the workaday stuff of life. And for loveliness, for whatever we're to be given by the daily walk."

Doty has remarked on his ambivalent attitude toward writing during such a painful time, yet on the necessity of writing. "To write," he says, "was to court overwhelming feeling. Not to write was to avoid, but to avoid was to survive. Though writing was a way of surviving, too: experience was unbearable, looked at head on, but *not* to look was also unbearable. And so I'd write, when I could." Ultimately, the writing became a powerful inspiriting and a profound act of restitution and love.

In Jamaica Kincaid's memoir of her brother's death, she reminds us that after a loved one dies, our lives are temporarily in serious jeopardy. "I became a writer," she says, "out of desperation, so when I first heard my brother was dying I was familiar with the act of saving myself: I would write about him. I would write about his dying. When I was young, younger than I am now, I started to write about my own life and I came to see that this act saved my life. When I heard about my brother's illness and his dying, I knew, instinctively, that to understand it, or to make an attempt at understanding his dying, and not to die with him, I would write about it."

She wrote *My Brother* because she believed his death threatened her life; she feared that she might follow him to the grave. Because her relationship with her family was complex and difficult, she felt she needed to unburden herself of conflicting feelings, many negative, about a brother whom she both loved and despised. Though he had enormous potential as a child, he had been involved in a murder and was a heavy drug user. And Kincaid was furious at him for that.

Born many years after Kincaid, Devon Drew was an unwanted child; her mother had tried to abort her pregnancy. After his birth, Kincaid was often put in charge of him. Once, when he was two and Kincaid didn't change his diaper, her mother took all Kincaid's beloved books and burned them. Later, Kincaid was sent away to work to help support the family, for with the birth of Devon Drew, Kincaid's stepfather couldn't afford to support them. Still, when he was dying, Devon Drew asked Kincaid if what he'd read in one of her books was true: that his mother had tried to abort him. Kincaid said, "No, the book he read is a novel, a novel is a work of fiction; he did not tell me that he did not believe my reply and I did not tell him that he should not believe my reply."

When, at his funeral, the minister preached a sermon about the family being reunited in an afterlife, Kincaid bridled: "I did not want to be with any of these people again in another world," she says. "I had had enough of them in this one; they mean everything to me and they mean nothing."

Yet reaching for a metaphor to describe her brother, she was surprised at what appeared under her pen, for the metaphor was hopeful, and it connected the two of them, she believed. He was like, she wrote, "the bud of a flower firmly set, blooming, and then the blossom fading, the flower setting a seed which bore inside another set of buds, leading to flowers, and so on and so on into eternity." For, she learned, the process of remembering him and memorializing him enabled her to remember herself—who she had been, who she became, who she was becoming. Writing his life helped ensure that she would stay alive.

"My own life," she concluded, "is still ongoing, I hope, and each moment of its present shapes its past and each moment of its present will shape its future and even so influence the way I see its future; and the knowledge of all this leaves me with the feeling: And what now, and so, yes, what now. *What now?*"

Kincaid wrote the work, in part, too, because she wanted to describe the wasted nature of her brother's life and her negative feelings about him. Too many works of literature, she believes, are too facile, too uplifting, too predictable in their sentiments. They misrepresent the painful reality lived by many. Her brother's life, Kincaid says, was never lived: "He sort of died all the time." Kincaid wanted to write his life to show that "if circumstances had been different, that might have been my own life."

What saved Kincaid's life is the awful paradox that, while her mother loved her brother, "my mother didn't like me. . . . I seemed to repel her. I had to learn to fend for myself. I found a way to rescue myself."

The terrible truth of *My Brother* is the potentially lethal effect of a mother's love. "Americans," Kincaid believes, "find difficulty very hard to take. They are inevitably looking for a happy ending. . . . I think life is difficult and that's that. . . . I am not interested in the pursuit of positivity. I am interested in pursuing a truth, and the truth often seems to be not happiness but its opposite." Kincaid is committed to telling the unpleasant, painful, difficult truths about her family. It is the only way she feels she can survive.

People who write about their loved ones' deaths are paradoxically engaged in a search for the meaning of their loved ones' lives. They want to make a record; they want to describe their loss and their grief. But they want to discover, too, an overarching meaning for this death so that it will not have been for naught.

This seems especially necessary if the death was a violent one, if it was a suicide or an accident, or if it was the death of a child. For these deaths greatly threaten our sense of order. They shake the foundations of our belief in a meaningful, beneficent universe; they make us question whether any actions we undertake have meaning.

The apparent waste or senselessness of violent, accidental, or suicidal deaths, though, can often be redeemed (albeit in small measure) through writing. Writing, too, can become a healthy substitute for unhealthy rumination about a loved one's death, says Esther Dreifuss-Kattan; it can offer comfort for loss by creating something new. For

James W. Pennebaker, writing is especially necessary for the kin of people who have killed themselves or have been the victims of accidental or violent deaths: the aftershocks of these deaths adversely affect our immune system, and any measures that make us healthier, including writing, we would do well to undertake.

In her preface to *Wrongful Death,* Sandra Gilbert describes her response to her husband's unexpected and unexplained death during a routine radical prostatectomy as akin to that of a trauma survivor. She felt "indelibly marked by a shock I still haven't assimilated even while I also feel I must bear witness to the reality—and the fatality—of an experience against which my whole self still protests." After his death, she was "stunned" by her unanticipated grief—"unable to grasp what had happened to my husband and *why* it had happened."

She wrote her book, she attests, because no one from the hospital where Elliot Gilbert died could explain the reasons for his death, no one expressed compassion for her pain. She wrote it, too, because her friend, Toni Morrison, told her that she must do "the *real* mourning things." And what would they be? Gilbert asked Morrison. "*He'll* tell you," Morrison replied.

And he did, says Gilbert. "In whatever strange way the dead communicate with the living . . . my husband spoke to me and told me to write this book."

She began writing one night after Elliot's death when, as usual, she couldn't sleep. "I went into the kitchen with a notebook," she says, "and began, weeping as I wrote, to try to write. Began to try to remember what happened to Elliot and me and the kids so people . . . might understand the impact of medical negligence on one 'real-life' family."

She has learned to live, against her will, in a world where there is no answer, no conclusion. "Somehow, someone killed my husband," she says. "And indeed, there is no closure." But writing transformed her from the "zombie" she was when she began writing to someone who defines, if not masters, her trauma.

While writing, Gilbert discovered that she could understand her husband's death only in the context of the modern practice of medicine as a business and as an industry. *Wrongful Death* is a powerful political protest against this. Though Gilbert understands that her writing can't resurrect her husband or assuage her and her children's loss, pain, and rage, she wrote, she said, to try to make the health care system more accountable, for accountability is "morally and emotionally crucial." She wrote so that his death will not have been wasted. She wrote so that she could one day say that there was nothing more that she could do to make his death meaningful.

Seven weeks after Peter Handke's mother killed herself, he decided to write her life. The work became *A Sorrow Beyond Dreams,* the story of his mother's life. The news of her suicide left him, he said, with a "dull speechlessness." Her suicide threatened his sense of reality. It was, he realized, something "incomprehensible and incommunicable." His day-to-day world fell apart. What he felt was not so much horror as "unreality." His mind "became so empty that it ached."

Once he began to write, though, "these states," he said, "seem to have dwindled and passed, probably because I try to describe them as accurately as possible." The work of describing his feelings, "of remembering and formulating," kept Handke so busy that the worst effects of his mother's death diminished. He was writing, he realized, because he knew more about why his mother died than did anyone else. Also because he wanted to describe his mother's suicide as an "exemplary case." But he was writing, too, in his own self-interest: "because having something to do brings me back to life."

Handke, in remembering his mother's life, started to understand something of the reasons for her death. Important was the horrific life led by poor women in Austria, where she was raised. "The girls in our town used to play a game based on the stations in a woman's life," Handke says. "Tired/Exhausted/Sick/Dying/Dead." His mother's future followed that pattern: "She was; she became; she became nothing." More important was her deep depression, caused, it seems, by living for years with a man who brutally beat her.

After a brief period of obsessively desiring something—to learn— and having her dreams denied her by her father, who told her that going to school was out of the question, she ran away from home to learn cooking, for the only choices open to her were becoming a scullery maid, a chambermaid, or a cook. With her move to Germany and Hitler's rise to power, though, Handke's mother temporarily felt that she was part of an important cause. But Hitler's legacy to Germany, Handke suggests, was also responsible for his mother's death.

Her first lover was a married German party member, with whom she conceived a child. Shortly before Handke's birth, she married a German army sergeant so that her child could be legitimate. After the war, living in East Germany, her life was hellish: trying to care for a family (there were now three children) in a one-room hovel in the impoverished postwar German economy. Her husband was alcoholic and constantly beat her. Her mistreatment was indubitably connected to the savage and brutal ethos established during Hitler's rule.

Though, initially, Handke's writing helped him organize the chaos that descended upon him after his mother's death, he also discovered that there was an even more complex meaning to the story of her suicide than he had initially imagined—the larger story of that war, which, itself, was tremendously destabilizing. Her suicide was connected to the shameful, horrifying history that was his painful legacy.

In a dream, though, near the end of his writing, he came upon "something cheerful" that indicated his new willingness to face this. "I saw," he says, "all sorts of things that were intolerably painful to look at. Suddenly someone came along and in a twinkling took the painful quality out of all these things. LIKE TAKING DOWN AN OUT-OF-DATE POSTER. The metaphor was part of my dream."

The last line of *A Sorrow Beyond Dreams* suggests that this work is only the beginning of the real work of understanding, which remains before him. "Someday," he says, "I shall write about this in greater detail."

Forms of Wounded Body Narratives

When our loved ones are dying, when our bodies are acutely ill, when we are facing death, we are living in the midst of the disintegration of everything that has marked our lives as normal and meaningful. When our bodies require our ongoing attention, as Nancy Mairs's body does (which she describes in *Waist-High in the World*), as the poet Kenny Fries's does (which he describes in *Body, Remember*), we question what others believe it means to be normal and to have a meaningful life.

Writing in crisis, as Arthur W. Frank says in *The Wounded Storyteller*, is a primary vehicle for resisting the seeming chaos of our lives. Sometimes it is a vehicle, too, for integrating our new feelings and experiences into our psyches, which are forced, often against our will and desire, to change. Writing is one important way to discover the meaning of our lives during these difficult times or to express what seems meaningless and threatening. Writing when we are living with wounded bodies is a primary vehicle for resisting cultural prejudices about who we are, what is possible, and what wellness and wholeness mean.

After reading scores of works, Frank has identified three major types of wounded body narratives: the chaos narrative, the restitution narrative, and the quest narrative. In preparing to write mine, about asthma, I found these categories extremely useful. They suggested some possibilities for the form my narrative might take.

The Chaos Narrative

In the chaos narrative, there is often no coherent sequence, no discernible order to events because the person is in such profound crisis or is replicating such profound crisis that distance and judgment from the lived events is impossible. The story is told in an "and then and then and then and then" way. Often, the events or the narrator's feelings seem unclear if survival (of torture, of extreme physical brutality, for example) has depended upon dissociation.

Feelings, when present, might be inappropriate to the events narrated. Or they might be overwhelming and might flood the narrative. Often, feelings of vulnerability, futility, and impotence are expressed. Always, there is an immediacy to the narrative; events are described as they're evolving, before they've been understood or integrated.

Chaos narratives are difficult to hear and are threatening to readers. This is especially so in a culture that insists on happy endings, that believes people can always find a way to triumph against adversity, that thinks that something good can always be wrested from tragedy. Because chaos narratives have their source in extreme anxiety and deep pain, they often elicit these states in the reader.

Several readers of my memoir *Breathless* told me that the initial pages made them so anxious they could barely continue reading. What I wrote was this: "I am alone. . . . I try to ignore the trouble I'm having breathing, the coughing attack that has continued, unabated, for the past two hours, the slamming inside my head, my fatigue. . . . For the next few seconds, I try to ignore this body I inhabit that has declared war on me. . . . Ignore the chronic cough, the pain in my chest, the lump in my throat, the rasp in my breath. And can't. . . . I'm aware of every breath I take. Inhale. Cough. Sputter. Exhale. Inhale. Exhale. . . . Inhale. (Can't get enough air into my lungs. Feels like I'm suffocating, feels like I have a tomcat sitting on my chest and that I'm breathing against its weight. Feels, too, like I'm drowning in mucus.) Clear my throat. Choke. Exhale. Inhale. . . . Clear. Swallow. Exhale. Inhale. Drowning. Mayday. Mayday."

I explained that I *wanted* to make the reader feel what it was like for me, what it's like for millions of asthmatics. Asthma is a serious, life-threatening, incurable illness that has reached epidemic proportions throughout the world. I wanted the reader to recognize what it feels like to be aware of every single breath you take.

What the writer of a chaos narrative desires, says Frank, is for the reader to recognize that states of chaos exist. If the wounded body narrative is told retrospectively, the writer wants the reader to understand that the narrator has survived times during which chaos prevailed.

Many wounded body narratives, even if they aren't thoroughgoing chaos narratives, have chaotic moments in them. Moments where there are one-sentence paragraphs, one-word sentences, long lists of unintegrated phenomena. Often, this broken speech is the only way we can accurately describe what we've experienced. "Narrative wreckage," Frank says, often attends such times in our lives. Formally, chaos narratives approximate this wreckage.

At the beginning of Catherine Kapphahn's "Thin Ice," a memoir of her mother's dying, Kapphahn uses a long list to show how unassimilated her experiences were. "Her cravings for eggrolls and hashbrowns / Writing letters / Rewetting the sponge, pink lollypop looking thing / Morphine on the medicine spinner / sleeping on the wide couch / Listening to them while I pretend to sleep / Oxygen humming / closed curtains / Moving the TV / Winter Olympics / Pulling Mama up, making everyone happy, / I'm the only one who can do it without hurting her / Giving away Mama's clothes / Hospice workers trying to prepare us / Usually they find it too late / High mortality rate / Time changes, every minute filled."

We resist chaos narratives. We resist reading them. Sometimes we resist writing them, penning a neater, more hopeful though fraudulent version of events we've survived. We want narratives that demonstrate the resilience of the human spirit. We don't want to admit defeat.

Once, when a student writer, whose body bore the scars of her physically abusive childhood, wrote as a chaos narrative a memoir sequence describing her violent relationship with her husband, some listeners expressed dissatisfaction and disgust with what she'd written.

"I know you don't want to hear this," she said. "But it's the truth, and I have to write it. Everyone wants to hear how, if you're abused, you survive, and you triumph over the evil of your childhood. But, until now, I haven't. This is my life right now. I'm not proud of it. But it's true that some of us don't escape. Some of us continue the patterns of our past. And this is the story I have to tell."

Restitution Narratives

If our culture resists the chaos narrative, it welcomes the restitution and recovery narrative, with its storyline of health restored and adversity overcome. We expect, says Arthur W. Frank, that for every suffering there must be a remedy; that for every illness there must be a cure.

The implication of a restitution narrative is that our bodies can be restored to what they were like before illness struck. Its deeper, perhaps unconscious, meaning is that dying is avoidable and that if someone dies it means that enough hasn't been done—the right doctor or the right medicine hasn't been found; the person hasn't fought hard enough. Writers like Nancy Mairs and Audre Lorde challenge these assumptions while critiquing a culture that promulgates them. But Mairs and Lorde, too, want to describe the ways in which illness has helped them learn about themselves and our culture. Narratives about *living with* illness, disease, dying, and disfigurement, they argue, must supplant falsely hopeful triumphed-over-all narratives as norms in our culture.

This means writing precisely what our lives are like—how we shower, dress, eat, make love, excrete, or move from place to place. It means writing precisely what bodies are like, as Kenny Fries does in the poems in *Anesthesia,* where he describes the "three toes on each twisted foot. / . . . the rough skin. The holes / where the pins were. The scars."

When writing a wounded body narrative, it's essential that we not misrepresent our experience, that we not write what we think the culture wants to hear, that we not spare our readers the sight of our bodies. If our story contains aspects of the restitution narrative, it's important that we relate them. But it's important, too, to be accurate in describing what we've lost and what we feel about it, including our fury. In *Breathless,* I found it necessary to quarrel with cultural assumptions about recovery. I describe how, after a year of constant care during which I'd gotten much better, I met a friend who congratulated me on my recovery. I was furious at her because I hadn't recovered. I had lost irrevocably the ability to do simple things that most people can do unthinkingly. I was dealing with asthma daily. She wanted to think that, though I had been broken, I was now fixed. This meeting made me realize I took issue with the comforting arc of the recovery narrative, and I wrote this into my work.

Many wounded body narratives take on the assumptions of the restitution narrative and critique them to expose the underlying fallacies of how our culture understands bodily ills. The narratives in

David T. Mitchell and Sharon L. Snyder's *The Body and Physical Difference: Discourses of Disability*, for example, expose the fallacious assumption that people with incurable illness aren't normal—that they can't be happy, productive, satisfied, irritable, short-tempered, generous, forgiving, accepting, protesting, depressed, married, adulterous, orgasmic, maternal, selfish—just like anybody. They articulate, too, how simple descriptions of bodily appearance and bodily functions challenge our culture's tendency to hide from the realities of life. An important part of wounded body narratives is to demystify the life of a people living with wounded bodies.

Quest Narratives

Quest narratives, like Audre Lorde's *The Cancer Journals,* Kenny Fries's *Body, Remember,* and Nancy Mairs's *Waist-High in the World,* are "open to crisis as a source of change and growth," says Frank. Unlike restitution narratives, which assume that we can reclaim the lives we led before illness, quest narratives assert that everything changes, that everything is always changing, and that we can learn to live moral, ethical, deeply meaningful lives in the midst of extraordinarily difficult circumstances.

In quest narratives, we search for something to be gained through the journey of the experience our wounded body provides. We describe the moment when we suspect that something is amiss; we describe our woundedness accurately; we describe the challenges we experience—those we rise to, those that make us despair, those that mark us irrevocably. We relate how our sense of the world has changed and how we make meaning of a life that has been utterly transformed.

Quest narratives strive for accuracy and unflinchingly honest narratives. But they also assert that though we are ill, disabled, or dying, we can put this experience to good use and can create something worthwhile for ourselves and others. So they often take on political overtones (as manifestos). Lorde and I both believe that pollution helped cause our illnesses. Both of us believe, too, that though people with wounded bodies must take responsibility for healing themselves, still, people must work in concert to correct, say, the fouling of our air, the poisoning of our water.

Quest narratives, of course, can be written in a variety of literary forms—fiction (as in Lynne Sharon Schwartz's *The Fatigue Artist*, about chronic fatigue syndrome); journal (as in May Sarton's *After the Stroke*); poetry (as in Sandra M. Gilbert's *Ghost Volcano*).

Sometimes, the form we choose is determined by what we can do with our bodies as they are—short poems or diary entries, say, because we can't manage more sustained forms. After I became ill, I began, as many writers with wounded bodies do, to keep a record of my illness in diary form, largely because no matter how sick I was, I could always manage to scratch out ten minutes of writing while propped up on pillows. I desperately needed to write; I needed some contact with a self that seemed to be slipping from me. These early entries sounded like clipped and cryptic wartime reports from some battle where the outcome is uncertain. "Today was awful." "Collapsed." "This has been one hell of a siege." "Close to despair, wondering if I'll ever get better." "I truly hope this stops." "I can't take much more."

Sometimes, illness launches people into writing. Writing, for many writers who've never written before illness, often feels like embarking upon a quest for life's meaning, for one's personal history. Facing mortal illnesses, people often feel that they must review their lives and establish a symbolic meaning for them, creating, perhaps, as Audre Lorde did, a "biomythography"—a life story with mythic dimensions.

Philip Sandblom, M.D., in studying the relationship between illness and creative activity, discovered that "by preventing other activity, disease may be a factor that awakens artistic creativity in those with dormant talents and offers the opportunity to develop them." Michel de Montaigne began writing his famous essays only after developing kidney disease. Flannery O'Connor believed that having lupus erythematosus gave her wisdom about the life cycle denied the well: "Sickness before death is a very appropriate thing," she wrote, "and I think those who don't have it miss one of God's mercies." Marcel Proust's gargantuan *Remembrance of Things Past* seems to have been impelled by his asthma; it is testimony to Proust's strength of will and endurance that he wrote despite his illness and in heroic defiance of its threat to deny him the ability to work.

When Michele Murray, at thirty-five, discovered she had cancer, she began to write poetry. She wrote four books before her death; seven months after her death, her first collection, *The Great Mother,* was published. "Working on poetry again," she wrote, "I know in myself the meaning of *vocation,* because that is the sense I have, of an inner directing voice assuring me that I am touching the center of *my* existence."

And sometimes, we try new forms, new combinations of forms, new voices, or new styles. It's as if what we've experienced, though it constrains us in many ways, makes us freer in others. As my student Tony remarked, "Hell, I've had everything thrown at me—a stroke, blindness, my father's death. Funny that it took all this for me to loosen up in my writing."

Often, part of the quest narrative is devoted to the significance of writing and art and how they help create order and meaning in a chaotic time. Erica Pedretti's prizewinning novel, *Valery and the Illbred Eye,* described in Esther Dreifuss-Kattlan's *Cancer Stories,* is a quest narrative about how the painter Ferdinand Hodler made portraits of his lover, Valentine Gode-Darel, as she was dying from breast cancer. The novel was written while Pedretti herself was being treated for breast cancer. In it, she meditates on how the process of creating functions for her: while creating, she remarks, through her fictional painter mouthpiece, "I still breathe, draw, draw my horror, my fear of death. . . . While drawing I am not afraid of anything other than my inability to record on paper what my eyes perceive."

Sometimes the quest narrative describes how our work has changed because of our illness. In writing *Breathless,* I discovered I was no longer writing long sentences punctuated by semicolons, containing lots of dependent clauses. I started writing very short sentences. Then fracturing my sentences. Because my body and my writing were different, my writing was different. Sentences that chopped and sputtered, I discovered, were the only ones I could write.

Writing as Self-Repair: The Restorative Potential of Wounded Body Narratives

Esther Dreifuss-Kattan, in *Cancer Stories,* and Emily F. Nye, in " 'The More I Tell My Story': Writing as Healing at an HIV Clinic," describe how writing has been used by people with cancer and people with HIV and AIDS to ward off the potentially emotionally destabilizing effects of living with these illnesses or with the certain knowledge that our death is imminent. People with illnesses that make the future uncertain and people who face death say they write for many reasons. Through writing, we can maintain control over our lives; create a work of art that will live on after our death; express our feelings (especially anger, grief, rage, jealousy of those who are well); keep disabling fear at bay; fight the idea that our illness has robbed our life of its meaning; resolve unresolved issues in our lives; share with others what we have learned about illness and, perhaps, what we've learned about effective treatment. Dreifuss-Kattan suggests that "perhaps there is something inherent in creativity that enables one to be braver than one otherwise would be" while facing "emergency conditions" that threaten us.

People with cancer who have turned to writing as they faced the likelihood of death—Audre Lorde (who wrote poetry, essays, fiction, and journal), Ruth Reichstein (who wrote poetry), and Alice James (who kept a diary) among them—have seen writing as a safe haven, somehow removed from illness, to which they could retreat to console themselves and gather courage and strength to face their illness anew, but from which they could witness their illness at a safe distance. They wrote, too, to prepare for death, to achieve a sense of wholeness and completeness within the time that remained, to remember how much they loved life. Writing, then, served as reparation in the face of death by transforming a threatening experience into a creative activity.

When our future seems filled with danger, we become fearful. Fear, unless it can be managed, leads to panic, powerlessness, and hopelessness. Because cancer and AIDS often engender a sense of "catastrophic anxiety" and of terror, a way must be found to defend the self against despair and depression when we feel least able to do so. But through writing, we can express our fears; we can mourn what we have lost and what we will lose in a way that doesn't overwhelm us.

Reviewing our life through writing as we face illness and death often enables us to achieve a healing sense of wholeness. Through writing, says Dreifuss-Kattan, we connect with the intact, healthy, generative parts of the self. This counterbalances the overwhelming losses we experience with illness.

In working with a group of nonprofessional writers in an HIV clinic, Emily F. Nye learned that the stories they created served several essential functions for them. The most significant was to tell the story of one's life up to and including the illness narrative, to make sense of life's meaning and purpose. Doing this made writers aware of the pattern of their lives: the impact of their upbringing, of meaningful events and people, of obstacles encountered, and of a turning point (often their illness) that give their lives new meaning. Frank Ostaseski, a writer at the Zen Hospice Project in San Francisco, says that telling stories is a crucial way we can prepare for our death: "Telling our stories can give us distance and help move us through the process. Often this is the way we make sense of our lives and discover meaning."

The second most significant reason they wrote was to discuss their feelings, wishes, and regrets about life and about having AIDS. People with AIDS, these writers maintained, must have a safe place to express their rage—at family, at society, at religion, at doctors and hospitals, at friends and lovers, at the person who infected them, at the illness itself. Expressing rage figured as a far, far more important function of writing than expressing fear. Expressing humor was important, too. But they also wanted to write about what might have been: their hopes, dreams, and ambitions; their regrets and longings. Writing was a place to mourn what was lost and a place to learn about what had been learned, like the necessity of living in the present and appreciating it.

And finally, these writers believed that an important function of AIDS storytelling was to share information about AIDS and tips about survival. In writing about AIDS in this way, writers felt empowered because what they had learned and shared, they knew, might help another. As a student once told me, "I've never been an expert about anything before; but now, at thirty-one, I'm an expert on AIDS." Many people writing with Nye expressed the belief that people with AIDS often knew more about the efficacy of various treatments than their doctors. They believed that writing about their experiences with drugs, with treatment, with navigating the health care bureaucracy and discussing the help available in their community and the behavioral changes they made performed a vital public service for the AIDS community.

Most stories written by people with AIDS, Nye learned, were powerful and positive. As one group member, Josh, reported, writing "changes me as to how I look at the disease. As I change the story, I change myself. I'm evolving."

During a summer session at Hunter College, I had a writing student whom I believed to be especially talented. I called him into my office to say that I wanted to work with him on an independent project and that I thought he had a great career ahead of him, that he could publish before graduating.

My words, which I thought would cheer him, made him weep.

He composed himself then said, "Let's start right away. Now. This afternoon."

I told him not to rush, to take the rest of the summer off, rest, relax. In autumn, we'd have plenty of time.

"I don't have a great career ahead of me," he said, "though I want to write more than I can say. But whatever work we do will have to be done quickly. I have AIDS."

During a summer meeting, Geoff decided that he had to teach me about AIDS, not by talking about it, as we had been doing, but by writing a story about it that could be published and that many people could read. Geoff's writing became, for both of us and for his readers, a "place of safety," as the critic Joshua Fausty has put it, where we could explore Geoff's world—one in which there was no safety.

Geoff's first piece was an award-winning elegy called "Passing

Time." In it, the central character, nicknamed "Angel" by his lover, Terry, witnesses Terry's death—the same death that Angel suspects he, too, will experience.

"When I work," Geoff told me that autumn, "time stands still. I'm not a man with AIDS, though I am a man with AIDS. I'm not going to die, ever. I'm just a writer. I'm writing for hope and sanity. I know my subject—the most significant subject of our time. And I have something important to say."

Geoff taught me about the *necessity* of writing as resistance, as reparation for the writer with a wounded body. But Geoff taught me, too, something about the moral value of such writing. He showed me that works of art make the act of listening possible. That though listening to wounded body narratives is difficult, it is also, as Arthur W. Frank puts it in *The Wounded Storyteller,* fundamentally a "moral act." Works of art make the overwhelming experience of trauma, suffering, bodily pain, and the inevitability of death bearable and so render them partially comprehensible.

All this Geoff taught me—and all who read his work—before he died.

WHAT YOU CAN DO NOW Is there a wounded body narrative that you feel ready to write? Can you write it, enacting the suggestions made here and in part 2, "The Process/The Program," and heeding, especially, cautions in chapter 6, "Caring for Ourselves as We Write"? What form might your narrative take?

Epilogue

From Silence to Testimony

Write it down, girl. Tell everyone how much
it hurts. Sharing will make it easier to bear.

TERRI L. JEWELL, in Valerie Jean, "Writing Survival"

This writing is what I was brought here to do.
And my purpose is to get out the word, to witness,
and give testimony. So I'm on a mission. . . .

SAPPHIRE, "The Artist as Witness"

What is important . . . must be spoken,
made verbal and shared, even at the risk
of having it bruised or misunderstood.

AUDRE LORDE, *The Cancer Journals*

It is spring, and my students at Hunter are sitting in a circle, waiting for class to begin. There's a festive spirit in the room, and not just because some of us have brought treats. For today we'll enact an end-of-the-semester ritual, making public the results of our private toil. Today we'll begin sharing our finished work, reading several pages we've chosen, saying something about our writing process, about what working on the piece accomplished for us. Our audience will listen carefully, paying close attention to our words. After, they'll share responses—what they liked, what it made them ponder, how it made them feel.

Today it's Catherine Kapphahn's turn. She's reading from "Thin Ice," about her mother's death from cancer. Before reading, Catherine is usually nervous. But I know her work is ready and that she's ready. She's dressed for the occasion in a pastel sweater. She knows how to focus on her breathing to compose herself. She's chosen her passage carefully, and has practiced. She knows how to engage her audience by making eye contact, how to pace herself so that she conveys the rhythm and meaning of her prose. She knows how to pause to give her listeners time to absorb the beauty or shock of her work. All this she's learned in her years of study.

Yes, Catherine is ready, and I am excited and proud.

Catherine reads a section about how her dog, Sasha, plunged through the thin ice of a pond near their house and nearly died, and her mother's feelings as she stands by helplessly, urging the dog to save himself, knowing that she can't help him, that if she treads the ice, she, too, will fall in and surely die. It prefigures how Catherine will attend her mother's dying.

I see how absorbed her listeners are. This is, I think, a privileged moment. When an audience is utterly captivated by someone's experience because a writer has communicated her meaning in a way that makes it directly apprehensible. A moment when there is no "I," no "you," only "we." One of connection and communion, of "conspiracy"—a breathing together.

I teach toward making this possible. I write to make this possible.

After Catherine has heard the response of her listeners, I congratulate her and ask her how she feels.

"Wonderful," she says. "They understood." *They understood.*

Building Community

People working with groups of writers, like Emily F. Nye (working first in Ann Arbor, Michigan, with groups of elders and later in Denver,

Colorado, with groups of people with AIDS), like Edvige Giunta (working at Jersey City State College, New Jersey, with working-class students), like myself (working at Hunter College), soon realize that sharing our work in a group setting helps us immeasurably. For we are using our writing to help build community. And this reinforces our ability to do our work well and to use our work to heal.

As we share our early scratchings, our thoughts about our works in progress, we realize that we have much to give others, much to gain from them. Writing in groups makes us more aware of our writing as a potentially public document. We become responsible for the words we write in a way we might not if we didn't anticipate sharing.

This doesn't mean we censor ourselves. But it does mean that we consider what it takes to make our personal story understood, as our listeners make us aware of the gaps in our story we haven't yet expressed. It means, too, that we discover how to make our writing understandable to those not sharing our experience.

Sharing our work removes us from a solitary brooding on our personal hurts as we listen to other people's struggles, learn of other people's triumphs. For those of us who find intimacy difficult, sharing work becomes a bridge to sharing ourselves. As an elder who wrote with Nye remarked, "When I started . . . I was in depression, lacking direction. During the course I found relief from the depression—in my own writing and from the writing of others in the groups." Nye found that feeling part of a writing community "decreased individual isolation, and increased a feeling of solidarity with others." Laura McKeon, writing with Giunta, said this: "We all suffer from certain degrees of historical, social, and familial amnesia. . . . The greatest gift I received was the sense of validation, trust, and community I garnered. . . . Our personal struggles, although different in detail, bound us together as survivors of our own life experiences."

In life, we have evolved social rituals for comforting and supporting a mourner through the necessary process of grieving a loss. As we come together to mourn, we reassert our need for community, for having others recognize the magnitude of what we've experienced, the emotional journey we've traversed. The most significant stage, then, of grieving is public recognition that we have sustained a loss and public recognition that we ought to be deeply feeling our loss. Making our work public can become this kind of ceremonial sharing, this kind of public recognition of our private experience. And it can be as healing as writing the work itself, though initially sharing might not be easy.

After I finished "Personal Effects," the essay about my mother's dying, I tried to print it, but nothing happened. At first I thought my computer had broken. Then I discovered I'd typed in a "0" for the number of copies I wanted to print. Unconsciously, I was no doubt reluctant to go public with much in that essay—my wanting my mother to die after she became completely paralyzed; my shame at having those feelings. Still, sharing brought peace; I learned others felt as I had during similar experiences.

Throughout her life, Virginia Woolf maintained that her work—that any work—was incomplete until it was shared with readers. Readers completed the meaning of a work and echoed it back to the writer, so the writer could fully understand, perhaps for the first time, the significance of the words she or he had penned to her own life and to others.

Woolf needed an audience to listen to the testimony she made about her life, to witness and validate the meaning she had made of her experience, to let her know that she was not alone. Only with an audience, Woolf believed, can we transcend the limits of the self, can we understand our life's true meaning. As Maya Angelou has said, through writing the "I" becomes "we."

Sharing with empathic witnesses our work about the shocks we've survived is, for me, an essential part of the process of using writing as a way of healing. Writing our story and keeping it locked away where no one can read it repeats the lethal pattern of silencing and tyranny and shame that so often accompanies trauma. And the deadliest feature of trauma is that its aftereffects are suffered solitarily and in silence. Dori Laub has written that for Holocaust survivors, "repossessing one's life story through giving testimony is itself a form of action, of change, which [one] has to actually pass through, in order to continue and complete the process of survival after liberation."

The Healing Benefits of Sharing Our Work

To be sure, we must care for ourselves as we make our work public. We must choose our witnesses carefully. Whomever we share our work with, while it's in process, we expect to be empathic. We share only when we're ready and only when we're prepared to share. But making our story accessible to others (through writing groups, writing partners, and eventually through publication, perhaps) can evoke a healing moment that's a logical outgrowth of the writing process.

As we prepare to share our work, I suggest that we think carefully about what this process entails, what we expect to gain from it, and what we won't allow to happen. Sharing our work with unempathic witnesses (or, worse, with mean-spirited or sadistic listeners, with those who don't understand or who refuse to recognize listening involves an ethical responsibility to the writer) can surely retraumatize us. Ask students in a writing program who have had their work savaged by peers or ask published writers who have had their work axed by a reviewer how it feels. Vicious criticism reinforces the writer's deep-seated fear that the story shouldn't be told, that the story isn't important, that the story won't be believed. Vicious criticism can silence stories that must be told.

I believe that it is our responsibility to ourselves and to our work to control the conditions whereby we share our work so that we do not foreclose our need to tell our story.

We can suggest that our listeners not tell us whether they like our work or they don't, for whether they like it or not can't help us heal. It is impossible to "like" important survival narratives that nonetheless must be told.

We can ask our readers to help us by letting us know if we are reaching them. We can say, "As you read, please tell me what you don't understand." That a reader understands our work, that we, in time, write in a way that a reader *can* understand, is far more important than that a reader likes what we've written.

How and Why Empathic Listeners Can Help

In my many years of working with groups of writers, I have learned that empathic listeners can help us in many ways while we're writing.

First, they can act as a caring presence to enable us to really hear what we've written. As we read our work with them, simply because they are listening and they care, we often immediately know what else we need to write and what we need to change. Often, witnesses must proceed slowly; they must feel, too, that they can be alone while in someone's presence. After hearing a description of a brutal mugging a writer had survived, I asked, "Do you want me to respond?" "Not yet," the writer said. "Later. For now, I just need to read this with you here." Often, only when we know that someone is listening can we feel the impact of what we have described.

Second, they can reflect back to us what we have written. They can tell us what, based upon their reading, we have communicated. Hearing their response enables us to judge whether we've told the story we've desired to tell.

Third, our empathic listeners can tell us what they like in our work or what works for them. (This is different from their telling us that they like or don't like the work.) When we learn, specifically, what makes our readers respond positively, we can make more accurate judgments about our work. Often in my classes, after a student has read and empathic listeners have reported what they've liked, the student is pleasantly surprised. Sometimes, they say something like, "I thought what I had written was completely worthless. But hearing that someone liked that one paragraph makes me see that what I've written is better than I imagined. And it suggests how I can improve the rest of the work."

Fourth, our listeners can tell us when there are what I call "holes in the narrative"—those places where we're so close to the story that we don't realize that our listener can't possibly understand something. These often indicate parts of our story (of our lives) that confuse us, that upset us, or that we deny. After a student read a piece describing her brother's violence, a listener asked, "Where were your parents while this was happening?" In time, the writer discovered this was the most significant, unanswered question in her narrative and in her life. After a student read a piece about how her parents divorced when she was sixteen and how she shared an apartment with a teenaged friend after both left town and how, soon after, she turned to prostitution to support herself, I asked, "Why didn't either take you with them?" This, she said, was the "big" question she couldn't ask herself. Asking it, answering it, dramatically changed her sense of why she'd lived as she had.

Fifth, when we share our work, our listeners can tell us where they would like to hear more. I have discovered that writers whose stories traditionally have been silenced usually don't take much time in telling them. What merits ten pages, twenty pages, a full-length book, even, is often described in a paragraph or two. When the work is read aloud, the writer races through it. But writing a detailed narrative, as I have described, is an important part of using writing as a way of healing. Reading work carefully allows us to hear ourselves. Our empathic listeners can help show us where our narratives need development. They can help us move slowly enough through our work and through our lives so we can fully comprehend. In time, we will learn that we have the right to take as much time as we need to tell our complex story.

Sixth, our listeners can tell us what they observe about how we have survived—our victories, our defeats, and our struggles. I learned, through empathic witnesses, that retreating to a world of books and writing were essential to my survival.

And finally, listeners can help us see the patterns in our narrative and in our lives. They can help us, too, see the images and metaphors we use, the form we've chosen, to construct reality. Until an empathic reader responded to my memoir, I wasn't aware that many people I had known as a girl had died in fires. This, coupled with my father being a fireman, was a significant pattern that explained much about my terrors and fears. Similarly, when Catherine Kapphahn read early versions of "Thin Ice," her listeners helped her see that, because of her mother's death, Catherine often felt that *she* was on thin ice—that she was in imminent danger of dying as her mother had.

When we share our writing, someone else knows what we've been through. Someone else cares. Someone else has heard our voice. Someone else understands. We learn that we are no longer alone and that we no longer need be alone.

But because our stories evoke feelings in our listeners, our listeners must be alert to what happens to them emotionally as they hear our stories. Often, our listeners will learn, through hearing our stories, what they must describe in theirs. This is one reason why Virginia Woolf said that no work of literature is a single birth: each work written depends on our having witnessed another work, on our opening to our own experience by, first, hearing another's. Hearing others' works in progress is an important part of our development as writers and as human beings.

But sometimes, as Nancy Venable Raine writes in *After Silence,* a memoir about her rape (which treats, too, the inability of society to hear the survivor's testimony), listeners whom we trust to be empathic instead may try to silence us. Raine was often told indirectly that her subject was disagreeable. She learned that listening must have awakened a sense of vulnerability. Raine decides to make listeners' resistance to her story the subject, too, of her narrative. She explores the impossibility of keeping silent, the cost of telling, the need of survivors having empathic witnesses. As Raine observes, by quoting Henry David Thoreau, "It takes two to speak the truth—one to speak, and another to hear."

Responsibility and Loyalty

After I published *Vertigo,* interviewers often asked me if I didn't feel disloyal to my family for telling its secrets. And my students often ask me whether I think it's unethical or irresponsible to make private stories like mine and theirs public. I say I believe my primary loyalty is to other survivors and not to the person who harmed me. And that telling my story is an ethical act.

In *Three Guineas,* Virginia Woolf writes that an important agent of our personal growth is "freedom from unreal loyalties," by which she means freedom from loyalty to oppressive institutions or people. She writes, too, that one of the most important agents of our culture's growth is just such freedom.

This is how the novelist Mary Gordon framed this dilemma in writing *The Shadow Man,* her memoir about her father. In it, Gordon describes her conflict about whether she should publish the truth she had learned about her father. Though Gordon thought her father was born a Catholic, he hid from her that he was born a Jew and converted to Catholicism. After, he became a vicious anti-Semite, a man who supported Mussolini and Franco, who said he saw no difference between the Nazis and the English, who thought that the worst thing Hitler did was to close Catholic schools in Bavaria. As a writer, he published his views in periodicals Mary Gordon only discovered after his death while researching her book.

Gordon says that she grappled with whether she should expose these painful truths about her father. But she took the biblical injunction "Thou shalt not bear false witness" literally. This meant that if you *don't* tell the truth when you've learned it, you are committing a sin. So, protecting her father was impossible. Keeping his story hidden would be immoral. Telling it served a larger purpose: exposing the anti-Semitism of a man who could influence others and the anti-Semitic publishing practices of certain periodicals in the United States. She believed it was essential, given the Holocaust, that stories like his not stay hidden, that, posthumously, he be held accountable for his actions.

How Making Our Stories Public Can Further Healing

There are many stories about how making our work public can initiate profound changes for ourselves and others. Here are just two.

After Susan J. Miller gave her mother a piece of her memoir that appeared in *Granta* prior to the publication of her full-length *Never Let Me Down,* Miller's mother started therapy. Miller's work is about the hidden emotional, physical, and sexual violence in her family; it's about the effect of her father's heroin addiction and her brother's physical and sexual abuse upon her, and it's about her mother's denial and failure to protect her daughter. Miller and her mother had never before discussed these issues.

But after reading her daughter's work, Miller's mother could no longer deny how damaged her daughter was by what had transpired. She continues therapy and is now a prominent speaker on family violence. Miller's writing helped Miller heal. It helped her learn, for example, that she needn't forgive her father or her brother; that unless people who've harmed us apologize and change their behavior to us, we are under no moral obligation to forgive them.

The poet Richard Hoffman published a memoir, *Half the House,* about how he had been raped repeatedly by his coach. After Hoffman's father read his son's memoir, he tried to locate the man Hoffman named in his work. Hoffman's father learned the man had been arrested twice on sexual abuse charges, that he was currently a volunteer coach in a local youth organization, and that his pattern of abusing children hadn't ended. Soon after, because of Hoffman's story and his father's persistence, the man was arrested for molesting an eleven-year-old.

Hoffman was stunned that his work led to the arrest. After, Hoffman spoke to the eleven-year-old boy. "The boy thanked me for the book," Hoffman related, "and said, 'You made it stop.'"

Arthur W. Frank believes that the proper name for writers like Richard Hoffman is not "survivor" but "witness." Survival, Frank says, does not imply any particular concern for others. Survival simply means "continuing to survive."

Becoming a witness to our experiences, though, means taking on the responsibility of telling what happened to us—writing a historical record, a public document. The "witness," says Frank, "offers testimony to a truth that is generally unrecognized or suppressed." Hoffman's truth was how he and other boys are often sexually abused by trusted male elders. When his work became a public document, it enabled others to understand their history; it enabled others to see their experience wasn't theirs alone. Hoffman's story is a dramatic case of how making testimony public can change lives.

Isabel Allende has said, "Being a witness is my mission in the world and this is what I do when I tell stories." Alice Walker, too, sees her role this way: "In writing," she has said, "I see myself in the role of this witness." Audre Lorde believed that it was her responsibility to continue writing until all those who were still silent could speak. She witnessed the suffering of others: she spoke *with* but never *for* them. Sapphire, too, said that when she was writing *Push,* she was writing because she was an incest survivor, but also with the experiences of certain of her students in mind (one, especially, who had given birth to a child by her father, like her character Precious). All see their private work as having a public purpose.

Scores of other writers frame their work in this way; they write about what they have lived through—experiences that might not be commonly known—to heal themselves. But they also write to help heal a culture that, if it is to become moral, ethical, and spiritual, must recognize what these writers have observed, experienced, and witnessed. All are writing to right a human wrong—one that affected them, surely, but one that affects others, too.

Writing testimony, to be sure, means that we tell our stories. But it also means that we no longer allow ourselves to be silenced or allow others to speak for our experience. Writing to heal, then, and making that writing public, as I see it, is the most important emotional, psychological, artistic, and political project of our time.

Sources and Further Reading

Chapter 1: Why Write?

Aftel, Mandy. *The Story of Your Life.* New York: Simon & Schuster, 1996.

Allende, Isabel, Alice Walker, and Jean Shonowda Bowlin. "Giving Birth, Finding Form: Where Our Books Come From." Creative Conversations Series. Recorded at Grace Cathedral, San Francisco, California, April 10, 1995, Sounds True Productions.

Bradbury, Ray. *Zen in the Art of Writing.* New York: Bantam, 1992.

Cheever, John. *The Journals of John Cheever.* New York: Knopf, 1991.

DeSalvo, Louise. *Conceived with Malice.* New York: Dutton, 1994.

———. "Eudora Welty." In *Writer in America Film Series.* Produced and directed by Richard O. Moore, 1979.

Doty, Mark. *Heaven's Coast.* New York: HarperCollins, 1996.

Feraca, Julia. Interview of the author. "Conversations with Julia Feraca." Wisconsin Public Radio, May 17, 1995.

Goleman, Daniel. *Emotional Intelligence.* New York: Bantam, 1995.

Martin, Jay. *Who Am I This Time?* New York: Norton, 1988.

Miller, Henry, Alfred Perles, and Lawrence Durrell. *Art and Outrage.* London: Village Press, 1973.

Muller, Wayne. *Legacy of the Heart.* New York: Fireside, 1992.

———. "Toni Morrison." In *Writer in America Film Series.* Produced and directed by Richard O. Moore, 1979.

Seligman, Martin E.P. *Learned Optimism.* New York: Knopf, 1991.

Chapter 2: How Writing Can Help Us Heal

Harber, Kent, and James W. Pennebaker. "Overcoming Traumatic Memories." In *The Handbook of Emotion and Memory: Research and Theory,* edited by Sven-Ake Christianson. Hillsdale, New Jersey: Lawrence Erlbaum, 1992.

Kinkaid, Jamaica. *My Brother.* New York: Farrar, Straus and Giroux, 1997.

Krystal, Henry. "Integration and Self-Healing in Post-Traumatic States: A Ten Year Retrospective." *American Imago* 48, no. 1 (1991): 93–118.

Lawrence, D.H. *The Letters of D.H. Lawrence*. Vol. 1, *September 1901–May 1913*, edited by James T. Boulton. Cambridge: Cambridge University Press, 1979.

———. *The Letters of D.H. Lawrence*. Vol. 2, *June 1913–October 1916*, edited by George J. Zytaruk, James T. Boulton, and Andrew Robertson. Cambridge: Cambridge University Press, 1981.

Pennebaker, James W. "Confession, Inhibition, and Disease." In *Advances in Experimental Social Psychology*, Vol. 22, edited by Leonard Berkowitz. New York: Academic Press, 1989.

———. *Opening Up: The Healing Power of Confiding in Others*. New York: Morrow, 1990.

———. "Writing Your Wrongs." *American Health* 10, no. 1 (1991): 64–67.

———. "Writing About Emotional Experiences as a Therapeutic Process." *Psychological Science* 8, no. 3 (1997): 162–66.

Pennebaker, James W., and Sandra Klihr Beall. "Confronting a Traumatic Event: Toward an Understanding of Inhibition and Disease." *Journal of Abnormal Psychology* 95, no. 3 (1986): 274–81.

Pennebaker, James W., Michelle Colder, and Lisa K. Sharp. "Accelerating the Coping Process." *Journal of Personality and Social Psychology* 58, no. 3 (1990): 528–37.

Pennebaker, James W., Janice K. Kiecolt-Glaser, and Ronald Glaser, "Confronting Traumatic Experience and Immunocompetence." *Journal of Consulting and Clinical Psychology* 56, no. 4 (1988): 638–39.

Pennebaker, James W., and Joan R. Susman. "Disclosure of Trauma and Psychosomatic Processes." *Social Science and Medicine* 26, no. 3 (1988): 327–32.

Petrie, Keith J., et al. "Disclosure of Trauma and Immune Response to a Hepatitis B Vaccination Program." *Journal of Consulting and Clinical Psychology* 63, no. 5 (1995): 787–92.

Chapter 3: Writing as a Therapeutic Process

Aberbach, David. *Surviving Trauma: Loss, Literature, and Psychology*. New Haven: Yale University Press, 1989.

Allende, Isabel. *Paula*. New York: HarperCollins, 1995.

Allison, Dorothy. *Two or Three Things I Know for Sure*. New York: Dutton, 1995.

Brink, Andrew. *Creativity as Repair*. Hamilton, Ontario: Cromlech, 1982.

Busch, Frederick. "My Brother, Myself." Review of "Imagining Robert," by Jay Neugeboren. *New York Times Book Review* (February 9, 1997).

Crystall, Elyse, Jill Kuhnheim, and Mary Layoun. "An Interview with Isabel Allende." *Contemporary Literature* 33, no. 4 (1992): 585–600.

Dearborn, Mary V. *Henry Miller*. New York: Simon & Schuster, 1991.

Ellroy, James. *My Dark Places: An L.A. Crime Memoir.* New York: Knopf, 1996.

Frame, Janet. *An Autobiography.* Vol. 1, *To the Is-land.* New York: Braziller, 1991.

———. *An Autobiography.* Vol. 2, *An Angel at My Table.* New York: Braziller, 1991.

———. *An Autobiography.* Vol. 3, *The Envoy from Mirror City.* New York: Braziller, 1991.

———. *Plaintext.* Tucson, Arizona: University of Arizona, 1986.

———. *Remembering the Bone House.* Boston: Beacon, 1989.

———. *Voice Lessons.* Boston: Beacon, 1994.

Fussell, Betty. "Isabel Allende's Fantasy Life." *Lear's* (May 1993): 51–53, 80–81.

Mairs, Nancy. *Carnal Acts.* Boston: Beacon, 1996.

Martin, Jay. *Always Merry and Bright: The Life of Henry Miller.* Santa Barbara, California: Capra, 1978.

Miller, Henry. *My Life and Times.* New York: Playboy, n.d.

———. *Stories, Essays, Travel Sketches.* Edited by Anthony Fine. New York: MJF Books, 1992.

Mishara, Aaron L., Ph.D. "Narrative and Psychotherapy." *American Journal of Psychotherapy* 49, no. 2 (1995): 180–95.

Neugeboren, Jay. *Imagining Robert: My Brother, Madness, and Survival.* New York: Morrow, 1997.

Roth-Hano, Renée. *Touch Wood: A Girlhood in Occupied France.* New York: Four Winds, 1988.

Sengupta, Somini. "More Orchard Beach Than Elaine's: Tales of Dominican Life Made Junot Díaz the Darling of the Literati." *New York Times* (September 15, 1996).

Woolf, Virginia. *A Passionate Apprentice, The Early Journals 1897–1909.* Edited by Mitchell A. Leaska. New York: Harcourt Brace Jovanovich, 1990.

———. "A Sketch of the Past." In *Moments of Being.* New York: Harcourt Brace Jovanovich, 1985.

Chapter 4: Writing Pain, Writing Loss

Cohen, Mark Francis. "The Healing Poets' Society." *New York Times* (September 15, 1995).

Cormier, Robert. Letter to author, June 17, 1997.

———. *Now and At the Hour.* New York: Dell, 1960.

Donnelly, Daniel A., and Edward J. Murray. "Cognitive and Emotional Changes in Written Essays and Therapy Interviews." *Journal of Social and Clinical Psychology* 10, no. 3 (1991): 334–50.

Herman, Judith Lewis, M.D. *Trauma and Recovery.* New York: BasicBooks, 1992.

Hughes, Cheryl F., Carmen Uhlmann, and James W. Pennebaker. "The Body's Response to Processing Emotional Trauma: Linking Verbal Text with Autonomic Activity." *Journal of Personality* 62, no. 4 (1994): 565–85.

Hussey, Mark. *Virginia Woolf A to Z.* New York: Facts on File, 1995.

Lorde, Audre. *The Cancer Journals.* New York: Spinsters Ink, 1980.

Maisel, Eric. *Fearless Creating.* New York: Putnam's, 1995.

Morris, David B. *The Culture of Pain.* Berkeley, California: University of California Press, 1991.

Mydans, Seth. "Maria Rose Henson, 69, Dies; Victim of Japanese Brothels." *New York Times* (August 27, 1997).

Nathan, John. "Ōe Kenzaburo: Mapping the Land of Dreams." *Japan Quarterly* 42, no. 1 (1995): 89–98.

Ōe, Kenzaburō. *A Healing Family.* Translated by Stephen Snyder. New York: Kodansha, 1995.

———. *Hiroshima Notes.* Translated by David L. Swain and Toshi Yonezawa. New York: Grove, 1965, 1985.

———. *A Personal Matter.* Translated by John Nathan. New York: Grove, 1960.

———. *The Silent Cry.* Translated by John Bester. New York: Kodansha, 1967.

———. *Teach Us to Outgrow Our Madness.* Translated by John Nathan. New York: Grove, 1977.

Pennebaker, James W., et al. "Levels of Thinking." *Personality and Social Psychology Bulletin* 16, no. 4 (1990), 743–57.

Raine, Nancy Venable. *After Silence.* New York: Crown, 1998.

Sarton, May. *Recovering: A Journal.* New York: Norton, 1980.

Scarry, Elaine. *The Body in Pain.* New York: Oxford, 1985.

Senick, Gerard J., ed. "Robert (Edmund) Cormier." In *Children's Literature Review,* Vol. 12. Kansas City, Missouri: Gale, 1987.

Taylor, Daniel. *The Healing Power of Stories.* New York: Doubleday, 1996.

Terr, Lenore. *Too Scared to Cry.* New York: Basic Books, 1990.

Williams, J. Mark G. "Autobiographical Memory and Emotional Disorders." In *The Handbook of Emotion and Memory: Research and Theory,* edited by Sven-Ake Christianson. Hillsdale, New Jersey: Lawrence Erlbaum, 1992.

Chapter 5: The Healing Power of the Writing Process

Awakawa, Yasuichi. *Zen Painting.* Translated by John Bester. Tokyo: Kodansha, 1970.

Bayles, David, and Ted Orland. *Art & Fear.* Santa Barbara, California: Capra, 1993.

Frame, Janet. *An Autobiography.* Vol. 1, *To the Is-land.* New York: George Braziller, 1991.

Gardner, Howard. *Creating Minds.* New York: Basic Books, 1993.

Grumbach, Doris. *Fifty Days of Solitude.* Boston: Beacon, 1994.

————. *Life in a Day.* Boston: Beacon, 1996.

Hyde, Lewis. *The Gift: Imagination and the Erotic Life of Property.* New York: Random House, 1983.

Lydon, Susan Gordon. *The Knitting Sutra.* New York: HarperSanFrancisco, 1997.

Mairs, Nancy. *Ordinary Time.* Boston: Beacon, 1993.

O'Brien, Tim. "The Magic Show." In *Writers on Writing,* edited by Robert Pack and Jay Parini. Hanover, New Hampshire: University of New England Press, 1991.

Plath, Sylvia. *The Journals of Sylvia Plath.* New York: Ballantine, 1983.

Robbins, Anthony. *Awaken the Giant Within.* New York: Simon & Schuster, 1991.

Sarton, May. *Journal of a Solitude.* New York: Norton, 1973.

Schiwy, Marlene A. *A Voice of Her Own.* New York: Simon & Schuster, 1996.

Suzuki, Shunryu. *Zen Mind, Beginner's Mind.* New York: John Watherhill, 1973.

Truitt, Anne. *Daybook.* New York: Penguin, 1982.

Ueda, Makoto. *Literary and Art Theories in Japan.* Cleveland, Ohio: Western Reserve, 1967.

Chapter 6: Caring for Ourselves as We Write

Fitzgerald, F. Scott. *The Crack-Up.* Edited by Edmund Wilson. New York: New Directions, 1945.

Hall, Donald. "The Art of Poetry XLIII." *The Paris Review* 33, no. 120 (1991): 154–93.

————. *Life Work.* Boston: Beacon, 1993.

hooks, bell. *Sisters of the Yam.* Boston: South End, 1993.

————. *Wounds of Passion.* New York: Henry Holt, 1997.

Maisel, Eric. *A Life in the Arts.* New York: Putnam's, 1994.

Rothenberg, Albert. *Creativity and Madness.* Baltimore: Johns Hopkins, 1990.

Storr, Anthony. *Churchill's Black Dog, Kafka's Mice.* New York: Ballantine, 1988.

————. *Solitude.* New York: Ballantine, 1988.

Woolf, Virginia. *The Diary of Virginia Woolf.* Vol. 3, *1925–1930.* Edited by Anne Olivier Bell. New York: Harcourt Brace, 1980.

————. *The Diary of Virginia Woolf.* Vol. 4, *1931–1935.* Edited by Anne Olivier Bell. New York: Harcourt Brace, 1982.

————. *The Diary of Virginia Woolf.* Vol. 5, *1936–1941.* Edited by Anne Olivier Bell. New York: Harcourt Brace, 1984.

Chapter 7: Stages of the Process, Stages of Growth I

Axelrod, Steven Gould. *Sylvia Plath*. Baltimore: Johns Hopkins, 1990.

Didion, Joan. "Why I Write." In *The Writer on Her Work*. Edited by Janet Sternburg. New York: Norton, 1980.

Gray, Paul. "Paradise Found." *Time* (January 19, 1998): 63–68.

Kreilkamp, Ivan, "Jamaica Kincaid: Daring to Discomfort." *Publishers Weekly* 243, no. 1 (1996): 54–55.

Miller, Henry. *Henry Miller on Writing*. New York: New Directions, 1964.

———. "They Were Alive and They Spoke to Me." In *The Books in My Life*. New York: New Directions, 1969.

Morrison, Toni. "The Art of Fiction CXXXIV." *Paris Review* 35, no. 128 (1993): 82–125.

O'Connor, Flannery. *The Habit of Being*. Letters edited and with an introduction by Sally Fitzgerald. New York: Farrar, Straus and Giroux, 1979.

Raudsepp, Eugene. "A New Look at the Creative Process." Part 1, in *Creative Computing* (August/September 1980): 48–51.

———. "A New Look at the Creative Process." Part 2, in *Creative Computing* (August/September 1980): 82–90.

Silver, Brenda R. *Virginia Woolf's Reading Notebooks*. Princeton: Princeton University, 1983.

Smith, Felipe. "Alice Walker's Redemptive Art." *African American Review* 26, no. 3 (1992): 437–51.

Tyler, Anne. "Still Just Writing." *The Writer on Her Work*. Edited by Janet Sternburg. New York: Norton, 1980.

Walker, Alice. "Saving the Life That Is Your Own: The Importance of Models in the Artist's Life." In *In Search of Our Mothers' Gardens*. New York: Harcourt Brace Jovanovich, 1983.

———. *The Third Life of Grange Copeland*. New York: Harcourt Brace Jovanovich, 1970.

Chapter 8: Stages of the Process, Stages of Growth II

Epel, Naomi. *Writers Dreaming*. New York: Vintage, 1993.

Hirst, Barbara. "How Artists Overcome Creative Blocks." *Journal of Creative Behavior* 26, no. 2 (1992): 81–82.

Hughes, Ted. *Birthday Letters*. New York: Farrar, Straus and Giroux, 1998.

Kolodny, Susan. "Writing and the Psyche's Assessment of Danger." *AWP Chronicle* (March/April 1997): 21–25.

May, Rollo. *The Courage to Create.* New York: Norton, 1975.

Rosenwald, George C., and Richard L. Ochberg, eds. *Storied Lives.* New Haven: Yale University Press, 1992.

Schank, Roger C. *Tell Me a Story.* New York: Scribner's, 1990.

Shengold, Leonard, M.D. *Soul Murder.* New Haven: Yale University Press, 1989.

Vitz, Paul C. "The Use of Stories in Moral Development." *American Psychologist* (June 1990): 709–20.

Chapter 9: Writing the Wounded Psyche

Alcoff, Linda, and Laura Gray. "Survivor Discourse." *Signs* 18, no. 2 (1993): 260–90.

Alvarez, A. *The Savage God.* New York: Norton, 1990.

Angelou, Maya. "The Art of Fiction CXIX." *Paris Review* 132, no. 116 (1990): 144–67.

Berman, Jeffrey. *The Talking Cure.* New York: New York University Press, 1985.

Bonn, Maria S. "Can Stories Save Us? Tim O'Brien and the Efficacy of the Text." *Critique* 36, no. 1 (1994): 2–15.

Brewer, William D. "Mary Shelley on the Therapeutic Value of Language." *Papers on Language and Literature* 30, no. 4 (1994): 387–407.

Caruth, Cathy, ed. *Trauma: Explorations in Memory.* Baltimore: Johns Hopkins, 1995.

Champagne, Rosaria. *The Politics of Survivorship.* New York: New York University Press, 1996.

DeSalvo, Louise. " 'Justice, Not Revenge:' Djuna Barnes and *The Antiphon.*" In *Conceived with Malice.* New York: Dutton, 1994.

Dreifus, Claudia. "Alice Walker: 'Writing to Save My Life.' " *The Progressive* 53 (August 1989): 29–31.

Ellenberger, Henri F. *The Discovery of the Unconscious.* New York: Basic Books, 1981.

Gilman, Charlotte Perkins. *The Living of Charlotte Perkins Gilman* (Madison, Wisconsin: University of Wisconsin Press, 1935, 1990).

Grady, Denise. "War Memories May Harm Health." *New York Times* (December 16, 1997).

Haberman, Clyde. "An Unofficial but Very Public Bearer of Pain, Peace and Human Dignity [Elie Wiesel]," *New York Times* (March 5, 1997).

Hendricks-Matthews, Marybeth. "Survivors of Abuse: Health Care Issues." *Primary Care* 20, no. 2 (1993): 391–446.

Henke, Suzette. *Shattered Subjects*. New York: St. Martin's, 1998.

Herndl, Diane Price. "The Writing Cure." *NWSA Journal* 1, no. 1 (1988): 52–74.

Horowitz, Mardi J., and Steven P. Reidbord. "Memory, Emotion, and Response to Trauma." In *The Handbook of Emotion and Memory,* edited by Sven-Ake Christianson. Hillsdale, New Jersey: Lawrence Erlbaum Associates, 1992.

Jamison, Kay Redfield. *Touched with Fire*. New York: Free Press, 1993.

———. *An Unquiet Mind*. New York: Knopf, 1995.

Lane, Ann J. *To Herland and Beyond*. New York: Pantheon, 1990.

Laub, Dori. "Truth and Testimony." In *Trauma,* edited by Cathy Caruth. Baltimore: Johns Hopkins University Press, 1995: 61–75.

Ludwig, Arnold M. "Mental Illness and Creative Activity in Female Writers." *American Journal of Psychiatry* 151, no. 11 (1994): 1650–56.

———. *The Price of Greatness*. New York: Guilford, 1995.

Mellor, Anne K. *Mary Shelley*. New York: Routledge, 1988.

Michaels, Anne. *Fugitive Pieces*. New York: Knopf, 1997.

Miller, Alice. *The Drama of the Gifted Child*. Translated by Ruth Ward. New York: Basic Books, 1981.

———. *For Your Own Good*. Translated by Hildegarde and Hunter Hannum. New York: Farrar, Straus and Giroux, 1983.

———. *Thou Shalt Not Be Aware*. Translated by Hildegarde and Hunter Hannum. New York: Farrar, Straus and Giroux, 1984.

Mines, Stephanie. *Sexual Abuse, Sacred Wound*. Barrytown, New York: Station Hill Openings, 1996.

O'Brien, Tim. *The Things They Carried*. New York: Houghton Mifflin, 1990.

———. "The Vietnam in Me." *New York Times Magazine* (October 2, 1994).

Pennebaker, James W., et al. "Disclosure of Traumas and Health Among Holocaust Survivors." *Psychosomatic Medicine* 51, no. 5 (1989): 577–89.

Pennebaker, James W., and Amina Memon. "Recovered Memories in Context." *Psychological Bulletin* 19, no. 3 (1996): 355–89.

Redmont, Jane. "Praying in a Time of Depression." *America* 173, no. 5 (1995): 14–20.

———. *When in Doubt, Sing*. New York: HarperCollins, 1999.

Salter, Anna C. *Transforming Trauma*. Thousand Oaks, California: Sage, 1995.

Styron, William. *Darkness Visible*. New York: Random House, 1990.

Sunstein, Emily W. *Mary Shelley*. Baltimore: Johns Hopkins, 1989.

Walker, Alice. *To Hell With Dying*. New York: Harcourt Brace, 1993.

Witztum, Eliezer, M.D., et al. "Use of Metaphor in the Treatment of Combat-induced Posttraumatic Stress Disorder." *American Journal of Psychotherapy* 40, no. 3 (1986): 457–65.

Chapter 10: Writing the Wounded Body

Broyard, Anatole. *Intoxicated by My Illness.* New York: Ballantine, 1992.

Campo, Rafael. "AIDS and the Poetry of Healing." *Kenyon Review* 15, no. 4 (1993): 93–105.

Cotter, Holland. "Not Just for Viewing, But Also for Healing." *New York Times* (February 14, 1997).

Coulehan, John L. "The Word Is an Instrument of Healing." *Literature and Medicine* 10 (1991): 111–29.

DeSalvo, Louise. *Breathless.* Boston: Beacon, 1997.

Doty, Mark. *Heaven's Coast.* New York: HarperCollins, 1996.

Dreifuss-Kattan, Esther. *Cancer Stories.* Hillsdale, New Jersey: Analytic Press, 1990.

Frank, Arthur W. *The Wounded Storyteller.* Chicago: University of Chicago Press, 1995.

Fries, Kenny. *Anesthesia.* Louisville, Kentucky: Advocado, 1996.

———. *Body, Remember.* New York: Dutton, 1997.

Gilbert, Sandra M. *Ghost Volcano.* New York: Norton, 1995.

———. *Wrongful Death.* New York: Norton, 1995.

Handke, Peter. *A Sorrow Beyond Dreams.* Translated by Ralph Manheim. New York: Farrar, Straus and Giroux, 1974.

Kenyon, Jane. *Otherwise.* St. Paul, Minnesota: Graywolf, 1996.

Kincaid, Jamaica. *My Brother.* New York: Farrar, Straus and Giroux, 1997.

Mairs, Nancy. *Waist-High in the World.* Boston: Beacon, 1996.

———. "When Bad Things Happen to Good Writers." *New York Times Book Review* (February 21, 1993).

Mitchell, David T., and Sharon L. Snyder. *The Body and Physical Difference: Discourses of Disability.* Ann Arbor, Michigan: University of Michigan Press, 1997.

Murray, Michele. "Creating Oneself from Scratch." In *The Writer on Her Work,* edited by Janet Sternburg. New York: Norton, 1980.

Nye, Emily F. " 'The More I Tell My Story': Writing as Healing at an HIV Clinic." Ph.D. diss., University of Michigan, 1995.

Pennebaker, James W., and Robin C. O'Heeron. "Confiding in Others and Illness Rate Among Spouses of Suicide and Accidental-Death Victims." *Journal of Abnormal Psychology* 93, no. 4 (1984): 473–76.

Sandblom, Philip. *Creativity and Disease.* New York: Marion Boyars, 1995.

Sarton, May. *After the Stroke.* New York: Norton, 1988.

Schweizer, Harold. *Suffering and the Remedy of Art.* Albany, New York: SUNY Press, 1997.

Selzer, Richard. *Raising the Dead.* New York: Viking, 1993.

Woolf, Virginia. "On Being Ill." In *The Moment and Other Essays*. New York: Harcourt Brace Jovanovich, 1948.

Wyatt-Brown, Anne M., and Janice Rosen, eds. *Aging and Gender in Literature*. Charlottesville, Virginia: University Press of Virginia, 1993.

Epilogue: From Silence to Testimony

Bell-Scott, Patricia. "Sapphire: The Artist as Witness" In *Flat-Footed Truths*, edited by Patricia Bell-Scott and Juanita Johnson-Bailey. New York: Henry Holt, 1998.

Felman, Shoshana, and Dori Laub, M.D. *Testimony*. New York: Routledge, 1992.

Giunta, Edvige. "Teaching Memoir at Jersey City State College." Unpublished paper given at Berkeley College, New York, June 1997.

Gordon, Mary. *The Shadow Man*. New York: Vintage, 1997.

Jean, Valerie. "Writing Survival." In *Flat-Footed Truths*, edited by Patricia Bell-Scott and Juanita Johnson-Bailey. New York: Henry Holt, 1998.

Miller, Susan J. *Never Let Me Down*. New York: Henry Holt, 1998.

Raine, Nancy Venable. *After Silence*. New York: Crown, 1998.

Sapphire. Interview by Dinitia Smith. "For the Child Who Rolls With the Punches." *New York Times* (July 2, 1996).

Tabor, Mary B.W. "Memoir Provokes Arrest [about Richard Hoffmann's *Half the House*]." *New York Times* (November 22, 1995).

Woolf, Virginia. *Three Guineas*. New York: Harcourt, Brace & World, 1938.